DATE			

1/14 S

DEVOTION
and
DEFIANCE

DEVOTION
and
DEFIANCE

My Journey in Love, Faith and Politics

HUMAIRA AWAIS SHAHID

with KELLY HORAN

 W. W. Norton & Company
New York • London

This is a work of non-fiction, and the events it recounts are true. However, in the interests of protecting the privacy and security of real people, I have changed the names of everyone except those in my family and those who are already known to the public.

For information about permission to reproduce selections from this book, write to Permissions, W. W. Norton & Company, Inc., 500 Fifth Avenue, New York, NY 10110

For information about special discounts for bulk purchases, please contact W. W. Norton Special Sales at specialsales@wwnorton.com or 800-233-4830

Manufacturing by RR Donnelley, Harrisonburg, VA
Book design by Lisa Buckley
Production manager: Anna Oler

ISBN: 978-0-393-08148-0

W. W. Norton & Company, Inc.
500 Fifth Avenue, New York, N.Y. 10110
www.wwnorton.com

W. W. Norton & Company Ltd.
Castle House, 75/76 Wells Street, London W1T 3QT

1 2 3 4 5 6 7 8 9 0

I dedicate this book to my three children Nofal, Fajr and Hafsa, three pieces of my heart who transform my life with their uncon- ditional love and who are the greatest gift of God, my solace and strength. This is our story, of our smiles and our tears.

I also dedicate this book to all those who faced injustice, violence and exploitation in their lives. To all those who are vulnerable and deprived, those who lost their loved ones and who stood up with resilience and courage.

Contents

DEVOTION

and

DEFIANCE

CHAPTER ONE

Before and After

EVERY LIFE HAS ITS LINES of demarcation, those signposts of experience that, like town line markers on a country road, herald that we are leaving one realm—before—and entering another—after. This is the story of the accumulated befores and afters of my life to date; of meeting, falling in love with and marrying Ednan Shahid; of becoming a mother, a journalist and a legislator, as well as an advocate for those who don't have political power and a thorn in the side of some who do. It is the story of passages both planned and unforeseen, and of all the tiny changes that, to paraphrase Tolstoy, add up to a true life lived.

Such is the domino effect of chance, by turns haphazard and fraught, fortuitous and well timed. In the chain reaction of seemingly random and unrelated events on stages large and small, personal and public, obstacles emerge, openings appear, and a life's journey is carved, a legacy forged, a fate sealed. I have come to recognize in the fallen dominoes of my own life evidence of the hand of God. Sometimes, as when Ednan first crossed my threshold, I have felt favored, and other times, as the reader will come to know, I have not.

This is very much a Sufi notion. In the thirteenth century, Jalal ad-Din Muhammad Balkhi, the Sufi mystic and poet better known to the West as Rumi, wrote, "Though Destiny a hundred times waylays you, in the end it pitches a tent for you in Heaven.

It is God's loving kindness to terrify you, in order to lead you to His Kingdom of safety."* Over the course of my life, Destiny has waylaid me, and God has terrified me. Neither, I believe, has finished with me yet. I have come to believe that this is the point of life's crossings: joyous or trying, they shape who we become and show us who we are.

RAISED WITH AN APPRECIATION of personal responsibility and an aversion to politics, I married into a family where the country's most influential decision-makers are frequent guests. This was my husband's normal growing up. Scion of a newspaper mogul, Ednan was reared to know the names, party affiliations and political loyalties of men most people knew only from headlines, not family dinners. Headed for the quiet life of an academic teaching Western literature to graduate students, I found my way into the fray of Pakistani politics, where I sometimes had to shout to be heard. Brought up with no conception that my gender might lessen my worth as a human being, I have devoted much of my adult life to correcting that calculus for women and girls who have not been so fortunate. While at first glance I might judge that nothing in my upbringing could have prepared me for the work I do or the life I live today, I see upon closer inspection that, in fact, everything has.

I was raised in Kuwait. My father, Abdul Hamid Bhatti, worked for the Al Ahleia Insurance Company and had lived there since 1959, when he left Pakistan at nineteen to join his father, who had a tailoring shop. He had returned to Pakistan for several weeks in 1967 only to marry my mother, Musarat Hamid. After their wedding, my parents made Kuwait their home. Each of their four children was born there; second in line, I arrived in

---

Mathnawi of Jalaluddin Rumi, trans. Reynold Nicholson (Cambridge: Gibb Memorial Trust, 1990), Book 1, Verse 1, pp. 260–61.

1971. From my earliest days, I remember that my father used to say to me, "There is power in the individual." One day, I would know well what he meant, but when I was girl, I was ever more taken with something that my maternal grandfather, Muhammad Nazir, my Nana Ji, used to say. "Bloom and be blessed, Humaira. Bloom and be blessed." It made me imagine myself as a beautiful flower.

I cherish the memories of my upbringing in Kuwait. Though I had nothing to compare it to at the time, hindsight tells me how fortunate I was to have been raised in such an open society. Kuwait was safe, secure and secular. The international community that we lived in was as diverse in national origin as in religious faith. We played with the children of Christians, Hindus, fellow Muslims and others. If our parents differentiated among them, held one group in higher regard than another, we didn't know it. That we spent many afternoons walking unsupervised the two kilometers to the nearest beach illustrates a freedom that I didn't even know I had until I was a teenager, living in Lahore, and as a girl not allowed to go anywhere on my own. How wistful I would one day be for the simple pleasures of an unfettered childhood.

THE PAKISTAN THAT my parents left in the late sixties was very different from the one I would discover upon moving there to live for the first time in September 1985.* We moved for my education. My parents had foreseen that there would be more

---

*When General Ayub Khan came to power in 1958, he sought such a distance between Islam and the state that he tried to have the country's name changed from "The Islamic Republic of Pakistan" to "The Republic of Pakistan." He wasn't successful, but his commitment to keeping an Islamist agenda at bay defined his regime. His was the Pakistan in which my parents came of age. While it wasn't without conflict, the general tenor of the age was one of tolerance. Being progressive didn't rule out religious faith, and vice versa. By the time I was born, religion had come to play an increasing role in Pakistan's state affairs.

expatriate children in booming Kuwait than there would be places for them at the International School there, and so, years earlier, they had come up with a contingency plan: We would move with my mother to Lahore when the time was right, and my father would keep his good job in Kuwait and visit us every other month. Summers we would spend as a family in Kuwait.

The question of where to live in Lahore had long been settled. In the early eighties, my father and a younger brother, Khalid Mahmood Bhatti, spent their vacations building an eight-bedroom duplex in Garden Town. By the summer of 1985, their work complete and my place not assured in the International School of Kuwait's eleventh-grade class, my parents decided it was time to move.

My father and uncle were devoted to each other and to their families. I attribute this in great part to the fact that they lost their mother when they were still boys. My father, the fourth son of six, was fourteen when his mother succumbed to tuberculosis in 1955. He was tasked by his overwhelmed father with looking after my uncle, the youngest, who was just five. My uncle told me often that my father fussed over him with all of the doting, worried attention of a mother and father combined. He felt a debt of gratitude to my father that went beyond a fraternal bond, and my father's love for him ran as deep as that of a father for his son. That one day their families might live together under one roof was a dream they shared.

Literally overnight, our family of six grew by four, when we joined my aunt and uncle—we called them Chachi and Chacha, respectively—and their two young sons, Ziad and Zain. In coming years, our numbers would swell and contract: My cousin Amna would be born the following September; my older brother Samir would attend college in Texas, where he would eventually settle, and my father would travel between his two homes in Kuwait and Lahore.

Life was boisterous with nearly double the Bhattis. My

brother Samir's departure left me the oldest, at fourteen, of a funny, noisy, pain-in-the-neck brood. My brother Muhammad, a year old, was the youngest, followed by Zain, who was three, Ziad, who was five, and my sister Aisha, who was eight. It helped to have such young and lively charges to care for at home because, frankly, there was so little that I was permitted to do outside of it.

My new existence was a chaperoned one. I could no longer walk to the ocean or succumb to a wanderer's idyll, as I had done in Kuwait. Perhaps in response, I read a lot. I had always loved reading, but it was only after moving to Lahore that I discovered novels as magic carpets, able to transport me to the far-flung reaches, where not even the worried eye of protective elders could find me. My bookshelf at the time was heavy with two genres in particular: Gothic and Romantic. If I tended toward a dramatic flourish or two in those days, I came by it honestly; it would be impossible to read *Wuthering Heights*, say, or *Emma*, without at least once flinging oneself upon a sofa in a show of despair.

For as much as Lahore had become my home, I remember always thinking of it as a temporary one. In spite of the fact that my father had built a house for us there, I always assumed that we would one day return to our real home, in Kuwait. Late in the summer of 1990, however, one particularly frightening and random twist of fate intervened: Saddam Hussein invaded Kuwait on the second of August. Without it, my family might never have remained in the city that I call home, and the arc of my story might look very different indeed. None of what came after that summer, I am convinced, would have happened had a power-hungry Iraqi dictator not decided to invade the tiny gulf state to the south of his country, and, in so doing, throw my family's life into upheaval and redirect the course of mine.

We spent that summer as a family in Kuwait. My father cherished our summers together; he missed us awfully when we were away in Lahore. On the thirty-first of July, I ended my summer holiday early to return to Pakistan to sit for my bachelor's exams.

My mother and younger siblings were to follow a week later. Two days after I left, however, Saddam Hussein's army invaded the country. It would be three excruciating weeks without word from my family before a letter from my father arrived. My Chacha read it aloud to us: My family was safe, but conditions in the country were deteriorating. My father had judged it less risky to flee Kuwait than to stay. My family would join a ten-car convoy of six Pakistani families making the overland journey of thousands of miles across Iraq and into Turkey, through Iran and into Pakistan. By the time we received this news, my family was already on the road. Several more weeks without contact with them followed.

My brother Muhammad was only six years old at the time, my sister Aisha just thirteen. I imagined what their world must have looked like from the back seat of a car for many hours on end along dusty, unfamiliar roads. I felt suspended in time, unable to sleep or concentrate. It was my first experience of that particular agitation that accompanies a desperate need for news when there is a vacuum of it. We were all worried for them. I had never seen my uncle, a tall, handsome man, look so haggard and upset.

At last, my family arrived safely in Lahore on the nineteenth of September. They were thin, ragged from exposure to the desert's scorching days and freezing nights, and exhausted. Their car had broken down somewhere in Iraq, so they had abandoned it. They had no money because Hussein's army had seized all expatriates' assets and bank accounts. But they were safe, and we rejoiced at their return. I remember watching as my Chacha took my father into a tight embrace and patted the back of his head tenderly, tears streaming down his face.

Days and nights of homecoming celebrations ensued, with relatives and friends descending on our home bearing sweets, cakes and warm tidings. I have always considered Punjabis the Romans of the subcontinent: intensely social, forever sharing a meal, and valuing kinship and the expression of it above all else.

The outpouring that accompanied my family's return made us all feel much loved and well rooted. Lahore had never felt more like home.

Our spirits were still high on Thursday, the twenty-seventh of September, as we readied the house for a fourth birthday party for Amna, who was waiting impatiently for her father to come home. He had promised to take her out to buy a party dress. When my father's cousin Najam appeared in our doorway sometime around one o'clock in the afternoon, we welcomed him as we had all the others who had turned out to join the fray of the ongoing reunion. But Najam's expression was grave.

"There has been an incident," he said, gathering us all in the living room. "A shooting. There is word that Khalid . . . "

The phone rang, and I ran to the kitchen to answer it. I did not recognize the man's voice down the line. He asked if we had received any news. "What news?" I said. There were a few moments' pause before he said, "I am calling to confirm that Khalid Bhatti was shot in the head and is near death." Without asking him to identify himself—he was most likely calling from the hospital—I hung up and ran to join the others in the living room, where everyone was silent.

I had no experience of death or of the delicate matter of disclosing news of an impending one, and so I blurted out what I had just heard. I realized in retrospect that Najam knew when he entered our house that my uncle was not going to live, but he was trying to prepare us. Perhaps he was also searching for the nerve to tell us. Very quietly, in response to what I said, my aunt replied, "If he is shot in the head, then he cannot recover." People began to cry.

Soon after, we saw my father coming through the garden gate. We ran to him, and he gestured with his hands that his brother was dead. At that, my aunt appeared to go into shock. Her eyes were unblinking, her face expressionless. She was unable to speak. "Arifa!" Najam said, calling my aunt by her first name.

"Arifa, do you understand? Khalid is gone, Arifa. Can you understand me?" Najam, a medical doctor, had seen shock before and was concerned that my aunt might have had a stroke. He must have repeated his questions twenty times before my aunt snapped out of her trance and began howling. It was the purest expression of anguish that I had ever witnessed.

I looked around and saw my cousin Ziad, who was just ten years old, standing alone, crying. I didn't know what to do but take him into my arms and hug him hard. His little brother Zain appeared in the doorway, clutching a small chalkboard. Zain was eight and had just learned to write in Urdu's complicated script. I saw that he had written "Allah, save my father. Give him life." He had drawn flowers around the words. I took him onto my lap and, one arm around each of my cousins, squeezed them both as I wept. The four-year-old birthday girl had no clue what had happened. Amna's frightened tears were in response to ours; everyone was seized by grief. For years, we would celebrate Amna's birthday two days later, the twenty-ninth, until she was mature enough to understand that her birth date was also the anniversary of her father's death.

The motive in my uncle's murder was robbery. He and his partner, Mian Amjad, a prominent Lahori businessman who was also killed, had just withdrawn thousands of rupees to invest in a factory to make children's garments. The police told us that there had been a string of deadly robberies outside banks in the days before the incident. They surmised that the bandit had witnessed the withdrawal inside the bank and then followed my Chacha and his partner out onto the sidewalk. Pakistan's business economy was almost entirely cash-based in those days, and my uncle and his partner would have made for easy marks as they left the bank with briefcases full of money. Their murderer was never apprehended.

Friends and relatives who had heard the news began to arrive at our home. Some had been planning on attending Amna's birthday celebration that evening. Instead, those gathered mourned a tragic, sudden and profound loss. My uncle was forty-one years old.

When his beloved brother was killed, my father had just begun to face the uncertain prospect of earning a living in a city that he hadn't worked in since he was a teenager. Now, he found himself consoling a young widow—my Chachi was just thirty-four—and her three young children while taking on the burden of caring for not just one family, but two. Just as he had been my family's steady hand during their uncertain weeks of flight from Kuwait, my father remained strong now. Though stoic, his heart was broken. I noticed that he would quiver for minutes on end, as though his body struggled to contain all of the sorrow he did not express. He grew even taller in my eyes for the grace with which he steered us all through that terrible time.

I TRACE THE PATH of my religious devotion to the painful aftermath of my uncle's sudden death. Home that morning, he was dead by afternoon. My sense that my family's lives had hung in the balance just weeks earlier was replaced by the realization that all lives do.

With my uncle's death, God ceased being for me the source of intellectual musing; he became real. All of a sudden, I felt His presence. He was the decider, the one who gives life, the one who takes it away. Until then, my faith had served my curiosity more than it had served my core. I approached it in much the same way as I had approached literature, as a means to exploring an idea. Before, God was an abstraction. He was an invention that served a story or pushed forward a narrative, like Beckett's Estragon or Brontë's Heathcliff. No longer. As I grappled with the notion of mortality and the meaning of life when it can so suddenly and violently end, God became a central presence in my life.

For the first time, I began to pray with regularity. It was then that I understood the transformative power of prayer. It is a grounding practice, literally, to place one's forehead on the earth. It is impossible to bow to God's will and still harbor pretensions. I prayed five times a day, as is the Muslim tradition, but I did so in secret, so as not to unsettle my nonpracticing family. Because I was the eldest of the children at home, I had adopted my father's habit of offering comfort in spite of my own hurt and questions. I took care not to reveal to my cousins and siblings the turmoil I felt over my uncle's murder. Instead, behind closed doors, I found peace in submission to God and in acceptance of His will.

At the same time, my studies took on new urgency. I read everything—literature, history, religious texts—in search of answers about mortality, the meaning of life, and the evidence of an afterlife. Once naïve and carefree, in my effort to come to terms with my family's ordeal in escaping Kuwait and our collective struggle to accept my Chacha's death, I became a serious and spiritual young woman. I recognized the overarching omnipotence of God's will and our powerlessness in the face of it. I realized, too, that the one choice I had in life was how I lived mine.

CHAPTER TWO

Finding Ednan

WHEN EDNAN AWAIS SHAHID walked into my office one day in January 1996, I didn't for a moment consider that he might upend everything I had ever thought about love, family, commitment or myself. Marriage was the furthest thing from my mind that winter. I was twenty-four years old and a recently minted master of English literature, happy in a new job working as a liaison between the students and the administration at the Imperial College of Business Studies in Lahore. My longer-term plan involved pursuing my literary crushes—Sartre and Beckett chief among them—in further graduate work. Pursuits of any other nature, especially the romantic, did not factor into my plans.

This was so in spite of the fact that my parents had begun to receive marriage proposals for me. It didn't matter that the concept of an arranged marriage struck me as a relic that belonged in a novel set in Victorian England; the practice was common enough in modern-day Pakistan that as soon as I graduated from college, families in my parents' acquaintance started expressing an interest in me for their sons.

There was a man in his early thirties from Chicago whose Pakistani-born parents had sent his photo. If I liked his face, they suggested, perhaps they would arrange for a visit. "How do you expect me to marry a photo?" I said to my mother, waving her and the offending picture away. He might have been perfectly nice. He might even have been handsome; I don't remember. I knew only that I could never imagine finding a husband by picking a photo. *How ridiculous!* I thought.

Another proposal came from the family of a son who, when we met, seemed genuinely perplexed—and not just a tad condescending—about why anyone would want to study books for a living. I ruled him out right away.

My parents resisted pressing any one particular suitor's case, even though their own arranged marriage had been a long and happy one by any measure. Their fathers, tailors, had met as young men in Burma, where they contracted others to sew uniforms for Indian soldiers during the Second World War. When conditions in the Japanese-occupied country grew too dangerous, Ismail Bhatti, my paternal grandfather, and Muhammad Nazir, my maternal grandfather, fled on foot. For four months they traversed jungles and wilderness, risking their lives, but they survived the trek from Burma to India. Over the course of their shared ordeal, they became such great friends that they vowed that one day their families should unite through marriage. When my parents married on the twenty-second of January 1967, my grandfathers made good on that promise.

Given the success of my parents' arranged union, I realized how fortunate I was that neither of them—well, perhaps my mother just a little bit—was fretting about my indifference to my prospects. Many young women of my age might have received tremendous pressure from their families to consider the offers, which brought with them a promise of wealth or status or both.

Restraint such as my parents' was not a widely shared trait among certain of my family's acquaintances and extended relations, however. After being warned repeatedly of the disaster that loomed—namely, my expiration date—by people who had no stake whatsoever in my future happiness, graduate study abroad held increasing appeal. I felt the urge to flee; I was beginning to have enough of Lahore.

Nearly a decade in that city had given me a distaste for the judgments and status-conscious values of our segment of society, where competition, ostentation and social one-upmanship are the paradoxical side effects of an essentially conservative, herd-mentality culture. No doubt because of the fact that it was considered a given that I should marry by a certain age, I recoiled from the notion.

There was also the not insignificant question of my heart. I had always made it clear that if I married one day, I would do so for love. I did not yet know what love was or what solace marriage would bring, but I knew that I would recognize love when it gripped me. My heart was alive. I believed then as now that my heart beats to a cosmic rhythm, that it responds to a divine music. While some descriptions of being in love that I read in novels left me with the impression that it was an impaired state, I knew that when the right person came, I would not lose my senses like some swooning romantic heroine, but feel them more acutely than ever. My heart would know love when it found it.

So there was the matter of love, as yet unresolved, and there was something else, as well: My long-held doubt about whether or not I was cut out to be someone's wife at all. That a marrying woman should exchange her father's four walls for those of her husband seemed in my case to have the potential to be a less-than-favorable swap. As I would learn in my work as a journalist and legislator much later, for many women, such a bargain amounted to captivity.

It wasn't just that I had spent my formative years in a freer society than the one of my nationality. It's that in a patriarchal society, I was born to a man who encouraged all of his children, not just his sons, to be independent and self-sufficient. I thrived on that freedom as a girl. I couldn't envision dispensing with it as a woman for the sake of finding a husband. I had an upbringing rooted in the assurance of unconditional love. How, I wondered, would I ever replicate such good fortune in another man's house?

If I questioned whether I could be a man's wife, I knew that I could not be a housewife. My mother lived for her husband and children, or so it appeared to me. Her love and support of us were the definition of selflessness. Such was my connection to her that when I was seven or eight years old and took a bad fall down the stairs of our home in Kuwait, it was only when my mother did not also feel my physical pain that I realized that I was separate from her. Before that moment, I had believed that we were extensions of each other, if not one being. Her devotion gave me no reason to doubt that. As I grew up, my gratitude to my mother was laced with uncertainty about whether or not I'd ever manage or want to do what she had done for her family.

Ednan Awais Shahid was an M.B.A. candidate at the school where I worked. Because he was working toward his second graduate degree—his first was a master's in economics—and had spent a couple of years working for his father's newspaper, he was older than most of the students in business school and, at twenty-six, my elder, too.

Yet, slightly built, he looked boyish in jeans and a cardigan sweater. He wasn't tall, but he had presence. He had a kind, open face, an easy smile and, as I would come to learn, an impish sense of humor. "I heard there is a new student liaison," he said, "so I thought I would drop by and see."

Behind his wire-framed glasses, his eyes were the color of caramel, a trait that set him apart in our dark-eyed culture. I would come to know that plenty of far greater significance set him apart, as well.

"I see they have brought in a pretty new face to deflect our concerns," Ednan said. I heard what he said as a challenge, not a compliment, and I was determined that this affable but needling fellow should take me seriously. In assuring him of my commitment to working with the students and not against them, I adopted a tone of slightly haughty reserve. And in case it gave me an edge, I made certain to let him know that I had a master's degree in literature.

I also told one lie: When Ednan asked my age, I told him that I was twenty-seven. I thought my being older than he might give him an impression of seriousness. Ednan could have cared less. "I don't know if you are twenty-seven or twenty-two," he said. "You look twenty-one!"

Of everything that we discussed that first day, he seemed most interested in learning more about my taste in reading. This went to his eternal credit.

Thereafter, whenever Ednan would drop by my office, as he did with increasing frequency, our official chitchat about school business always gave way to long conversations about authors and novels. We discovered a shared affinity for Sufi writers and mystical poets, such as Bulleh Shah, Sultan Baho, Waris Shah, Imam Ghazali and Rumi. Coming from Punjabi culture, this discovery was not so surprising. What impressed me more was that we were drawn to the same Western writers, as well. We talked about Thomas Hardy and his tragic protagonists, notably Tess of the D'Urbervilles and Jude Fawley of *Jude the Obscure*, and about Joseph Conrad's exploration of hearts of darkness both real and metaphorical.

"I can't believe that someone who wears such frivolous, bright clothing is so death-obsessed!" Ednan said one day.

He was right, but I hadn't realized it until he said so. At the time that we met, I favored a wardrobe of bright, saturated colors and ornate embroidery. Meanwhile, the stories I most loved seemed woven from shadows. I didn't have to explain their appeal, however, because Ednan favored them, too.

We were under the spell of Dostoyevsky, Sartre and Nietzsche, existentialist writers whose questions about the meaning of life and the imperative of living with passion appealed inherently to us. This is important, because it spoke to something larger in each of us. I recognized in Ednan a sincerity and an integrity. He had values, he knew what they were, and he lived by them.

In his work on the student council, Ednan had a clear, strong voice. He wanted to change things for the better. I loved that about him. I remember thinking once: *He is a revolutionary that has walked into my office!* Our belief in our ability to fix things around us was integral to our relationship from its earliest days.

WHEN MY NEW FRIEND EDNAN and I discussed our futures, I told him that, as my brother Samir had done, I planned to study abroad. Those conversations always led to talk of my marriage proposals, because my desire to study abroad was also my escape plan. I knew that if I stayed in Lahore long enough, I would have to marry *someone*. I also knew that nothing would dim a suitor's interest quite like my choosing to live on a different continent.

Ednan was very curious about my suitors, a fact that I was slow to realize was a dead giveaway of his interest in me. He wanted to know everything. What families did they come from? What did they do for a living? What kind of an arrangement were their parents offering me? Were they kind? Handsome? Intelligent?

"On paper, there is little not to like," I told Ednan.

"Why are you refusing them, then?" he asked.

"Because there is 'on paper,' and then there is 'in the flesh.'"

I'm afraid my ambivalence about the entire prospect of married life gave my poor husband-to-be a terrible complex. He was almost convinced he could never get anywhere with me. How fortunate I was that he was determined. Ednan used to say to me, "Humaira, it was very clear to me that you were the one, but you had your hang-ups, so I said to myself, 'Okay, let her grow up.'"

I should have known, given all of my reading of the Romantics, that what was happening to me was love—the anticipation of his visits, the rare ease of our interactions. Now it seems to me that "love" is a deficient word to describe what I felt for Ednan. Our hearts recognized each other, but so did our minds and our spirits.

BY THE TIME EDNAN was in business school, his father, Zia Shahid, presided over a small but successful media company. In a country where the leading newspapers had been established by conglomerates and dated to Partition, Zia's privately run newspaper group was a fledgling in comparison. That it held its own against the competition was a tribute to Zia, a workaholic who had proved his chops as a hard-charging journalist and businessman.

Zia founded the newspaper the *Daily Khabrain*, which means "news" in Urdu, in September 1992. *Khabrain*'s mission— to give voice to the voiceless—set it apart. So did its editorial independence.

As a middle-class-born player in a rich man's game, my father-in-law had learned the hard way to back his paper with small, private investors, not influence-peddling entrepreneurs. Pressured to toe the government line by backers of his first news-paper, *Kahani*, which he founded in 1971, my father-in-law chose instead to walk away. In 1973, he went to work as an editor at the daily newspaper *Mashriqi Pakistan* and bided his time until he had amassed the funding and the staff to launch his next newspaper, a political weekly he called *Sahafat*, the Urdu word for journalism, in 1975.

Over a long career as a reporter and editor, Zia had distin-guished himself for his fearlessness in rooting out and exposing corruption at every level of society, from the local waterworks department to the Prime Minister's office. In the mid-1970s, a frequent target of his investigations was Prime Minister

Zulfikar Ali Bhutto, which made him, in turn, a frequent target of Bhutto's. In 1977, when *Sahafat* published an exposé of corruption in Bhutto's government, the Prime Minister seized the paper's printing machinery and license to operate, shutting it down. Not long after, Zia and the source behind the damning document, Hanif Ramay, a prominent Bhutto defector, disappeared. Both men, it turned out, had been imprisoned, a fact that their worried families would learn only after their release three months later.

That Zia survived months of torture in the notorious underground dungeons of Lahore Fort is a testament to his strength. That he did so to return to the fray of Pakistani journalism signaled his commitment to exposing the rot in the country's political structures, regardless of the personal risk of doing so.

Following Zia-ul-Haq's overthrow of the Bhutto government in July 1977, which marked the beginning of eleven years of martial law in Pakistan, Zia reopened *Sahafat*. In a country where the press is free in name only, my father-in-law was determined that his paper would be the exception. His courage and defiance made him a hero to aspiring journalists. To anyone who might find himself on the wrong side of Zia Shahid's inquiring mind, he was a threat. Thirty-five years later, *Khabrain*, his fifth and most successful newspaper, is renowned in Pakistan as a training ground for enterprising journalists. It is said that if you can survive the tutelage of Zia Shahid, you can work anywhere. I would learn this to be true.

The Shahid family was not rich by the standards of Pakistan's most wealthy; Zia put every rupee his newspapers made back into the business. What they lacked in wealth they made up for in influence, however. Of course, I didn't know any of this about Ednan that first time he crossed the threshold of my office in 1996. I knew only that, increasingly, I listened for his footsteps in the hall outside my door.

ONE DAY A FEW MONTHS after we met, Ednan called my brother in Dallas, where he had settled after graduating from the University of North Texas at Denton. I hadn't thought much of Ednan's asking for Samir's phone number in America; I had assumed it was to find out more about studying abroad. Of all my character traits apart from stubbornness, naïveté must be my most enduring.

Samir called me later that day, chuckling. We had always been close. I was the imperious little sister to his indulgent big brother. I was fond of repeating to him something that my maternal grandfather always said to me: "You are the most special girl in the world." I had believed him, naturally. My brother, for his part, always seemed unimpressed by this news. Even so, indulged as I was by both my father and my grandfather, I got away with a lot when we were kids. Samir was always big-hearted enough to let me. He was big-hearted still.

"I have had an interesting conversation with your friend Ednan Shahid," Samir said.

"Oh?"

"He wants to marry you, Humaira."

I held my breath.

"And he wondered if I would have any objections."

I was shocked by the news that Ednan wanted to marry me, and, even more so, by my inclination to say yes. My heart, I realized, was glad. I had never had such an instant and easy rapport with someone, and my intuition told me that I might never have it again.

"What did he say?" I asked.

Samir began to laugh. "Humaira," he said, "what did you do to this guy? He's terrified of you!"

According to Samir, Ednan had said, "I am so afraid of your sister. When I go to her, she is full of philosophies and ideas and concepts and just talks and talks and talks. I have no idea how to approach her, let alone propose to her. Please, help me out."

Samir appreciated that Ednan had reached out to him about his intentions toward me. He also understood why. Ednan might have gone directly to my father with his desire to marry me, but he knew that having Samir on his side increased his chances that my father would agree to the union. He was right. In addition, it was not Samir's prerogative, as it would have been my father's, to reject Ednan's proposal outright if he didn't consider it worthy.

Just one thing bothered Samir about Ednan: his profession. Ednan explained to Samir that he planned to return to his father's newspaper as editor of *Khabrain* after receiving his master's degree. Samir was concerned. In Pakistan, journalists are targets for what they write. Shooting the messenger has particular meaning in a country ranked the second-most-dangerous for journalists by UNESCO in 2012. Only Mexico claimed more murdered journalists. The same year, the Committee to Protect Journalists estimated that since 1992, at least 42 reporters had been killed in Pakistan for doing their jobs.

Samir's fears for my safety should I marry into one of Pakistan's highest-profile newspaper families were not unfounded. He might have been concerned, too, that as the son of one of Pakistan's most outspoken journalists, Ednan might share Zia's bold manner and penchant for stirring things up, thereby putting himself and his family at risk. On that count, Samir needn't have worried. As I would come to know and marvel at over the years, few people were as gentle, self-effacing and comfortable behind the scenes as my husband.

Ednan acknowledged Samir's worry. He said simply, "I will always do all in my power to protect your sister and any family that we have together." That he brooked Samir's concern without a trace of defensiveness is what really assuaged my brother, and impressed him, too.

So from worrying about me, Samir moved on to worrying about Ednan.

"What did you tell him?" I asked. His response caused me to wonder whether he was trying to prepare Ednan for a life with me, or to determine whether or not he scared easily. Perhaps he was trying to do both.

"I said, 'Do you have any idea of what you are getting yourself into if you marry my sister? Are you ready for a woman you can never convince? Who is going to be extremely independent? Who will do what she feels like? Who will have a career of her own and be very serious about it?'"

Again, Ednan found the right response. His mother had always worked, he told Samir, and his sister had become a medical doctor before joining their father's newspaper. "I like a professional working woman," he assured my brother.

"Let's get serious, Humaira," Samir said. "He's into you. So what are you going to do? Spend your life with him or go with one of the arranged proposals?"

I asked Samir what he thought.

"I told him I would have no objections if you didn't," Samir said. "He wanted me to speak to you about it. So what do you say?"

Samir suggested that he tell our parents and bring the question of my marrying Ednan to both of our families. He also suggested that I go on a date with Ednan. Samir's suggestion was the nudge I needed.

A MONSOON ACCOMPANIED our first date on the thirtieth of June 1996. Dramatic weather has always held a power over me. The image of Jane Eyre crossing a windswept, rain-soaked moor in a haze of hurt bewilderment is for me one of the most enduring images from Western literature. Our evening would produce nothing so dramatic, unless soaking downpours count.

Ednan met me in Lahore at the home of my friend Farina, who offered me her unvarnished counsel before he arrived. "Don't be so anti-male, Humaira," she said. "Try to have an open mind. If you feel something for him, be honest with yourself." Farina was older than me by three years, and we were great friends. She knew me well. She had seen me vanish into depression after my Chacha's death. At a time when an innocent flirtation might have proved diverting, I was praying and reading the Qur'an. Farina wasn't alone in wondering if I'd ever acknowledge the existence—the appeal, even—of the opposite sex. She urged me to be openhearted and to focus on the here and now.

She also suggested that I wear red lipstick. "Don't overdo it, but look like you made a little effort at least!" she said. I took her advice. And so, in addition to the black kohl that always rimmed my eyes, I wore a casual but colorful cotton tunic in a print of black, red and beige, and I smudged a bit of red on my lips. I did not cover my head in those days, and so I wore my long, layered hair loose around my shoulders. Ednan would tell me much later that he loved my hair that way.

Ours wasn't a traditional first date. For one thing, the rains were so heavy I didn't want to get out of the car. By wanting to stay dry, I'm afraid I was a bit of a wet blanket. I declined Ednan's offer of dinner. I declined, too, his offer of tea and sweets. What was he to do? We drove to the tony Lahore suburb of Gulberg, just twenty minutes from downtown Lahore. Parked outside a florist's shop, his idling car's windshield wipers losing pace to the torrents of rain, Ednan said, "Wait here." Fleet as a rabbit, he dashed into the shop. A few moments later, he emerged bearing a single long-stemmed red rose. With that gesture, Ednan established himself as the romantic in our relationship.

Eventually, the weather forced us off the road. Ednan pulled over in the parking lot of a shopping plaza. The rain fell with such force that water seeped through the car's floorboards, and droplets gathered at the edges of the sunroof. Every so often, one mighty drip would plop onto my head. So much for staying dry.

Ednan ran back out into the rain and into a market. When he came back, he had bought water, Coca Cola and juice. "Are you expecting us to die out here?" I asked, trying for lighthearted but embarrassing him instead.

"I just wanted to make sure that you had everything you need," Ednan said, blushing. I felt bad for teasing him. That aspect of our relationship would change; in little time, Ednan would excel at dishing it out and I would have to get better about taking it.

If our rendezvous lacked a destination, our conversation during it returned again and again to a single point: my marriage prospects. Ednan wanted to know what I planned to do about the arranged proposals; I wanted to know how to make them go away. My irritability on the subject seemed to amuse him. Regarding my thoughts on marriage in general, I quoted George Bernard Shaw. "Marriage is legalized prostitution," I said. No wonder Ednan was afraid to propose to me.

EDNAN NEVER FELT like a stranger to me. With each new interaction, I felt that I had always known him. I feel such relief in retrospect that I let that feeling prevail over my instinct to flee romantic entanglement. I thank God for having given me the wisdom to recognize without knowing it that, in Ednan, I had found my soul's other half.

Ednan and I had two more dates after that first in the monsoon rain. Since we saw each other every day at the university and worked alongside each other on the school's magazine and student council, we had many hours in each other's company. In spite of how seldom we went out together, we had grown almost inseparable by the time we went on our second date.

One day, I returned to my office from a faculty meeting to find a white envelope and a red rose on my desk. When I opened the envelope, my heart racing from the thrill of this unexpected find, I saw that Ednan had typed a poem and signed his name. Something about seeing his name written in his hand gave me a frisson. The poem was Shakespeare's "Who Is Silvia?":

> Who is Silvia? what is she,
> That all our swains commend her?
> Holy, fair, and wise is she;
> The heaven such grace did lend her,
> That she might admired be.
>
> Is she kind as she is fair?
> For beauty lives with kindness.
> Love doth to her eyes repair,
> To help him of his blindness,
> And, being helped, inhabits there.
>
> Then to Silvia let us sing,
> That Silvia is excelling;
> She excels each mortal thing
> Upon the dull earth dwelling:
> To her let us garlands bring.

For Ednan, I was Silvia—a thought both flattering and frightening, for surely I would inevitably end up shattering his idealized notion of me.

DURING OUR SECOND DATE, Ednan proposed. "Humaira, if I make my bed every morning, if I don't leave the cap off the toothpaste . . . "

This was the man who quoted Shakespeare? I had anticipated Ednan's proposal as evoking rather more sublime images than uncapped toothpaste and an unmade bed. Even so, I knew that what he was trying to tell me was that he wouldn't expect me to be his domestic keeper. During one of our many talks about marriage, I had railed about the indentured servitude that seemed inherent to the bargain of marriage for so many women. He had taken my fears of becoming his maid to heart, and so he was leading with a disclaimer.

"Why are you saying this?" I said. I wanted to give him a chance to spell out his intentions a bit more. To summon the Bard, again, perhaps, if he felt so moved.

"Would you please consider spending the rest of your life with me?" Ednan's gaze was intent. In it, I saw hope, but worry, too. He wasn't at all certain what my response would be. What I said next couldn't have reassured him.

"Ednan," I said, "I am not anti-love, but I need time to absorb this." In truth, I was elated that Ednan had asked me to marry him. I just had to make certain that my elation wasn't relief in disguise, and that I wasn't latching onto Ednan's proposal as a way of running away from the others. My heart told me that my feelings for Ednan were genuine; my head needed to confirm it.

I had another concern, as well. Ednan had always maintained that genuine friendship could exist between a man and a woman. I considered our falling in love with each other the upending of that notion. In my mind, there was friend, and there was lover, and there was a dividing line between. If we married, I worried whether our friendship could survive romantic love. Now, of course, I recognize what Ednan was trying to convince me of when he urged me to watch the films *When Harry Met Sally* and *When a Man Loves a Woman*: that love rooted in friendship grows the strongest of trees.

After a couple of days' reflection, and in a move as evocative of a Victorian past as the arranged marriages I dodged, I sent Ednan a letter accepting his proposal.

MARRIAGE IS A FAMILY AFFAIR in Pakistan. Two individuals merge, but so do their families. So when my somewhat disbelieving, possibly relieved, parents had my assurance that I would accept, they invited Ednan's parents and extended family, including aunts, uncles, siblings, in-laws and cousins, to our home so that they could offer a formal proposal. I felt humbled by the outpouring; it is an honor in our culture for elders to partake of such events, and Ednan's relatives did so with generosity and grace.

Ednan's parents had married for love, and Ednan's father had always told his son that he wanted him to do the same. Zia and Yasmine were delighted for us. My father, after conducting a little fatherly detective work to make certain that Ednan's reputation in the world lined up with my view of him, was also very happy. His "sources" had confirmed that Ednan was every bit the good, intelligent and kindhearted man that I had made him out to be. My mother, who had quietly weathered exasperation over her elder daughter's refusal to marry, might well have been happiest of all. Before giving her consent, however, she turned to her father, my Nana. In keeping with a Sunni tradition laid out by the Prophet Muhammad, praise be upon him, he prayed for guidance from God. When my Nana returned from the religious scholars that he had consulted, the word was good: Ours would be an extremely fortunate union, they had told him, to the abiding joy of us all.

OVER FOUR DAYS that began with our vows and culminated in my moving in to my in-laws' home, Ednan and I were married. It was December 1996, less than a year after we met. Already it felt to me that I had never not known Ednan. It seemed impossible to me that I had lived for so long without him. What a relief, after suffering such profound ambivalence about marriage, to know that he was my destiny.

When I watch the video of our walima, the lavish celebration that marked the final event on the last day of our wedding, I am struck by what I see: a couple radiant with youth and the prospect of all that is to come. We also look a bit dazed. Had it been left to us, Ednan and I would have been married under considerably humbler circumstances. Given his father's stature in Pakistani media and political life, however, there was no way around a guest list that exceeded two thousand and counted various stars of sport, cinema and television among our well-wishers.

When I watch this video, I also see that I did less well than I thought I had at masking my disbelief over being one-half of the center of all that fuss. Whereas Ednan, next to me on a stage bedecked with ornate arrangements of chrysanthemums and roses, manages to look at once giddy and serene, I, with my curling half smile, appear as inscrutable as the Cheshire cat. When I try to decode my expression by recalling what I was thinking at the time, I can't. It was all a whirlwind—our courtship, our romance, our wedding, that day.

When I pause the video on a particular moment when Ednan and I have our eyes turned away from the crowd and fixed on each other, however, that instant and everything that I was thinking and feeling during it come back. I see the false eyelashes that made my heavy-lidded eyes itch and look as though lowered to half-mast. In contrast, Ednan's are wide and keen behind his glasses. I see the forward tilt of my head betraying my fatigue as I struggled under the weight of the gold that I wore, in contrast to Ednan's posture, which was so upright it looked as though he might leap up at any time. I see that my hennaed hands are clasped in my lap, in submission to my nerves, whereas Ednan's are outstretched, palms-down, on each knee, the embodiment of repose. For all of the ways that our physical selves differed, however, in that freeze-framed moment, I see—I recognize—that we were thinking the same thing: *Isn't this silly? Isn't this fun? I can't wait to get out of here.*

What I see most of all in watching video footage from the ceremonies that marked our wedding is our dreamy ignorance. We were in love, full of hope and untested, awash in that particular brand of invincibility for which only experience is the corrective.

CHAPTER THREE

Trials

OUR WEDDING CHRYSANTHEMUMS fading like the henna on our hands and feet, Ednan and I settled into our new life together. After four days of celebrations, it was a relief to retreat to our digs at Zia and Yasmine's house in the Model Town suburb of Lahore, where we had the entire ground floor to ourselves. When the last of the well-wishers had finally come and gone, we both exhaled.

It was a happy time, and one of adjustments. I had grown accustomed to the hum and chaos of life in my family's Garden Town duplex, where privacy, like solitude, was scarce. I had become used to the ever-present din of a busy family: the clattering of pots and pans in the kitchen that seemed always to be in the process of turning out another meal; the squabbles and laughter of adolescents who adored and annoyed each other in equal measure; the chatter of the television and radio and our mothers, who were never, it seemed to me, at a loss for words.

The Shahid home was of a similar size, but that was all. For one thing, the gleaming kitchen was a male domain, ruled by a pair of professional cooks who managed all of the meals. For another, I had almost too much quiet. The tranquility was such that I realized I could barely read in absolute silence; I needed a happy cacophony for concentration. With my in-laws and husband at work until late in the evening, the house didn't come alive until after ten o'clock, when high-profile guests would turn up for dinners that often lasted into the wee hours. That was another difference between my new and old homes: Whereas dinnertime conversation with my mother, aunt, cousins and siblings was a wide-ranging free-for-all grounded in the amusing minutiae of our days, discussion around the Shahid table often had the air of a summit. There was talk of newspaper business and the day's headlines, and there were debates about political questions and the fitness of our country's decision-makers to answer them. It was not uncommon for the newsmakers themselves to be there. Imran Khan, the politician, cricket star, and, in 2013, candidate for prime minister, was a frequent guest, for example, as were prominent opinion writers and leaders from various of Pakistan's political parties, including Jamaat e Islami, the Pakistan Muslim League and the Pakistan People's Party.

Late in the winter of 1997, a particular topic of conversation was the political fortunes and future of a frequent guest, Pakistan's eighth President, Sardar Farooq Leghari, a close friend of my father-in-law. Quite unbeknown to me at the time, this soft-spoken, Oxford-educated man would be instrumental to my entrée into a political career of my own several years later.

At the time, Leghari's political power and what would come of it was a great preoccupation around Zia's table. As President during his political ally Benazir Bhutto's government in the early nineties, Leghari was considered by many to be a figurehead. That changed when he dissolved Bhutto's government in 1996 over suspicions that she and her husband, Asif Ali Zardari—"Mr. Ten Percent," as he became known—were guilty of accepting bribes and kickbacks. In fact, Zardari would be arrested and spend the next eight years in prison on corruption charges.* Of a sudden, Leghari looked like a very strong President, indeed.

In the general elections on the third of February 1997, Bhutto

---

*Zardari would be elected President of Pakistan on the sixth of September 2008.

lost to Nawaz Sharif, whose Pakistan Muslim League-Nawaz (PML-N) had won a two-thirds majority in the National Assembly. Some called Sharif's victory "decisive," but given that a mere 35 percent of Pakistani voters—and likely even fewer than that official estimate—turned out to cast their ballots, the true meaning of the results was subject to much debate around Zia's table.

Since as a democratic socialist and leader in Bhutto's Pakistan People's Party (PPP), Leghari was from the start at ideological odds with his new PM, Zia's table speculated about how long Leghari would last in Sharif's government. In fact, by December of that year, Leghari would be out as President, replaced by Sharif loyalist and friend, Rafiq Tarar.

Among the Sharif government's most controversial moves was to pass the Anti-Terrorism Law on the seventeenth of August 1997, which established Anti-Terrorism Courts and Special Appellate Tribunals. The law also broadened the definition of "terrorism" to include murder and robbery. Sharif's brother, Shahbaz Sharif, then Chief Minister of the Punjab, seized on the law as offering amnesty for extrajudicial killings and unleashed his police force to kill criminals. This caused a furor. The Supreme Court heard a challenge to the law on the grounds that it violated the normal administration of justice and was a step in the direction of authoritarian rule. On the twenty-eighth of November 1997, a violent mob of Sharif's supporters and assorted goons stormed the Court, so frightening the judges that they dropped the case.

In the Shahid home, of course, we didn't have to wait until the following morning to read about the day's events in the paper. When Zia recounted that evening what his reporters on the scene had witnessed, we were stunned. Not only had Pakistan been plunged into a constitutional crisis, its judiciary undermined and, literally, assaulted, our entire political system, it seemed to me, had devolved into farce.

I followed the siege on the Supreme Court and its fallout with a mixture of fascination and disgust. This was the pressing business of the government of Pakistan—to suppress the judiciary, upend the course of justice and permit our law enforcement to kill suspected criminals without consequence? It was clear to me that, flush with the triumph of being elected to the Prime Minister's office for the second time in his political career, Sharif intended to stay there.* His consolidation of power would ultimately bring about his downfall. Until then, however, Farooq Leghari would be just one of his political casualties; he would resign in December after his expression of support for the embattled Court's independence put him at irreparable odds with Sharif. Chief Justice Sajjad Ali Shah would be gone by year's end, as well.

The judiciary in tatters, I watched in consternation as Sharif undermined the parliament, too, by forcing through a constitutional amendment that required all members of the National Assembly to vote along party lines. And in case his old friend, the new President, Rafiq Tarar, got any ideas, Sharif did away with the Eighth Amendment to Pakistan's Constitution, thereby stripping the President of his authority to dissolve the government, as Leghari before him had done.

Sharif's adversarial relationship with the press hit ever closer to home. He arrested journalists and launched tax audits of editors who were critical of him. *Khabrain* and its reporters and editors would become particular targets during Sharif's government. After the comparative reprieve that had come during Benazir Bhutto's government (which is not to say she welcomed all criticism), the sudden return to a press that faced government intimidation and tacit censorship signaled trouble to Zia and his colleagues.

All of it made for a lively, if intense, nightly dinnertime ritual,

---

*Sharif secured an unprecedented third term as premier after his party won a solid majority in the parliamentary elections on the eleventh of May 2013. That election marked the first transition of power between two democratically elected civilian governments in Pakistan's nearly sixty-six-year history.

and the raising of my political consciousness. I was so uninterested in politics at the time I married Ednan that at our wedding, when a very distinguished-looking man approached the stage to speak, I leaned over to my new husband and asked, "Who is that?" Ednan was shocked. "Why Humaira!" he said. "That is Malik Meraj Khalid, our caretaker Prime Minister!"

If at the start of my marriage I was apolitical, it was impossible to remain so for long. Between the copies of *Khabrain* that were always scattered about our home, and those riveting dinners, I learned a great deal very quickly about the state of things in the homeland I had lived in for just over a decade. Zia's table offered a crash course in the fundamentals and the intricacies of Pakistan's social and political past, present and future—and failings. I was hooked. It was the beginning of my education about the extent to which the political system in my country is broken. With a few notable exceptions—Farooq Leghari being one—many of Pakistan's politicians could be divided into two camps: buffoons at best, gangsters at worst. If one had told me at the time that in just a few years I would be a sitting member of the provincial parliament, I would surely have feared for my scruples. Wouldn't I have to lose them, I might have wondered, to accept membership in such a club?

It was during those evenings at Zia's table, I believe, that my father-in-law first took real notice of me as more than just his son's wife. I asked a lot of questions and disagreed freely when I felt an opinion strongly. I might have thought that my speaking up and speaking out would displease Zia, a man of firm convictions and set opinions. On the contrary, he valued my forthrightness and saw in me something of his younger, rabble-rousing self.

He complimented my mind and expressed appreciation for what he said was the depth I brought to conversations. I believe that he liked that I was not easily intimidated, even by him. He said to me often, "Humaira, you are a swimmer. You will never drown."

LIFE IN THE SHAHID HOME was absorbing. So much so, in fact, that it verged on the all-consuming. All currents flowed into and out of one source: Zia's growing media empire. Even my mother-in-law, Yasmine, who had her own demanding career as a senior civil servant in the Provincial Information Department, spent her evening hours working at the newspaper. It was only a matter of time, I realized, before I, too, would be tapped. In fact, from those earliest days of my marriage, my father-in-law campaigned with not always subtle persistence for me to join *Khabrain*.

It is not uncommon in Pakistan for upper-middle-class children to follow their parents into the same profession; doctors' children become doctors, lawyers' children lawyers, and so forth. The Shahid children were no exception; even Ednan's older sister Nausheen, a medical doctor by training, eventually bowed to her father's wish that she work for the paper.

It happens less often in Pakistan, however, that a spouse joins the family vocation. In a country where the majority of upper-middle-class women, once married, don't work at all, it's even less common that a wife should do so. Zia wanted to safeguard the future of the organization that he built by staffing it at the top with his most loyal lieutenants, his family.

My response to Zia then and for a long time after was always the same: The boldface names that still mattered the most to me were writers.

How glad I was that, months before our wedding, I had had the foresight—and Ednan's encouragement—to apply to an M.Phil. program in Western literature. Even before starting my life in the Shahid home, I knew that I would need an outlet. Faced with the fascinating but relentlessly one-track quality of the conversation at home, I needed more varied fodder to satisfy my own intellectual interests. Once again, books would be my respite.

I saw my decision to return to graduate school as the natural next step on my path to becoming a professor of English literature. What's more, by staking my claim on an academic career, I was making it clear that I wouldn't just hold on to my individual identity, I would cultivate it. And so I did, beginning the M.Phil. program at the University of the Punjab in Lahore just ten days after our wedding. I did so to the dismay of some relatives who couldn't believe that a young bride might postpone her honeymoon in favor of being in the classroom. Graduate work was my passion. It was also my declaration of independence. Zia, meanwhile, made no secret of his opinion that the academic life was too sleepy by half for me.

On our first Valentine's Day as a married couple, I awoke to find that Ednan had filled our bedroom with roses. Subtle romantic gestures just weren't his thing. He had also made twenty-five valentines, one for each year of my life. When I asked him why, he said, "Because I missed the first twenty-four, and one more brings us up to date." Awash in this romantic spirit, we embarked on our honeymoon later that month, during my first academic break.

We had ten days, and while we might have preferred a tour of Europe, it wasn't possible with that length of time. So we passed our holiday in Dubai, which was just a two-hour flight away. In a city known for its nightclubs and opportunities for excess, Ednan and I retreated to our hotel room most nights by ten. Even early on, Ednan and I preferred the pleasure of each other's company to glittery diversions. We used to joke that we were a pair of elderly homebodies masquerading as lively twenty-somethings.

I have never found it easy to relax. Ednan, on the other hand, had a preternatural gift for doing so. Whereas he could have lingered on holiday and delayed our reentry indefinitely, I was eager to return. The pace of our lives was hectic, and the hours we kept were long, but it was never boring. Ednan loved his work at the newspaper, and I thrived on the rigor of my studies. Even the challenge of devouring hundreds of pages in a single evening delighted me. I drank too much coffee, stayed up too late and burned the candle at both ends. I loved it.

When in early April I began to feel waves of fatigue that seemed to emanate from my very bones, I chalked them up to hard work being done well. As I began to feel that I was dragging a lead weight along with me, however, I knew there was more to it than burnout. That is when I confirmed what I had begun to suspect: I was pregnant.

I was not immediately enchanted by this news. Ednan and I had not planned to start a family so soon. My first response was to worry about what a baby would mean for our relationship, which was serene and indulgent in the way that only being newly wed can be. We were enjoying our time as a couple and were greedy for more of it. I also fretted about what a baby would mean for my graduate work. I was determined to finish my degree.

Our families had no such concerns; they were elated. My father, showing his independent streak from Pakistani male culture at large, wished aloud for a granddaughter. My mother insisted that I start eating more—she knew that I was absent-minded at best and negligent at worst about such matters. Delighted by the notion of another heir, Zia pulled me close and squeezed my face lovingly in his hands; we had already given him a great gift. Down the line from Dallas, my older brother Samir was, perhaps, the most moved of all. "Oh, Humaira!" he cried when I told him the news. "I am going to pray for twins!" I cursed him in a good-natured way for wishing such a fate upon an inexperienced mother.

My exhaustion deepened as my pregnancy progressed. I am prone to anemia, so my obstetrician, considered one of the best in Pakistan, gave me an iron supplement to boost my energy levels. It didn't, but I pressed on nonetheless, devoted to my studies and spending long hours poring over my books and traveling back and forth to the university's campus. I managed through sheer force of will, until I couldn't.

In the first week of my seventh month of pregnancy, my belly huge and my body in considerable discomfort, I fainted. The diagnosis was thalassemia minor, a branch of anemia that causes iron resistance in the body and, as a result, extreme fatigue. No wonder the iron supplements hadn't worked; my body couldn't absorb them.

That wasn't the only surprise, however. Since my second trimester, my doctor had used a Doppler to track the fetal heart rate, but he hadn't performed any ultrasounds. After my collapse and the threat it posed to the baby, he decided to do one. That is when, in the spectral images from the waters of my womb, I saw that I was carrying not one baby, but two. They were identical twins, and they were overlapped in my uterus. For months, the Doppler hadn't picked up a second heartbeat, and my doctor hadn't known to listen for one.

I had been waddling around looking cantilevered and telling myself that I was blessed to be carrying one big fat baby. All the while, I should have been on bed rest, which is what my doctor ordered now. My condition might have required it, but my constitution resisted it. I had never in my life taken to my bed, and I didn't know how I'd endure it. I was devastated by my doctor's orders, which meant that I had to drop out of my M.Phil. program in my second semester. I was also struggling with the prospect of caring for two infants at once. When I told my brother Samir that his prayers for twins had been answered, he wept on the phone. His joy gave me comfort.

TEN DAYS INTO MY NEWLY imposed bed rest, I noticed that the babies seemed to be moving less. I had grown used to their somersaults and kicks. My hands on my belly one morning, I realized that I hadn't felt much of anything for hours. I called my doctor. "Should I be worried?" I asked. He told me to come to the hospital right away, which told me that I should be.

Ednan left the office to meet me at the hospital. As my doctor pressed the rounded end of the Doppler's wand into my belly, the otherworldly whoosh-whoosh of a single heartbeat came across the radar's speaker. Ednan watched the doctor's movements, but I watched his face. I knew that his expression would tell me everything. He moved the wand this way and that in search of the second heartbeat, but none was audible. As he did so, his eyebrows knit together and his mouth set. In spite of the concern on his face, I did not allow for the worst possibility. The fetuses were overlapped, after all, and he had missed the second heartbeat for several months running. It was only when my doctor ordered an emergency C-section that I knew that my babies' lives hung in the balance.

With one baby's heartbeat undetectable and the other's growing faint, my doctor would have to take the babies out right away, he explained, if there was to be any hope of saving them. Within forty minutes, I was under the blinding lights of an operating theater. As a tide of general anesthesia swept me under, Ednan was by my side. My limp hand dropped from his, and the doctor made the incision.

Hours later, when I came to, the first person I saw when my vision cleared was Ednan, who hadn't left my side. Tears in his eyes confirmed what I somehow already knew: at least one of my babies was dead.

"Humaira," he said, his voice weak, "we have a beautiful son." As he kissed my cheeks, I could taste the salt on his.

He told me next that our son's twin brother was stillborn. I felt a stabbing pain in my heart. Where was the baby, I wanted to know. Where were both of them? I wanted to see them, to hold them. My babies. God had given me two babies and taken one away. Had I not been grateful enough for this gift? Had I pushed my body too hard? Even in my postoperative haze, my guilt was sharp as a razor's edge.

It would be two days before Ednan let me see our surviving son. He hadn't wanted to tell me that he was unstable, and he feared that I might not be able to withstand the sight of his tiny, fragile body beneath a tangle of medical tubing. He had been born so prematurely that he could breathe only with the assistance of a machine that pumped air into and out of his lungs.

Ednan wheeled me to the window of the neonatal intensive care unit, where there were eight or nine incubators with tiny babies inside. "Can you tell me which one is our son, Humaira?" Ednan asked. He was astonished when I pointed right at him.

"But how did you know?" Ednan said. I wanted to let him believe that it was a mother's inimitable intuition, that spooky gift that my own mother possesses in spades, but it wasn't.

"Because," I said, "that baby's arms are outstretched in exactly the same position that you stretch yours when you are asleep."

Our son weighed just three and a half pounds at birth. When I held him for the first time on that second day of his life, I felt a gush of love unlike anything I had ever experienced. It was as though my heart had grown huge in my chest. I was overwhelmed by the mystery and the miracle of his flesh-and-blood existence. However small, this being in my hands possessed not only our physical traits, but our hearts and souls, as well.

His ears translucent, his nose a tiny unformed point at the center of his face, and blue veins visible across the lids of his eyes, he had the vaguely alien mien of so many premature babies. He was so beautiful, and so small. We named him Nofal, after a Christian mystic said to have been the first person to recognize the Prophet Muhammad, praise be upon him. It is also an Arabic word that means "handsome youth."

Of our handsome youth, the neonatal intensive care nurses said that he was feisty. "He does what he wants to, this baby!"

"He is from a journalist's family," Ednan replied.

"Oh, we can see that," said the nurse. "Anger is good in a

preemie," she continued. "It's the ones who have tempers that fight to survive."

Nofal was a born fighter.

WHEN I LOOKED AT NOFAL through the clear hard glass of the intensive care incubator, I felt so much love, but also despair. I was helpless in the face of my son's struggle to live, and I wished silently that I could give my life to save his. I wanted to pray for his survival and for the soul of my lost son, but I found myself at a loss. To whom would I offer my prayers? When my beloved uncle was murdered seven years earlier, prayer had been my solace. Not now. How could God do this, I wanted to know, as I watched compressors work to keep Nofal's lungs from failing. What was the point of sending us two babies only to snatch one away and leave the other clinging to life beneath a ventilator, with intravenous tubes jabbed into his tiny feet? I could not understand why or how God could do this.

I gave birth to one son and lost the other on the twenty-ninth of September 1997, a date that would mark the beginning of one of the darkest, most difficult passages of my life. It was a time during which I could not bring myself to pray.

IT WOULD BE TWENTY DAYS in a hospital incubator before Nofal would be strong enough to come home. As the doctor declared him stable, I knew secretly that I was not. I felt myself unraveling. I was wracked with guilt over his fragile state and his brother's death. I obsessed over the question of whether I could have done something differently. Had my body betrayed me, I wondered. Had I betrayed it? As I recovered from the surgery, my heart continued to ache.

Because Nofal's condition remained delicate and his immune

system extremely vulnerable, only Ednan, our mothers and I handled him during his first four months. To minimize his risk of exposure to infection, we did not take him out of our bedroom. Because I was nursing him and he could not take a bottle, Nofal and I spent the better part of every single day and night together. It was a time of almost disorienting fatigue made worse by my postpartum depression. In the middle of the night, I would find myself standing over Nofal in a panic, my heart racing. Was he breathing? Was he alive? I was terrified that he would die. I would check his pulse and return to bed, only to get up a few minutes later and do it again.

Throughout that time, Ednan was my stalwart. After a long day at the newspaper, he returned home to spend the night helping me. He did everything—diapers, baths, lullabies. When I pleaded with him to let me keep vigil by Nofal's bassinet during the night, Ednan assured me that our son the born fighter was fine—and then stayed up watching over him just to assuage my worry and let me get some rest.

If Ednan shared in caring for our newborn son during those early, trying days, he shouldered singlehandedly the burden of my depression and my detachment from my faith. When I raged that God had turned away from us, he would tell me that, on the contrary, God had blessed us with the miracle of a son. When I slipped ever deeper into despond, he was patient and also persistent with the message that I would feel joy again. And when I bewailed the end of my academic career, he would say that it was merely on hold, not over.

We had been married for less than a year when we faced this great trial, and through it, Ednan was the strong one. As I fumbled to get my bearings as a mother, he seemed always to know what to do. Where I was nervous and second-guessed all that I did, he was all calm self-assurance. Through everything, Ednan was an unwavering partner, a preternaturally gifted father and my spiritual ballast. Where some men might have come undone, I never once heard him complain. And where some marriages might have foundered, ours grew that much stronger.

Nofal grew stronger, too. In January 1998, our doctor gave us our first great news: Nofal had defied the odds of his rough beginning and was no longer in critical condition. That meant that, at four months old, he was at last strong enough to leave my constant care. I only wondered if I was strong enough to leave him. Regardless, the news was our first cause for celebration in a long while—we had even let our first wedding anniversary pass almost unnoticed. Ednan and I rejoiced. Our son was going to make it!

As Nofal grew plump and more robust, my worry and doubt gave way to delight. What had become the constant, dull ache of my depression began to subside. His gurglings and gestures and expressions became my sun, radiating warmth and light and healing into my wounded heart. I had been unprepared for the grinding physical and emotional fatigue that comes with caring for a tiny, premature baby, but I was also unprepared for the experience of that purest, most life-affirming joy. What a relief it was to feel that my grief might be a temporary condition, after all.

Nofal's gradual improvement brought me a measure of peace, but my connection with God remained lost. Whereas once I had found refuge and comfort in prayer and looked forward to it in the way that I would a conversation with a good friend, not even my gratitude for Nofal's survival inspired me to pray. Inherent in the act of bowing in prayer is submission, but I felt defiant and angry, unable to submit.

Ednan urged me to let go of my anger with God. I told him in response that mine was the visceral pain of a mother's for her lost child, that he couldn't understand. This must have hurt him. He could understand, of course. We had lost his son, too. But in the myopia of my grief, I could not see that. Nor could I hear what Ednan was trying to tell me: that by holding on to my anger, and by denying the spiritual side of my being, I was only prolonging my sadness.

God would test me twice more before another year had come to pass. On the second of December 1998, fire ravaged the quarters that Ednan and I shared in the Shahid home. I had gone to my mother's to give Nofal a late morning bath. Not long after I arrived there, one of my in-laws' cooks called to tell me that our rooms were burning. After Nofal's birth, we had traded our ground-floor apartment for Yasmine and Zia's on the top floor, so that we could have more air and light during the days when we were confined for the baby's sake to a single space. I rushed home to find the top of our house engulfed in smoke and flames. It was too late to save anything. The objects that I held most dear—the first rose that Ednan had given me, his Valentines, Nofal's first teddy bear—were lost. The fire department never determined the fire's cause. Somehow, this made it all the more menacing in my mind. In the absence of a concrete explanation, my imagination suggested sinister plots. The space that was left when the fire was extinguished was uninhabitable, so Ednan and I moved with Nofal and what remained of our belongings into my family's house in Garden Town. I felt a renewed surge of anger with God.

Six days later, on the evening of the eighth of December 1998, another shock: "Ednan has been in an accident," my brother-in-law called to tell me. "He is being taken to a hospital. I'm coming to get you." Ednan had been with me at my mother's house just twenty minutes earlier. We had been laughing as he left to drive a friend of his home. Now, Imtinan, Ednan's younger brother, told me only that he was on his way to pick me up. He couldn't tell me about Ednan's condition, because he didn't know.

I would later learn the facts of the accident. On a winding, one-lane roadway, Ednan pulled too far to the right to let another vehicle pass him on the left, and his car swerved off the road and down a steep embankment. His friend was thrown from the passenger seat but was not badly injured. My husband was found conscious but bleeding behind the wheel of the silver Honda Civic, now demolished, that he had bought just before we were married. It had slid eight feet below the roadway and landed in a grove of trees. Just a few feet further down, the waters of a canal rushed past.

There were suspicions, never proven, that the other vehicle had deliberately forced Ednan's off the road. The Shahid family had been receiving unspecified threats at the time, and given their status and the many enemies that the newspapers' reporting made them, such threats were an occupational hazard.

When I found Ednan in the emergency room at Jinnah Memorial Hospital, I could barely recognize his face for all of the blood. The paramedics explained that it had hit the steering wheel.

"Don't let her see me like this!" Ednan cried from the gurney where he lay, as a plastic surgeon prepared to sew thirty-four stitches into his face, tongue and neck. "She mustn't see me like this!" Nurses escorted me out while I shook from the second disaster in a week. It had taken the first tenuous year with our son to establish a semblance of a normal life. Now, in a matter of days, that was gone.

That there were miracles in these disasters eluded me for a long time. I appreciated that it all could have been worse. Lives, after all, not just sentimental trinkets, might have perished in the fire. Ednan's injuries might have been fatal. I was focused on Ednan's recovery, on rebuilding and returning to our home, and on resuming my studies in the New Year. God had spared me the worst, but I was of no mind to grant Him that. In the meantime, the near misses slapped me awake, reminding me, as my uncle's death had, that life can change—end—in an instant. I cherished my husband and son.

WHILE EDNAN CONVALESCED, I resumed my studies in January 1999. That had been my plan since getting the all-clear for

Nofal—to spend another year ensuring his continued progress, and then divide my time between home and school. More than once during the previous year, the promise of going back had lifted me out of some mournful, worried depth. Ednan saw in my return to school a lifeline, of sorts. He was right. While my hopes for myself were modest—I wanted merely to reestablish momentum toward my degree—a return to the life of the mind saved me.

My mother and my sister pitched in to help me with Nofal, and so did a nanny. My first day back felt like a triumph. I could almost not remember the carefree young bride I had been when I first began my studies. So much had happened in the two years since I last sat in those classrooms that it felt more like a decade had passed. I was changed. So was my passion for the work, which had a new urgency and for which I had a deeper appreciation. I took nothing for granted.

Such was my haste even to get to school every day that one afternoon I looked down at myself during class and saw that I was wearing my coat inside out. The memory of it makes me wince, less because of how ridiculous I looked in a sea of well-put-together students than for the feelings of desperation it brings back. I was desperate to revive that long-untended part of myself that was so vital to who I was, and desperate to escape, if for just a few hours a day, the unrelenting demands of motherhood.

In February, Zia assigned Ednan, who by then had recovered fully from the car accident, to take over management of *Khabrain*'s Islamabad bureau. Ednan was conflicted, but there was no question that he would go. It was his opportunity to shine, to show his father how ready and capable he was to rise to the challenge of rebuilding a troubled bureau from scratch, and he would do it well. For me, it was a blow. Nofal was entering chubby, energetic toddlerhood; I was learning to master my new juggling act as wife, mother and student; and Ednan and I were relishing what still felt novel and, given the blaze and his accident, all the more precious to us: leading normal if harried lives with a healthy child. What would it mean for Ednan to be four hours away? I considered dropping out of school again and joining him in Islamabad, but I banished the idea. I simply couldn't disappear into this marriage and this powerful family, no matter how much I would miss my husband.

Thus began yet another time of adjustments. During the nearly yearlong period that Ednan was in Islamabad, I spent weekends traveling to and from the city to join him. Nofal was a fussy traveler, so to the stress of leading a bifurcated life was added the challenge of calming the only toddler in the world—or so I was convinced—who was not susceptible to the lulling vibrations of a moving car. Often, to avoid interminable stretches of his crying, I flew. But during the rare drives when Nofal was calm, I was able to take in the majesty along the Islamabad–Lahore motorway, its sine curve road threading through vertiginous mountain ranges and along the lush landscape of the Punjab. The beauty calmed me, too: the Kallar Kahar Salt Range and the gardens where peacocks roam; the fields of mustard, wheat and rice that stretched out toward the horizon; and the orchards that teemed with fruit. It was a time of high anxiety and stress, but once in a while, the sight of a tree with branches that hung heavy with apples or citrus would yank me out of my head and into the moment, and remind me of the times when Ednan would pull the car over so that we could run among the trees and pluck their ripe fruit.

When I completed my last semester in December 1999—I had only to write my thesis to earn my M.Phil.—I moved with Nofal to Islamabad. It was time to be a family again.

CHAPTER FOUR

Coming Home

TO LEAVE ONE'S HOME can be to fall more deeply in love with it. Like a lover whose absence draws her more fully into her beloved's thrall, once away from Lahore, I missed it. Lahore for me is a city of ishq, a Sufi notion derived from the word "ashiqah," or vine, the idea that love taken root is love that endures to the exclusion of all else but God. Everywhere one looks in Lahore, there are symbols of that love, and nowhere more so than in the shrine of our greatest saint, Data Ganj Bakhsh, its soaring minarets reminders that the Sufis ignited love's fire in the people of the Punjab and made peaceful conquests of their hearts.

Witness to centuries, Lahore teems with chaotic, vibrant life and bears still the evidence of all that it has seen. One stands in the shadows of Mughal invaders and the majestic architecture they left behind. The Badshahi Mosque, Jahangir's Tomb, the gates that surround the Old City—they are unsurpassed by anything that has come since, and their allure endures in spite of the neglect and assaults of modern times. One inhales in Lahore the spores of memory, along with the aromas of cardamom, clove and cinnamon, black pepper, cumin and chili, that waft from kitchen windows and street vendor stalls and mask some unbearable stenches. It is an olfactory carnival.

Beyond Lahore's physical aspect and architectural treasures, the city for me is warmth and laughter, color and noise. It is a metropolis that cooks all day and stays up all night, a city that teems, for better and for worse, with passion. I am addicted to Lahore's passion.

Islamabad, by comparison, is the opposite of ishq, a tree without roots, a city without a past. Built in 1960 to replace Karachi as Pakistan's capital, it is sprawling and sleek and urban, but antiseptic and quiet, too. Despite its status as an international hub and a seat of government and wealth, Islamabad goes to sleep at ten o'clock. It is a city of hostels, diplomatic enclaves and convention centers, where so many people seem just to be passing through.

There is beauty in Islamabad, to be sure, but it is the beauty of clean, straight lines, modern edifices and tidy façades. It is not the beauty of a great stewpot of cultural influences or a hot mess of humanity, as one finds in Lahore, and it is not a beauty that stirred me. I appraised my city as I might a novel, mining it for those essential elements that invite me to linger: a sense of place, intriguing characters, complexity and heart. I would come to judge my new home wanting in every aspect. And as though to betray outright my feelings for Islamabad, my body reacted to the place with flaring asthma. I was literally allergic to that city.

The great compensation, of course, was that I was back under one roof with Ednan, and a comfortable roof it was. Before we arrived, Ednan rented and furnished a modern three-bedroom villa that had a lush green lawn where Nofal could play. It was in one of the city's newest sectors, more posh than soulful, more dwelling than home, but we were fortunate nonetheless to live there.

Separation had been trying for Ednan and me. Absence had fired our yearning, but it had also opened up a distance that felt strange and unfamiliar. It didn't help that I was falling over from fatigue every time I arrived in Islamabad, or that Ednan's work had no boundaries, with colleagues calling day and night needing his guidance and input. Our weekends together were so rushed and so dominated by exhaustion and competing demands that they took on the quality of a dream state. No sooner had I arrived than I was turning to go, Nofal wailing from his car seat, to make the long trek home. What a relief it was to land in one place and to feel settled at last, after having lived out of a suitcase during nearly all of the previous year. So while I lamented that our families and friends were far away and that I found myself in a city that left me cold, I was grateful. I decided to do as I had always endeavored and make the best of it.

It didn't relieve my itching eyes or shortness of breath, but it did help immeasurably that I arrived in Islamabad with a job waiting for me. Dr. Najma Najam, head of the psychology department at Punjab University when I was working toward my M.Phil. there, was a family friend and knew of my plans to move to Islamabad. After she became vice chancellor of the newly founded Fatima Jinnah Women University in nearby Rawalpindi, she offered me a part-time visiting post and gave me carte blanche to build a syllabus around the essay and the short story. After deferring for so long my desire to teach, I couldn't wait to get started. On the eve of a new year and at the dawn of a new decade, I was filled with anticipation about what the future might bring.

I began teaching two courses in January 2000. What had been normal, obvious, even, for me—that is, a syllabus loaded with activist and feminist authors—I learned was rather thrilling and surprising for my charges, who were working toward their bachelor's and master's degrees in literature. I would come to find out that they were used to a certain degree of tameness in both their literary fare and their instructor. I taught Mary Wollstonecraft's 1792 treatise *A Vindication of the Rights of Woman*, in which she espouses the power of the intellect and stirs the reader "to persuade women to endeavour to acquire strength, both of mind and body, and to convince them that the soft phrases, susceptibility of heart, delicacy of sentiment, and refinement of taste, are almost synonimous [*sic*] with epithets of weakness."* I taught D. H. Lawrence's *Odour of Chrysanthemums*, in which the long-suffering heroine, Elizabeth, recognizes her abusive husband's humanity only after his accidental death. Her epiphany about the late father of her children forces her to reconsider her own actions and free will. The lesson I taught is of the perils of fashioning one's self into a victim.

Talking to Ednan one day, Najma Najam said, "Oh my God, your wife is not teaching literature here, she is teaching activism!" This fact delighted her. Fellow faculty called me "firebrand," and my students greeted me with enthusiasm. The warmth and acceptance that I felt at the school gratified me fully. It was the perfect antidote to the lingering social chill I felt in haughty Islamabad. I just didn't know how to be Pakistan's version of a desperate housewife, a pretty but vapid creature who concerns herself mainly with shopping and whose chief worth is as arm candy for her husband. How fortunate I was to have married a man who would have found that incarnation of me repellent, and how lucky that I had a crop of students to whom I could show a more empowering vision of womanhood.

WHILE EDNAN WAS BUSY ESTABLISHING and running *Khabrain*'s Islamabad bureau, Zia was exploring another platform: television. By 2008, the Shahid family media empire would include Channel 5, its own national television news station. Early in the year 2000, however, Zia thought it more prudent to buy two-hour afternoon slots on Pakistan's state-run national channel, the Pakistan Television Corporation, PTV. He had a hunch that putting his reporters on TV would help sell more papers, which proved correct.

---

*Mary Wollstonecraft, *A Vindication of the Rights of Woman: With Strictures on Political and Moral Subjects* (London: T. Fisher Unwin, 1891), p. 34.

Not long after I began teaching, Ednan mentioned Zia's new television venture. "Humaira, you are always talking about wishing you could get the ear of this or that well-placed woman. What if you could interview her on national television?" Zia planned a series of interviews with women in public office on topics ranging from policy and agriculture to population, and Ednan thought I should conduct them. It was an appealing notion, but I demurred; my hands were full enough as it was. With Zia's fledgling television effort now underway, Ednan began campaigning for my involvement, too.

I was flattered, of course, and intrigued. What if I *could*, as Ednan suggested, get the ear of national role models and ask the questions I most wanted to ask? After all, I taught my students to seek to better understand the motivations and choices of the heroines in the stories they read. What an instructive and satisfying challenge it could be to explore the lives of real women. I agreed to do it.

In February 2000, I began training in the finer points of the televised interview. Television cameras and lights transformed our home's drawing room into a makeshift studio, where Sohail Zafar, a national TV presenter, taught me how to conduct a conversation in front of a camera as though none was there. Sometimes, the artificiality of it reduced me to laughter. Other times, I felt ridiculous and out of place. Over time, I learned little tricks to which I had never before given any thought, such as when to look directly into the camera and when not to, and how to use my voice and my gestures to convey authority and confidence, but warmth and accessibility, too. To my great amusement, a makeup artist showed me how to apply more foundation, blush, eyeliner and lipstick than I typically wore in a year so that my best features would pop on camera.

Zia left the actual conversations to me. He had remarked often at the end of one of his dinner parties upon the ease with which I established a rapport with a guest who had been a complete stranger to me just hours earlier. He trusted that that skill would serve me well before the cameras. I might not have known which camera to turn to when, but Zia knew that I had an instinct for getting people to open up by asking the right questions. I appreciated his vote of confidence, even as it would require many practice interviews, retakes and exorcisms of nerves to find my own.

Over the course of ten prerecorded interviews broadcast to a national primetime audience, I found my ease in front of the camera and with my guests. My on-air style might have lacked the slick polish of well-practiced TV presenters, but the informality worked to my advantage. My interviewees, all highly placed female ministers in the federal and provincial assemblies, opened up to me. I asked them the same questions I would have posed had they been seated across from me at dinner. We talked woman-to-woman, but with millions of viewers watching, about their professional careers and challenges, and about their personal lives and choices, as well. Viewers responded favorably to the broadcasts, some expressing an interest in hearing more from me about specific issues. That's when I began writing the odd opinion piece for the paper. In one, I wrote about Pakistan's shrinking middle class and the widening gap between rich and poor. In another, I wrote about the scattered focus of NGOs that purported to serve women; they were unable to have the impact they might otherwise have had if their vision had been unified and their efforts collective.

In the meantime, in April 2000, there was another, more immediate development at home: Ednan and I were expecting our second child. I welcomed this news with an open if cautious heart. The scars both physical and psychic of my first pregnancy remained, but this time around, I decided, I would approach pregnancy as the great gift it was, and accept the burdens that accompany it with gratitude. I would also be more vigilant and request every ultrasound and test that might provide important information. I would not seek God's blessing, however. My spiritual estrangement continued. In place of regular prayer, I made time for a practice of pause and reflection, the better to be present for myself and for my growing baby.

Finding that time wasn't always easy. There wasn't much to spare, not with teaching, television interviews, writing op-eds and helping Ednan at the newspaper—not to mention caring for Nofal and preparing for the arrival of his sibling. Even so, I was full of pep. I rejoiced at the return of my intellectual life. It felt glorious to be doing meaningful and varied work. I began to appreciate the difference between busy-ness that enervates, which I had come to know too well when caring for Nofal, finishing my degree and being a commuter spouse, and the kind that energizes.

Certain ghosts are hard to shake, however, and as my belly expanded and my due date drew near, I remained haunted by the circumstances of Nofal's birth. I did my best to keep negative thoughts at bay. When my allergies and asthma attacks worsened as my pregnancy progressed, I told myself this was normal. When in my sixth month I developed a mysterious pain in my appendix, I decided to put faith in my new doctor, who told me that while my pain was certainly inconvenient, she did not believe that it would prove harmful to my baby.

In December, I returned to Lahore; I wanted to be near my family when I gave birth. My due date was the tenth of January. Other than my anemia, which sapped my energy, nothing in recent days or weeks had caused me to fear for the health of our baby. Then on the twenty-first of December, our fourth wedding anniversary, it was as though the nightmare of Nofal's birth were repeating: At a routine checkup, my doctor detected fetal distress. Was the umbilical cord wrapped around the baby's neck? An ultrasound confirmed that it was so. The baby's heartbeat was growing erratic. She wanted to perform an emergency C-section.

That morning, Ednan had left to return to Islamabad. When

I reached him, frantic with the news that I was about to go into surgery, he reversed direction on the motorway and came speeding back to Lahore. Meanwhile, as I lay on the operating table under the unsparing glare of bright lights, I began to feel panic. I looked at the knives arrayed for the operation, and I thought, *I have been angry with my God for so long*. The familiar, frightening scene reminded me that my faith had died along with my son. For the first time in four years, I prayed. "God, I lost you in the fret and fever of my life. I lost you, and now I am looking at you and the door is closed. Maybe I am going to die in this moment. Maybe this baby will die in my belly. But I want you to know what I know: You didn't turn your back on me; I turned my back on you."

My doctor returned and prepared me for surgery. As I went under, I felt awash in darkness. I came to in a state of confusion, reliving Nofal's birth, believing that I had lost a baby. Ednan was there, and so that I would hear him over my crying, he had almost to shout, "No, Humaira! No! You have a beautiful daughter that looks like you! And didn't I always say that if we had a daughter, I would want her to look just like you?" I protested—I was convinced that I had lost my baby. And my dear Ednan, whose sense of humor seemed never to be far from hand, said, "Oh Humaira! I can't believe you come out of anesthesia with an argument!"

That our daughter Fajr was born healthy healed me more even than my once sickly son's astounding progress had. Her name means "light of the dawn," and that is what she was to me. With her came the rebirth of my faith. The joyful experience of nurturing from the first such a robust, undemanding baby would also remove my long-harbored fear that I wasn't really cut out to be a mother. With Nofal, I had been overprotective and nervous and virtually fused with him. With Fajr, who would take a bottle from anyone, sleep anywhere and gurgle in delight at the smallest thing, I was able to preserve—and give her—so much more of myself.

I returned to Islamabad after a month in Lahore, but I never returned to the state of guilt that dogged me after Nofal's birth. I attribute this not only to Fajr's serenity as a baby, but to mine as a prodigal daughter come home. I felt God's presence, and I felt my love for Him almost as a rush in my veins. I was at once grounded and flying, in a rapture and calm at my core. My doubts and resentment were gone, replaced by clarity and certainty. I eased back into daily prayer and resumed talking to God as though picking up the thread with an old friend. As I did so, I rediscovered the vitality and exuberance that I had once taken for granted in myself. In denying my spirituality, I had denied all that I was. Back in the glow of His luminous light, my world was restored to full color. There was liberation in submitting to Him—I had the freedom to love those most dear and to let my work be a manifestation of my devotion. My heart was full of gratitude and bliss.

Eventually, I began spending more time at the office with Ednan, helping in an unofficial capacity to edit stories and focus news coverage. I discovered that I loved the work, and also that it was great fun to be with my husband all the time. We got on each other's nerves—it is possible that I got on his more than he got on mine—but there was never a place where I would rather be.

Though busier than I had ever been, now with two children and a host of professional responsibilities, none of it felt like work. It was, rather, that feeling of ease that comes when you know without knowing why, exactly, that you are exactly where you need to be. This sense of flow built so that, eventually, I felt that I was being carried along by a swift but gentle current.

DURING THE FIRST YEARS of our marriage, Ednan and I watched as his brother and my sister fell in love with each other. Our two families had become close, and when Imtinan expressed his desire to marry my sister Aisha, it almost seemed like the obvious thing to do. In spite of this, I harbored misgivings. For one thing, they were so young, each in their early twenties. For another, I worried that part of what they were looking for in each other was an extension of Ednan and me. They idealized our marriage without, I think, knowing what work it had sometimes taken to survive the challenges that had come our way. But that March, when they married in a celebration that was every bit as beautiful and extravagant as ours had been, we rejoiced for them. The Shahids and the Bhattis, it seemed, were destined to fall in love. With their marriage came the reassuring notion that we would always be there for each other.

IN MAY OF 2001, the Islamabad bureau running well and no longer in need of Ednan's on-site guidance, and another semester at Fatima Jinnah wrapped up, Ednan and I returned to Lahore for good. Such joy to return! As productive, calm and healing as our time up north had been, it had still possessed the vaguely unresolved feel of a holding pattern.

Once back in Lahore, my allergies vanished. How curious, I thought, that in a city surrounded by mountains and filled with sprawling green space, I should choke on the air, while back in a place where the air can be a swirl of diesel smoke and so many simmering curries, I should once again—and in many more ways than one—breathe easy.

WE SETTLED WITH RELATIVE EASE into the familiar groove of life in Yasmine and Zia's home. With our return came the revival of a perennial topic of conversation: my joining the newspaper. In Islamabad, I considered the television interviews, op-eds and editing support I gave Ednan tangential to my real work as a college professor. Back home in Lahore, Zia made it clear that he thought differently. His full court press was on.

In the end, however, it was not my father-in-law who convinced me to join the newspaper in an official capacity. It was my husband. Where Zia, who is tall and striking with sharp, dark features and a kinetic, charismatic charm, can be insistent to the point of domineering, Ednan—slight, quiet and gentle—instinctively took a different tack. Zia had an impressive capacity to talk, by which I don't just mean speak, though he is a remarkable orator. Zia could talk, as in, go on for forty-five minutes without appearing to take a breath. Ednan, on the other hand, was a gifted listener. His talents for hearing between the lines and distilling the essence of a matter served him well in his role as editor, identifying the crux of a story with reporters who weren't always able to articulate it. They also served him well in his life with a woman who was constantly ruminating, ever philosophizing.

"Do you want to write things that will be relevant only within academic circles?" Ednan asked one evening, after we'd excused ourselves from a dinner at which the subject of my leaving teaching and joining *Khabrain* came up yet again. I listened without saying anything; we both knew the answer.

"You have to ask yourself if you want to work to change people's lives in a practical sense," he continued. "You want to effect change?"

"Of course I do," I said.

"And by teaching activist writers you just might be sowing the seeds of consciousness in your students?"

"Exactly. Yes."

"Humaira, where do you think you can have the greater impact?"

He let the question linger before continuing. "At the university, where anything you publish will be read by the handful of people interested in the subject and then be put back on a shelf to molder, or at a national newspaper that has a readership in the hundreds of thousands?"

Ednan made an irresistible point. I cherished exposing my

students to writing and writers that had the potential to expand their views of the world, but I had to admit that it all felt rather abstract to me; there was no way of knowing if my lessons would have an impact beyond the classroom. Journalism, on the other hand, had the potential to effect real change.

I considered journalism to be a jihad of the pen. "Jihad" has become freighted with sinister meaning, but the word translates literally as "struggle." For me, journalism and, later, politics, presented opportunities to struggle on behalf of ideals I believed in, namely human rights for the disenfranchised—the poor, children and women. As I weighed my decision to become a journalist, I did so from the vantage point of activism. I would not only report the news, I would expose the individuals, the systems and the structures that colluded to exploit and harm the innocent. I felt a responsibility to make a difference. That is what decided it for me: the promise of being able to have a positive impact on the lives of real people, and not just on the minds of students.

A month later, in June, I traveled to America with the children to visit my brother in Dallas while Ednan joined a journalists' exchange program in Washington, D.C. I planned to join *Khabrain*, by then Pakistan's third-largest Urdu newspaper, full-time in the fall. I did not require a soothsayer's gift to know that what lay ahead would change me. I just didn't know how. Lacking the oracle's future vision, I would train my eyes instead to where the view was clearest, within, and mine the experience of past transitions for clues to navigating the one to come. I would carry with me the girding protection of faith, and the grounding solace of family. Beyond that, I just didn't know.

CHAPTER FIVE

Righting the Women's Pages

I LEFT AMERICA in late August. Just days later came the attacks in New York, Washington, D.C., and Pennsylvania that would come to be known collectively as 9/11, for that day in September when airplanes crashed into buildings and fell from the sky, taking thousands of innocent lives with them. I couldn't have chosen a more interesting—or uncertain—time to begin my work at the newspaper. Nor could I have anticipated that events on the world stage would cast such a sharp, unsparing gaze on Muslims everywhere, and in my part of the world in particular, or that those terror strikes in America would lead to war in the country next door to mine, Afghanistan, or that Pakistan would be caught in the crosshairs of a conflict that would be dubbed the War on Terror but seems very much at times to be a war on Islam.

That fall, Pakistan convulsed with popular protest. There were some who cheered the attacks in America. There were many more who protested Pakistan President General Pervez Musharraf's ties with Washington; as civilian deaths from American-led air raids in Afghanistan mounted, many would accuse Musharraf of having blood on his hands.

Musharraf had seized power from Nawaz Sharif in a bloodless coup on the twelfth of October 1999. Like Pakistan's three military rulers before him, Musharraf claimed that his armed forces had stepped in so that democracy would flourish in Pakistan. The United States had denounced the coup, and they eyed Musharraf warily now. They also made their demands clear. They wanted access to Pakistan's border posts, as well as air bases for launching air strikes in Afghanistan. The American administration also demanded that Musharraf crack down on the domestic expressions of support for 9/11. In case any in Pakistan had missed the threat implicit in Washington's "with us or against us" message, U.S. Deputy Secretary of State Richard Armitage reportedly spelled it out. In September 2006, Musharraf told the CBS News program *60 Minutes* that in the run-up to the war in Afghanistan, Armitage had delivered a stark warning to Pakistan's Director of Intelligence should Pakistan fail to cooperate: "Be prepared to be bombed. Be prepared to go back to the Stone Age."

Meanwhile, headlines in our newspaper announced the identities and nationalities of the 9/11 hijackers. They told us, too, that the United States was setting its sights on Taliban and al Qaeda fighters in Afghanistan, which meant one thing: war loomed. The only question was when. Our front page carried updates of the Afghan Taliban's kidnapping of a British reporter, Yvonne Ridley, on the twenty-eighth of September, and of her continued captivity. I recall thinking at the time that the Taliban and al Qaeda had done more than just hijack innocents; they had hijacked Islam, as well. I feared that this distorted view of an entire religion would come to dominate foreign press reports of it—and thus define it. As reports about anthrax attacks in America made headlines in Pakistan, I cringed at the inevitability, given the tenor of the day, that the culprit should be assumed to be a Muslim. "Muslim," I noted, was fast becoming shorthand for "terrorist."

President Musharraf was pulled in opposing directions. On one side were the voices, growing louder and more numerous, opposing his cooperation with the United States. On the other side was the American government, with its demands for that cooperation and the threat of cutting off Western aid, military equipment and access to loans from international financial institutions. In late September, he called a meeting of Pakistan's top newspaper editors to discuss the dilemma he faced and to solicit their advice and support. Musharraf often held such meetings on important issues with editors to share sensitive information off the record. It was his attempt at transparency, but also his intention to tame criticism of the policies he made in the name of national security. His meeting with the editors after 9/11 was part of this strategy.

My husband and his father attended the meeting with Musharraf, and that evening at dinner they told me that Musharraf expressed exasperation over how best to serve Pakistan's interests. He worried about the opposition and the threat they posed to his tenure in office. He worried, too, that if he didn't go along with the United States, Pakistan's long-time foe, India, would offer its air bases to the Americans and amass its army along Pakistan's borders.

It was not this story unfolding in Pakistan and across its northwest border, however, or the specter of America's War on Terror that would be my focus. It was the "women's pages," a section of the newspaper that, with its features about celebrities and fashion and recipes, I had never read. From the start of my marriage, whenever I raised a criticism about the section's content or its portrayal of women, my father-in-law had the same reply: "Instead of complaining about it, why don't you come do something about it." I had at last agreed. In the wake of 9/11, as the world fixed its gaze with increasing intensity on Muslims and their faith, the section's lack of substance and relevance seemed to me to be especially glaring. I felt that I would not be able to stand it if the sum total of my day's work amounted to the journalistic equivalent of cotton candy—stories whipped and spun for fleeting delectation. I had spent the previous two years teaching a syllabus heavy with heroines of complex, independent natures; now I was meant to start overseeing content that assumed nothing of the kind about its intended readers. Zia knew me well; when he asked me to become editor of that section, he must have known that I'd venture in with a machete, not a scalpel.

Against the backdrop of terrorism and war, geopolitical endgames and upheaval on Pakistan's domestic front, the women's pages marched blithely on. In its photoshopped microcosm, there was no war, no collateral damage, no twisted interpretation of Islam to justify violence. Instead, there were airy morsels about the glamorous lives of two favorite Lollywood—the L is for Lahore—actresses, Reema and Meera. Fashion spreads featured handbags that could be had for a week's salary, as well as the latest in kameez and culottes. A page that offered readers interpretations of their dreams made me blush, not in the way a Freudian interpretation might have, but for the pure ridiculousness of it. And a recipe section offered tips for how to achieve perfectly thin, perfectly crisp jalebi, circles of deep fried wheat flour soaked in sugar syrup, a national favorite.

After a month observing the way various newspaper departments ran and worked with each other, I assumed my editor's post in October. A week into my new role, what the United States would call Operation Enduring Freedom, the war in Afghanistan, had begun. The front page on Monday, the eighth of October, carried news of the first air strikes on Kabul the previous day. As our paper printed images of the bodies of Afghan children killed by American bombs, Pakistani popular outrage grew. On the twenty-eighth of October, more than 50,000 members of the far-right religious party Jamaat-e-Islami gathered on the Mall Road, very near to our newspaper headquarters in Lahore. Eighty-nine civilians, including nine children, had been killed in airstrikes across three Afghan villages the day before. The protesters decried what they called Musharraf's complicity in those deaths.

Another voice of dissent emerged. Gulbuddin Hekmatyar, the leader of Afghanistan's Hizb-e-Islami party, an Islamic extremist group, issued a plea to Islamic countries not to join the War on Terror. Our newspaper, like those across Pakistan, carried Hekmatyar's plea. Religious extremist parties that had long been sidelined and given little credence beyond a zealous fringe began to gain in popularity. Pakistan would find out precisely to what extent after national elections that would take place one year hence. Even in the autumn of 2001, however, it was clear: In the struggle to control the message about the War on Terror and Pakistan's involvement in it, the religious right was finding traction with a disgusted people.

As protests raged in Lahore that twenty-eighth of October, in eastern Pakistan tensions over the war found a deadly outlet. Six masked men riding three motorcycles descended on St. Dominic's Church in Bahawalpur and opened fire with AK-47 assault rifles, killing one guard stationed outside before storming the church. Inside, the gunmen barred the doors and opened fire on the gathering of Protestant worshipers, killing 15 of them, including children who were at prayer. Survivors reported that the gunmen declared that Pakistan would become a graveyard of Christians to avenge deaths in Afghanistan.

Word of the attack reached our newsroom quickly. Even before it was known that at least two of the gunmen had ties to the outlawed Sunni organization Lashkar-e-Jangvi, it was understood that Islamic extremists had retaliated for the air strikes on Afghanistan by killing their own people for worshiping a different God. I ran to Ednan's office and found him holding his head in his hands, his posture of defeat.

The next day, Ednan published an editorial entitled "Whose Horrific Act Was This?" I had never been more proud of my husband. By standing up to the murderers, he was putting himself at risk. More than that, and the source of my pride, is that he was putting *Khabrain*'s hundreds of thousands of readers on notice:

This attack was not Islam, and these murderers did not deserve to call themselves Muslims.

Two days after the massacre at Bahawalpur, on the thirtieth of October, Ednan and I presided over a forum at the *Khabrain* headquarters in Lahore. We had invited Christian community leaders, including the Bishop of Lahore, to join us to discuss the violence and to express Muslim solidarity with them and with Pakistanis of all faiths. Simultaneous forums took place at *Khabrain* bureaus in Peshawar, Multan, Karachi and Islamabad.

At the forum in Lahore, Ednan cited a passage from the Qur'an in which the Prophet Muhammad, praise be upon him, exhorts Muslim soldiers entering Mecca to shed no blood, to harm no property, and to aggress no one unless in self-defense, even though Muslim followers had been slain there by the Prophet's opponent, Abu Sufyan. "He who enters Abu Sufyan's house would be safe, he who shuts the door upon himself would be safe, and he who enters the sacred mosque would be safe," the Prophet, praise be upon him, decreed.* The merciful messenger of God had forgiven the faults of even his worst enemy. In citing the passage, Ednan was making clear that the violence carried out at St. Dominic's in the name of Islam was, in fact, a pure violation of it and the Prophet's will. "Fight in God's cause against those who fight you, but do not overstep the limits," Muhammad, praise be upon him, says. "God does not love those who overstep the limits."†

MEANWHILE, I WAS LAYING the groundwork for my section of *Khabrain* as a niche for articles that made for tough but eye-opening, and also inspiring, reading. I wanted the women's pages

---

*Sirat e Ibn Hisham, *Biography of the Prophet*, Vol. II (Lahore: Idara e Islamiyat, 1998), p. 409.
†*The Qur'an: A New Translation*, trans. M. A. S. Abdel Haleem (New York: Oxford University Press, 2010), 2:190, p. 21.

to become a force for improving the lives of women. In a concession to the business side of the paper, which derived revenue from the features, I preserved some entertainment news, the dream interpretation page and the occasional recipe. What mattered to me, however, was that there would be no more airbrushing the lives of women.

I sought to balance our content: There were plights to expose, but there was also power to celebrate. I commissioned and also wrote profiles of noteworthy women, such as Dr. Attiya Innayatullah, a federal minister with expertise in population and demographics whom I first met when I interviewed her for television, and Shaheen Atiq-ur-Rehman, a literacy activist and provincial minister. We also profiled authors, entrepreneurs and other women whose lives offered models for what girls and women could achieve. My goal was that the women's pages should reflect the spectrum of realities for women and girls in Pakistan. Build awareness on the one hand, spark aspiration on the other.

Among my small staff, two women in particular proved willing allies in this work. Huma Sadaf was young and ambitious and just beginning her journalism career. That she was a gentle, sensitive soul was reflected in her delicate features, framed by a graceful hijab, and in the refined way she had of expressing herself in both written and spoken form. Attiya Zaidi was my newspaper veteran. Tall and slim and with features as strong as her personality, Zaidi was in her mid-forties and could have taught a master class in not taking no for an answer. If Huma Sadaf was my sweet-faced but capable ingénue, Attiya Zaidi was my seasoned nonsense detector.

One afternoon, we came up with the idea to host forums, free of charge and open to the public, to discuss populations, such as prostitutes and eunuchs,* who rarely received attention

---

*Known in the subcontinent as *hijras*, eunuchs are born male and identify as female. Some eunuchs were born with ambiguous genitalia; others have been castrated for

that wasn't prurient or condemning. We also wanted to examine the lives of women in contemporary Pakistani society, with a particular emphasis on the cultural restrictions that remained in place thanks to the Hudood laws, holdovers from Zia-ul-Haq's military dictatorship that had as their focus—obsession, I would venture—the total suppression of the rights of women. I sought immediately to recruit Ednan, my editor, toughest critic and staunchest backer, to support our efforts in this expansive new editorial direction. Armed with my team's ideas, I went straight to his office across the hall from mine one afternoon in late October.

I don't suppose that many women would welcome having a husband double as their boss, but this was not a concern of mine. I felt on such equal footing with my husband, and we shared such mutual respect, that I expected the ease of our private rapport to extend naturally into the workplace. It did. So did our habit of teasing each other, which we did as an expression of affection, but also as a corrective for the odd moment when self-righteousness or some other annoying tendency threatened to make one or the other of us unbearable.

I knew, then, what to expect that first day when I pitched our ideas along with several stories that I wanted to cover: Ednan clutched his head in his hands. As he did so, I indulged in a moment of admiring him. In the afternoon light that poured in from the windows of his office, his light brown hair and eyes looked almost golden. As I sat there that afternoon, I realized how rare it was that five years, two children and two unrelenting full-time jobs later, he could still distract me in that way.

---

medical or social reasons; still others are men who identify as women. There are an estimated 300,000 *hijras* in Pakistan, where they lead marginalized lives. They piece together livings by dancing at weddings and other ceremonies, offering blessings in exchange for money and gifts. Many eunuchs resort to begging and prostitution.

I read from my notepad the stories and subsequent forums that I wanted my reporters to pursue:

- Women incarcerated for zina—adultery—in Lahore's central prison, Kot Lakhpat, and the conditions for female prisoners there
- Prostitution in Lahore's famous red-light area, the Heera Mandi
- Eunuchs, their fight for legal recognition and their struggle to avoid lives of begging and prostitution
- Reports of child prostitution near Data Ganj Bakhsh, Pakistan's most important Sufi shrine
- Subliminal advertising that demeans women

As Ednan listened, head in his hands, he groaned as though in terrible agony. He was teasing me, but only partially. When I finished reciting my list, he said, "Oh, Humaira! But why are you so obsessed with violence and exploitation?" I crossed my arms across my chest and fixed my most defiant gaze on him. One advantage of being married to the man in charge: the ability to speak volumes without saying a word.

It was classic Ednan. "Lighten up!" he'd admonish me from time to time. But this wasn't one of my somber moods; this was the direction in which I planned to take the women's section of *Khabrain*. In spite of Ednan's feigned exasperation, I knew that I could count on his support. He knew better than to tell me no—I would only dig in harder. And I knew better than to rush things; I had to give Ednan time to embrace the ideas, not just resign himself to them.

I listened as he expressed his concerns. "These are very controversial and sensitive issues," he said, taking care not to sound dismissive.

In his opinion, the nature of the stories that I proposed called for the sensitivity of a female reporter, but it was out of the question that the paper could send a woman into the kinds of places where the reporting would have to be done. Even in the twenty-first century, Pakistani society restricts the movement of its women. If it were a threat to a woman's honor to be seen riding a bicycle along a city street, for example, or for girls to walk unaccompanied to school lest they be subjected to leering men en route, how could the newspaper send a woman by herself into a red-light zone? It was a conundrum I could not imagine any of my contemporaries in the Western press facing.

Ednan proposed a compromise: Male reporters would accompany the female reporters, but the women would write the stories.

I agreed, even though I knew precisely which female reporters I would send without a chaperone. If Ednan had underestimated the toughness of some on my staff, I hadn't. Attiya Zaidi was more than capable of doing the work. No-nonsense and utterly self-assured, she was so formidable that I'd give any man who dared impede her movements a medal for bravery. In order to get what I wanted—women's pages with depth and relevance, and work that held my interest—I knew I would have to bend, however. Attiya would be accompanied in her investigations by a male reporter (even if who was chaperoning whom might remain in question).

How well this early lesson in bargaining with men for even modest freedoms for women would serve me one day in parliament! But then, the notion of a life in politics was not even a twinkle in my eye.

CHAPTER SIX

Two Pakistans

IT IS WRITTEN in the Qur'an that injustice to a single soul is injustice to the whole of humanity. " ... if anyone kills a person ... it is as if he kills all mankind, while if any saves a life it is as if he saves the lives of all mankind."* This simple but profound notion informs my work. During my first months at the newspaper, however, I could not have foreseen how it would test me to translate that belief into action.

My overhaul of the women's section well under way, by late 2001 I turned my attention to *Khabrain*'s languishing Helpline, an editorial feature that invited readers from all over the country to air their grievances, report their plights and seek our paper's help in getting justice. *Khabrain*'s motto: "Wherever there is injustice, *Khabrain* is there." My father-in-law's vision was to make *Khabrain* the newspaper for the everyman and every-woman of Pakistan. The Helpline was a natural extension of that vision, a kind of outlet of last resort for those who either had no other options or had exhausted better ones. On a typical day at our Lahore headquarters alone, the Helpline received twenty-five to thirty letters, phone calls or drop-in visits from readers. It was the same for our bureaus all over the country,

---

The Qur'an, trans. Haleem, 5:32, p. 71.

from Islamabad and Muzzafarabad in the north to Multan and Faisalabad in Punjab Province, and Karachi in the south.

There was just one problem: More people sought help than *Khabrain* had staff to receive them—few wanted to spend their days listening to victims' woes. Every day from the window of my office, I saw queues of people who had come for an audience and wondered how many of them were being turned away. When stories did make it to beat reporters for verification, the absence of a protocol for handling their follow-up and investigation meant that many stories fell through the cracks. I worried that the paper wasn't living up to its mission to be the voice for the voiceless, and I expressed this concern to Zia. I should have known that not only would he agree with me, he'd put me in charge!

I began spending three hours at a time meeting with people who sought the Helpline's assistance. I considered the work a practical form of prayer, a way to put the tenets of my faith into action. Some cases were straightforward enough: a tap switched off by a spiteful landlord, say, or complaints that local civil services, from the power development authority to the police, demanded bribes to do their jobs. Others were not straightforward at all, particularly if they implicated powerful officials in wrongdoing. I referred those cases, such as one that ultimately tied the Secretary of Social Welfare to an embezzlement scandal, directly to Zia, who had the political connections and the clout to investigate, as well as the know-how to brook reprisal, when it inevitably came.

I brought cases that involved women, girls, and the rural poor to the women's pages. As my staff negotiated a new volume and kind of work, I developed a system for classifying the cases and coordinating the follow-up reporting with *Khabrain*'s eight bureaus and one hundred correspondents across Pakistan. In time, the Helpline went from the paper's most neglected department to the niche for which it is still known.

The more time I spent listening to the stories of the aggrieved, the more I realized how little I really knew about Pakistan beyond my tidy, privileged corner of it. What I had understood at an intellectual level I came to know at a visceral one: that swaths of Pakistani culture sanctioned the inhumane treatment of its women and girls—and, in many cases, boys. While this was a cultural practice based in clan and tribal culture, Islam was often evoked by perpetrators in their own defense. As I would come to understand, the misperception of Islam as a religion that permits and even calls for certain abuses is not only widespread in the Western world; among the populations of Pakistan's tribal regions, where adherence to tribal tradition prevails, practices such as honor killings and revenge rapes are so common, they are customs. If Pakistan's law enforcement agencies are ineffectual in urban areas where literacy rates and income levels are higher, in tribal regions, law enforcement isn't even recognized. Tribal councils set laws and determine punishments, and the question of what is or isn't prescribed in the Qur'an is moot in a population that cannot read it. In the tribal regions, the illiteracy rate is 71 percent for men and 97 percent for women.* Islam is not to blame for the crimes against women and children that are carried out in its name; ignorance is. A succession of encounters with victims of violence and those on the losing side of Pakistan's wealth-tilted economy revealed to me the depth of the misunderstanding of Islam so prevalent in the tribal areas.

The first such case came in early December, when the Helpline received a third-party tip: A young woman had sold one of her kidneys. I was aware of organ-selling in Pakistan, but the particular details of the woman's story were entirely new and

---

*Owen Bennett Jones, *Pakistan: Eye of the Storm*, 3rd ed. (New Haven: Yale University Press, 2009), p. 27.

shocking to me: She had sold the organ to get out of debt with a predatory moneylender, who was pressuring her for more money still.

The woman's name was Rehana. She and her husband, Hanif, were from Mandi Bahauddin, a district in northeastern Punjab, halfway between Islamabad to the north and Lahore to the south. In two installments, the couple had borrowed 175,000 rupees to pay for Hanif's sister's wedding. The loans' total before interest amounted to approximately US$2,700.

Like many in Pakistan whose only option is to turn to private moneylenders, Rehana and Hanif could not read the contract to which they had agreed; in lieu of a signature, they had marked the document with their ink-stained thumbs. They understood neither the terms of their arrangement nor how compound interest would swell their debt. In fact, the couple had unwittingly agreed to a rate of 100 percent interest, to be raised in the event of a late or missed payment to 140 percent. When the note came due, Rehana and Hanif were blindsided by the amount they owed, 430,000 rupees, or approximately $6,800. The lenders, a feudal family named Chaudhry with significant landholdings in the region and a history of predatory lending with violent outcomes, offered them a stark choice: Repay in full plus interest, or be beaten.

Rehana and Hanif's circumstances revealed not only the extremes to which economic hardship forces many in Pakistan to go, but also the readiness of a criminal network to exploit people like them. That the Qur'an forbids interest-based lending is a fact conveniently ignored by unscrupulous lenders who know well that the illiterate populations they prey on have never read the Prophet's teachings for themselves and are thus not aware of the prohibition. Even if prospective borrowers do know that "God . . . has forbidden usury,"* however, poverty lends itself

---

*The Qur'an, trans. Haleem, 2:276, p. 32.

to a desperate math. As would become clear, Rehana and Hanif were hardly the only ones engaged in the calculus of straitened circumstances.

I coordinated our Lahore and Islamabad bureaus' reporting of the case and was startled by one detail in particular that emerged: A well-respected hospital was at the center of Rehana's story. The revelation that Jinnah Memorial Hospital in Rawalpindi had arranged for the surgery and the sale of Rahana's kidney—thus acting as a kind of organ broker—was a bombshell. As the third point in a triangle that also included moneylenders and destitute borrowers, Jinnah Memorial Hospital was, then, complicit in Rehana's ordeal.* I realized that hers could not be an isolated case and urged our reporters to keep digging.

Rehana and Hanif's story went from being one of local interest to one of national importance. By the time *Khabrain* published a front-page account in all editions of the paper on the eleventh of December 2001, our reporters in Lahore and Islamabad exposed not only the couple's plight and the moneylenders' deceitful and intimidating tactics, but also a thriving black market for organs operating out of one of the country's best hospitals. The damning article led to investigations of both the moneylenders, who finally stopped harassing Rehana and her husband, and the hospital administration.

Pakistan would not outlaw organ-selling until 2007, by which point the country would already be a major destination for "transplant tourism," its hospitals and shady clinics serving as bazaars for wealthy foreigners willing to pay for what they could not buy outright in their own countries: healthy organs. It turned out that Rehana was just among the first to reveal what she had done, and why. As breadwinner, Hanif could not afford the downtime from surgery, so the sacrifice fell to Rehana, com-

---

*The hospital has since changed owners and management, and there is neither evidence nor suspicion that this practice continues there today.

pelled to sell a part of her body to get the couple out of debt. In coming years, I would meet similarly indebted women faced with the inhuman prospects of selling their bodies or, worse, those of their children. The awareness that such harrowing choices should be the consequences of poverty became the seed of my future legislation to ban lending that ensnares the poor and makes pawns of their dignity.

My optimist's heart beat with less conviction after those first months on the Helpline. I felt that my ignorance of certain hard realities made me an unwitting accomplice to them, and it weighed on me. At the same time, the more I learned, the dimmer my view of humanity grew. Ednan tried his best to lift my twin burdens of guilt over what I didn't know and despond over what I did. At home in the evenings, he would cajole me to join him on the couch. "You are so tired," he would say. "Put your feet up and come with me to Middle-earth!" The first movie in the *Lord of the Rings* trilogy was out on DVD, and the second had just arrived in theaters. Ednan was obsessed with Tolkien, a rare divergence in our literary tastes. I envied his capacity to leave work at work and escape for a few hours into a fantasy realm. "Come, my sweet," he would say. "You can't save all of the world tonight." Even when I humored him and joined him in front of the television, my mind churned over the details of Helpline cases in progress.

IN MARCH 2002, Ednan suggested that I accompany him on a work trip to Multan, in the southern reaches of the Punjab. He had to interview some prospective hires for the newspaper's bureau there, and he told me that he wanted my help in vetting candidates. I saw right through the pretext; he wanted to offer me a diversion, an antidote to my weary-making first months on the job.

Ednan knew that I loved Multan, a city famous for its mosques and shrines. Perhaps he hoped that time in the City of Saints, so named for the abundance of hallowed Sufis that hailed from there, would return me to my core view of the world as a place in which people are inherently good.

We so rarely traveled on our own in those days, with Nofal and Fajr still so little. My mother teased me that they would survive a few days with their grandmother, who had, after all, managed to raise four children without leaving them with scars literal or figurative. Besides, she said, she would be delighted to have them. I launched a few feeble protestations that I really ought to stay in Lahore for work, but I hoped even more than Ednan did that time away with him would refresh my spirit.

The day after our arrival, as Ednan and I sat in the office of Aleem Chaudhry, the Multan bureau's resident editor and a close friend of Ednan's father, a staff reporter named Masood interrupted. "There's a sad old man here with his teenaged daughter," Masood explained. "I think it might be a case for the Helpline to consider."

"Come on then," Ednan said to the young reporter, who led us to the pair in question. Among the mostly empty reporters' carrels we saw an elderly man clad in a kurta, a long cotton tunic, and a dhoti, an unstitched garment tied at the waist and resembling a sarong—garb favored by men in rural regions of the Punjab. He wore a turban fastened tightly around his head, and I saw that he had sad eyes that peered out from under immense bushy eyebrows. Next to him sat a young girl, her head bowed and covered by a tattered dupatta, or long head scarf.

Ednan and I sat down across a small table from the old man. The young girl with him never once lifted her gaze from the floor. The old man, a widower, told us that his name was Ilyas. As he began to speak, his voice quavered and tears filled his red-rimmed eyes. "I'm a poor farmer with a small patch of land about an hour from here," he said in Seraiki, the dialect that is spoken in southern Punjab. It is very close to Punjabi, but more mellifluous. "I have come to ask you for help in getting justice for my daughter, Parveen."

Ilyas began to weep. He explained that he had four sons and two daughters, the eldest of whom had been married off to a landowning man from their tribe a few years prior. When she fell ill a few months back, the village hakim—homeopath—had not been able to cure her, and she passed away. Not long after, Ilyas's son-in-law, Munawar, appealed to Ilyas for Parveen's hand in marriage. In the ledger book of his loss, Munawar had determined that he was owed a wife.

"I refused," Ilyas continued, his lips quivering. "I told him that my daughter was only fifteen and too young to be married." At that, Munawar went away. "He didn't look very happy," Ilyas said. "Neither were we, because my daughter had just died. Instead of trying to alleviate our grief, this man was just adding to it."

One day, when Ilyas had gone to a nearby town, Munawar abducted Parveen. "He held her captive for three weeks," Ilyas said, "and he violated her. He raped my poor child. He beat her up. He cut off her hair. He treated her like an animal."

Ednan shifted in his seat. We both knew that we had to do something. The old man, who had not taken his eyes from Ednan's, fixed his gaze on me now. "Please help me," he said. "I am a poor man, but I need justice for my daughter." He sobbed, and as he did, he removed his turban and placed it at my feet.

I was taken aback. Across the subcontinent, the turban—pagar—is a symbol of pride and honor. The man's gesture signaled his belief that he had lost both. Ednan bent forward, picked up and dusted off the turban and returned it to Ilyas. As he did so, he put his hands on his shoulders and said, "Your honor and pride are intact. We will do everything we can to bring this culprit to justice."

While we were meeting with Ilyas and Parveen, the newsroom filled with reporters beginning their workdays. Ednan gathered several of them and doled out reporting assignments. He planned team coverage for an article about Ilyas and his daughter. He assigned two reporters to return with the pair to the police station where the officers on duty had refused to file a First Investigation Report for the crime. "Don't leave until they have done so," Ednan instructed them. Meanwhile, Ednan enlisted Aleem Chaudhry to follow up with—and keep pressure on—senior police officials working the case to arrest the man in question.

I learned so much watching my husband that day. I was still figuring out how best to wrangle all the moving parts of turning around a story on a tight deadline, from managing a staff to making assignments. Ednan did it instinctively. He got the best from his reporters and editors by being at once demanding and authoritative, encouraging and supportive. I would strive to emulate his example and discover that he made it look easy.

The matter well in hand, Ednan returned to the work of hiring new staff for the Multan bureau. Two days later, he received an update from one of the reporters working the case. "There has been a development," the young reporter said. "We may need to go to the old man's village because the panchayat there is reportedly considering the accused's offer of a diyat."

In other words, the panchayat, or tribal council, was brokering a payoff between the accused, the son-in-law, and the accuser, the father-in-law. In Islamic law, a diyat represents a mutual decision by opposing parties to choose forgiveness over vengeance. That forgiveness is, in essence, bought. Such an arrangement can be effective in the case of accidental death, when the aggrieved might otherwise feel compelled to revenge. Nowhere is it written in Islamic law, however, that a diyat can be offered in the case of rape.

A common tribal practice, payment of a diyat has come, in recent decades, to be used cynically. Ednan and I feared that in

Ilyas's case, it was the equivalent of shut-up money. Worse, Ilyas had reportedly agreed to marry Parveen to Munawar once the diyat was paid.

This news surprised us. The farmer was considering marrying his daughter off to the man who had brutalized her—for compensation? What of the justice for which he had pled? We were off, wending our way in one car while a team of reporters followed in another, clouds of dust emerging in our wakes along the dirt tracks that led us to the village. After an hour or so, we arrived to find that we didn't have a moment to spare: the panchayat had already begun to assemble.

For Ednan, the scene that we took in through the car windows was nothing new. With experience reporting from all over Pakistan, he knew well that it took less than an hour's drive to find the Third World underbelly beyond every city's borders. The village consisted of a scattering of tiny mud and brick houses, some of which were no more than huts. There was no electricity. I didn't see a single woman; presumably, they were all indoors, tending to domestic chores while the men of the village gathered outdoors for the panchayat.

The men wore kurtas, dhotis and white turbans. The six older men who formed the village council sat on charpoys, four-legged hand-strung beds common across the subcontinent. The younger men, who were not part of the panchayat but were permitted to witness its proceedings, squatted on the ground across from their elders. Neither Ilyas nor his daughter was present. Ednan asked me to wait in the car, a fact that I fumed over as I sat idling in air-conditioned comfort, even as I understood that a woman's presence at such a gathering might not be welcome. Because a sexual assault was among the crimes in question, Ednan needed to ascertain how conservative the group was before presuming that I could join them. Many considered it inappropriate to discuss such matters in front of a woman.

The panchayat had been told to expect Ednan and his team's

arrival. Some of the men rose to greet their visitors, and two of the younger men disappeared behind a mud and brick house and returned with a charpoy, which they offered to Ednan and two reporters. I noticed that Ednan was looking at me as he sat down and leaned over to speak with a village elder. A moment later, Ednan gestured to one of his reporters to ask me to join them. After the stress of dealing with a village council, I suppose he realized that it would be a very long ride back to Multan, indeed, if he had, then, to deal with a furious wife who had been relegated to the sidelines.

I secured my dupatta over my head. I wore it out of respect; in those days, I was not yet in the habit of covering my head on a regular basis. That would come years later. Before I stepped out of the car, I also wrapped a chador around me, for modesty. The men stopped talking and watched respectfully as I approached to join Ednan on the charpoy. They were very polite and stood to greet me warmly.

Where abject poverty spares no one, tribal councils such as this one consisted of villagers who were distinguished not by wealth, but by other measures. In this case, age conferred status. The council's head appeared to be the oldest man in the group. He clasped a walking stick in one hand, and as he began speaking in Punjabi, the assembled men, save a few of the younger ones who stole intermittent glances in my direction, gave him their full attention. He explained that in recompense for the abduction and rape of Ilyas's daughter, the perpetrator offered a diyat of 125,000 rupees—approximately $1,270 at the time. The man also agreed to marry Parveen, who would be unmarriageable given her stolen honor.

As I followed the proceedings, I felt a queasy tension building within me. A group of men presided over by one in particular had determined, in essence, the price and grim future for an already traumatized fifteen-year-old girl. What kind of life would she have to look forward to? How on earth could her assault be forgiven with rupees, and how could her father possibly accept that money? I felt that the tribal elder couldn't have been more dispassionate in his decree if he had been deciding the value of livestock. I held my breath for whatever he might say next.

"The aggrieved party has accepted," he said with a finality that made it clear that he did not welcome further discussion of the matter. *What have we come for?* I asked myself. Panicked, I looked at Ednan for an answer. That is when the tribal elder, having read the look on my face, addressed me directly. "You from the city need to understand some basic facts about village life," he said. "You all are journalists and probably see a story in this situation. What you don't understand is that if incidents like this are publicized in the press, our lives are thrown into disarray. Rivalries that could otherwise be handled flare up and spiral out of control."

He gestured toward the men who sat impassively by. "We are the elders of this community. We have decided that the best way forward is reconciliation between the two parties. We understand that what happened to that young child is criminal and very unfortunate, but if we do not make that man marry her, there is no guarantee that anyone else will."

One of the younger men squatting on the ground sneezed. The tribal elder glanced in his direction without really looking at him. "You need to understand," he continued, turning his gaze back to Ednan this time, "that if we don't marry her to the man who assaulted her, there is every chance that, at some point in time, she will elope with another. That will bring more shame on this community and could incite a bloodbath, because someone from this village will want to seek revenge from the person who dared to steal one of our women."

He tapped his cane on the ground for emphasis. "That is why we, the panchayat, have decided that the father of that girl will receive a diyat from the man who treated his child so unfairly. You need to understand that our decision is not focused on ensuring that the old man receives financial compensation alone. Our decision focuses on the need to restore the honor of his family, his entire clan and this community. Our decision is based on the need to make the rapist pay for his actions. We believe that the strongest punishment for him is to make that young woman his honor." I noted that already he had stopped referring to her as a girl.

With that, he stood, his lanky frame and turbaned head cutting a striking silhouette against the setting sun. "I hope you understood everything I said," he said, turning to address our group as we got to our feet. "You journalists will return to your world, and we will remain to deal with the long-term effects of blood and revenge if we do not make the right decisions in the interests of this community."

He instructed the younger men to remove the charpoys. I stood by as the men in our group shook hands with him and the rest of the village council. Once they had dispersed, I leaned in to Ednan and whispered, "We have to find Ilyas."

A bit of asking around led us to a young boy who knew where to find Ilyas's tiny mud hut, which was about a five-minute walk to the outskirts of the village. Outside, we found the old man sitting alone on a jute stool called a moora. He tugged on a hookah, inhaling deeply of the water-diffused tobacco. He looked forlorn. Seeing him, I felt like crying.

"Salam Alaikum," Ednan said in greeting. Peace to you. The man looked up through glassy, listless eyes. One of our reporters knelt and offered him a cigarette, which he declined. It was only when I came into his line of vision that he acknowledged my presence. I asked him if I might speak with his daughter, and he gestured to the mud hut behind him.

I entered. In the absolute darkness of the hut, it took several seconds for my pupils to adjust so that I could see. When I could, I saw that the space was nearly empty except for a couple of charpoys. I made out a small form that was hunched and rocking back and forth on one of them. It was Parveen. I sat next to her and put my hand on her shoulder. She looked up at me and burst into tears. She clutched my chador and sobbed as I sat with my arms around her. After ten or so minutes, her body still twitching and her breath still uneven from hard crying, she rested her head on my shoulder. "I will speak with your father," I whispered to her. She nodded and let me go. I would wish later that I had not said anything; by doing so, I had given her false hope for a different outcome.

Back outside, I found Ednan and the reporters sitting cross-legged around the old man, who was still puffing on his hookah. "Why did you do this?" I asked in Punjabi, standing directly over him. "You had the chance to get justice and to see the culprit punished for what he did. Why did you agree to the diyat? Why are you selling your daughter?"

The old man didn't protest. He didn't even look at me. He spoke in the quiet monotone of surrender. "What could I have done?" he said. "I'm a poor man, very poor. You can see this is all I have, this bit of land you stand on. My daughter has been raped. My honor has been violated. I can't look anyone in the eye anymore. Now the same man who raped my daughter is offering me money and he says he will marry her. At least, this way, she will get his name.

"After a few years, no one will even talk about the shame that I suffered. I don't care about the money he is offering me. It will go to my daughter and to my sons, who are all very little. Their mother is dead. I will be able to feed my children with this money. You need to understand that no man will agree to marry her because she has been raped. I have accepted the diyat because I am afraid that if I die and she has no means, she will be forced into prostitution. I don't want her to suffer anymore. The panchayat cannot force anyone to marry her, except the man who violated her."

I tried to take in the convolutions of his reasoning. He spoke of his damaged honor, when just a few feet away sat his devastated daughter. And now he was sending her back for more? Tribal culture prizes honor above all and links that honor, like a currency's valuation to gold, to the chastity of its women and girls. It is an effective way to suppress them. Where virginity is gold, a raped virgin might as well be a prostitute for the dishonor she brings to her family, her clan, her village. Her plight is not factored into the equation, because her honor cannot be reclaimed.

I opened my mouth to speak, but Ednan caught my eye with a glance that said, *Leave it.* Ilyas had made up his mind. It dawned on me that he might have come to us not because he wanted to bring his son-in-law to justice, but because he knew that the threat of our involvement in the matter would force the panchayat to hatch a solution that benefited him. His daughter be damned? I did not know what to think, but in that moment I was overwhelmed by the possibility that this girl's own father might have used us and betrayed her.

After a few minutes of silence, Ednan said, "We are here if you decide to change your mind." There was no response. My last memory of Ilyas is of a broken man sitting alone in front of his mud dwelling, smoking his hookah.

I willed myself not to judge him. I could not know his pain or the weight that his decision would force him to carry. I could not know what it was to have one's choices decided by fear and survival. If Ilyas had chosen to avenge his daughter's rape, custom dictated that the other side would have to retaliate. Perhaps the specter of orphaning his children, or of losing one or more of them in a blood feud, made his only other option, accepting the diyat, preferable. With barely enough food to feed his family, Ilyas was a slave to his economic circumstances.

I asked myself what resistance Ilyas could have mounted, in a vacuum of economic security and the rule of law, to the panchayat's ruling. What resistance could the council itself have mounted to Munawar, the lone character in this story who possessed economic means? Had he bribed them?

What the panchayat considered justice I couldn't help but think of as a jettisoning of it. Because beyond that village, laws exist to punish kidnappers and rapists and to protect underage girls like Parveen from forced marriage. Beyond those laws, a higher authority still, as dictated in the Qur'an, forbids the treatment of women and girls as chattel. In that village, however, neither the law of the state nor the law of our shared faith, Islam, mattered.

I struggled to fit the panchayat's ruling and Ilyas's acceptance of it into a context where any of it became acceptable to me. I could not. My challenge, then, was to endeavor the next-best thing: to understand *their* context. Separate the sin from the sinner, the Qur'an says. In other words, venture understanding. I knew that if I could understand their thinking, then one day, perhaps, I might bring them or others like them around to understanding mine. Somewhere in that equation lay the prospect of changing minds.

On our drive back from the village, I thought of the tribal elder's admonishment about the divide between our worlds. I thought also of Rehana and Hanif. Their circumstances were different from Ilyas and Parveen's, but they were no less emblematic of that divide. I felt that we lived not only in different countries—the rural and the urban—but in different centuries. I felt that we lived in two Pakistans. To the divergent multitudes that exist within Pakistan—the rich and the poor, the educated and the illiterate, the believers and the zealots—could be added two more: the rural and the urban. It seems obvious to me now, but at the time, it felt like an epiphany.

OUR ATTENTION DIVERTED by Ilyas and Parveen's case, our projected three-day stay in Multan had turned into a longer one.

Ednan still had to wrap up the job interviews. I wanted to return to Lahore, but Ednan wanted me to stay. When his parents called to say that they were coming to Multan so that Zia and Aleem Chaudhry could discuss newspaper business, I asked them to bring our children along; I missed them terribly.

On our last day in the city, I convinced Ednan to take us to the shrine of Hazrat Bahauddin Zikriya, a twelfth-century Sufi whose mausoleum, with its blue ceramic tiles and soaring white cupola, is especially stunning. I looked forward to our visit there as a joyful counterpoint to the previous days' difficult reckonings.

I loved walking barefoot on the glazed tiles while, all around me, the faithful recited poetry and read aloud from the Qur'an. It is an ecstatic experience, and it is one that I particularly loved sharing with Ednan.

A man at the entrance sang a poem in Seraiki by another Sufi saint, Khawaja Ghulam Fareed:

> I lined my eyes with kohl
> I colored my lips with red gloss,
>   I decorated myself for love.
> I spent all my life scaring crows
>   but my beloved did not come.

My heart thumped to the rhythm of the earthen pitcher that the singer struck with a stone to keep time with the verse. As he did, I realized that poetry is embedded in the language of my culture, a gift from the Sufis. In the background, I could hear someone else singing.

> I wandered in the dry land
>   in desert and in woods and jungle,
>   I wandered for my love.
>   Never did I sleep well
>   Not for a moment,
> My fate did not give me the turn.

> With the name of Allah
> I uncovered my head
> And picked up the burden of love.

Hearing the passion in the singer's warble, it was clear to me that I was not the only worshiper intoxicated by being there.

Outside, Ednan was minding Fajr, who was in her stroller eating kulfi greedily—bribing her with sweets was our only way of keeping her in her seat for more than a few minutes on end. Nofal was feeding the pigeons, and I grabbed his hand and ran into the great flock to send them scattering up into the blue sky. Ednan laughed and called out, "Humaira! You are a bird yourself!"

I shouted back, "Yes! And I am flying! But am I a dove? A pigeon? An eagle?"

"You are my hansini!" Ednan shouted. It is the Urdu word that poets use for "swan," and it was one of his terms of affection for me.

I smiled at him as I stretched out my arms as though to take flight.

"Just don't fly away from me!" he called.

CHAPTER SEVEN

Bearing Witness

ON THE SIXTH of April 2002, President General Pervez Musharraf announced in a spirited and lengthy televised address that he would hold a referendum on his presidency, breaking his promise not to remain in office beyond the three-year term granted to him by Pakistan's Supreme Court. "I am not power hungry," he said. A referendum victory, though unconstitutional, would allow him to remain in power after the fall's general elections.

There was precedent, if not a reassuring one, for Musharraf's move: On the nineteenth of December 1984, General Zia-ul-Haq, who had deposed Zulfikar Ali Bhutto in a coup d'état during the summer of 1977, held a similar referendum to remain in power for another five years. Zia-ul-Haq had made Islam the centerpiece of his administration and the "Islamization" of civilian life in Pakistan his foremost goal. Pakistanis lived under martial law for eleven years with Zia-ul-Haq, whose Hudood Ordinances, enacted in February 1979, applied punishments decreed by the Qur'an to civilian transgressions. There was a narrow focus on sexual morality and behaviors, which aimed especially to punish and curtail the rights of women.*

---

*Islamist regimes the world over seek to control their people by first controlling women, and Zia-ul-Haq's Hudood Ordinances did just that. They gave cover to those who would invoke Islam to justify systematic injustices, especially violence against women. Thousands, the majority of them women, were jailed on trumped-up adultery

While Musharraf had no such agenda in mind, his announcement nevertheless undermined his pledge, delivered in the days immediately following his coup, that, "I will not allow the people to be taken back to the era of sham democracy, but to a true one. And I promise you I will InshAllah."

If Musharraf seemed untroubled by his flouting of democracy and the law, many others were not. Fifteen political parties, including the exiled Benazir Bhutto's PPP and the exiled Nawaz Sharif's PML-N, formed the Alliance for the Restoration of Democracy and called for a boycott of the voting. The Alliance argued, correctly, that Pakistan's president could be selected only by the elected members of the national and provincial assemblies and the senate, not by direct popular vote. Musharraf's move to extend his term would effectively place his presidency beyond the reach of those assemblies.

In a country with so well developed a tolerance for the moral failings, illegal moves and constitutional swerves of elected officials, Musharraf's referendum went ahead, on the thirtieth of April, in spite of the challenges to it. For all of his critics, there were as many, if not more, in Pakistan who were hopeful about his presidency. Unlike his predecessors, Musharraf came to power with a reform agenda. A top priority on it: to rid government bureaucracy of its rampant corruption. The memory of Benazir Bhutto and Nawaz Sharif's corruption-addled tenures caused many to embrace their new president as having the potential to be a vast improvement.

The sole ballot question that was put to voters: "For the survival of the local government system, establishment of democracy, continuity of reforms, end to sectarianism and extremism,

---

charges. Rape victims unable to meet the Qur'an's evidentiary requirement of four male eyewitnesses to their assault were convicted of fornication, which carried a punishment of lashings and hard labor in prison.

and to fulfill the vision of Quaid-e-Azam,* would you like to elect President General Pervez Musharraf as President of Pakistan for five years?" Musharraf secured the mandate that he sought.

The vote itself was widely criticized. Voter turnout numbers, said by Musharraf's people to be as high as 70 percent of Pakistan's 78 million eligible voters, were claimed by the opposition to be as low as 5 percent. There were no voter lists or constituencies, and there were few safeguards against fraud. Pakistan's Human Rights Commission reported instances of multiple voting, as well as pressure on state employees to go to the polls. Anyone who could prove his identity and age could vote at any of the 87,000 polling stations set up around the country. The opposition argued strenuously that Musharraf did not have popular support.

The controversy and doubt surrounding it notwithstanding, the referendum certified Musharraf's rule for another five years. It also alienated political friends and foes alike. Even those who had professed support for Musharraf's tenure and who believed that his goals were genuinely in Pakistan's best interest expressed concern that the referendum had weakened Musharraf, politically speaking. Now the President had only to hope that October's general elections would assure him the majority he would need to get anything done.

IN THE WAKE of the referendum and in the months preceding the October elections, Zia and Yasmine's home once again became a gathering place for politicians and other highly placed government officials. They discussed and debated Pakistan's

---

*Literally, "Great Leader," as Muhammad Ali Jinnah, the founding father of Pakistan, is commonly known. On the eleventh of August 1947, Jinnah delivered a speech laying out his vision for a forward-looking Pakistan, free from religious biases.

evolving political topography, as well as the motives of their President and whether or not his apparent comfort with reversing himself undermined his bold pronouncements about the future of democracy in Pakistan. All of it made for lively and diverting dinnertime theater, with his supporters and detractors alike wondering at what he might do next.

One evening that spring, when Ednan and I went downstairs to join Yasmine and Zia for dinner, we were pleased to find Farooq Leghari engaged in deep conversation with Zia. The old friends were in touch frequently, and it wasn't unusual that Leghari should visit, especially in the midst of an election season. Pakistan's former President broke off mid-sentence when he saw us and stood to greet us in his usual warm fashion.

Our fondness was mutual. I admired Leghari's elegance and intellect, and I appreciated that he always asked after our children and offered an amusing anecdote about his grandchildren. His lack of pretense and jovial mien made him excellent company, and Ednan and I looked forward to his joining us for dinner. On that occasion, however, it was clear that my father-in-law and his distinguished guest had matters to attend to in private. Ednan and I excused ourselves and sat down for dinner with Yasmine.

The day after Farooq Leghari's visit, I was meeting with Helpline staff in my office when my telephone rang. "Zia Sahib asks that you stop by his office when you have a spare moment," my assistant, Nauman Sheikh, said. "Okay," I said. "Please tell him to expect me in a few minutes."

My father-in-law was just wrapping up an editorial meeting in his office when I arrived. Once the last editor had exited, he asked me to close the door and got right down to business.

"Are you following what's happening politically?" he said.

I shrugged. "You know, Zia Sahib, that my interest in politics is cursory at best." In spite of the fact that we were family, I always referred to my father-in-law deferentially as "Zia Sahib," as everyone at *Khabrain* did.

Zia smiled. "That's what I thought you'd say," he said, peering at me over the top of his glasses. "But I think you should take a little more interest in political events that take place in this country."

I smiled and shrugged again. "With two children, the women's pages and the Helpline, I have little time for much else," I said.

Zia shuffled the papers on his desk. Without looking up, he asked what I knew about proportional representation. "There is talk of introducing it in parliament," he said.

I had listened as Zia and various dinner guests discussed Musharraf's proposal to introduce proportional representation, and I had read the editorials that our paper ran debating both Musharraf's motives for establishing the reserved seats and the merits of the seats themselves. There is little doubt that Musharraf sought to boost his popularity by advocating for women. I don't believe, however, that the impetus behind proportional representation was either that simple or that self-serving. Musharraf espoused a doctrine he called "enlightened moderation," the goal of which, in part, was to combat religious extremism and terrorism. He regarded women as peacemakers and, therefore, essential to helping do that. Musharraf also recognized that, at best, women in Pakistan are subjected to chauvinism; at worst, they endure physical and sexual violence. Political empowerment, he believed, is an essential step toward women's emancipation. Let women advocate for women's causes, he said, and change will come.

Because it was a matter relevant to the women of my country, I paid more attention to mentions of it than I did to most political developments. Proportional representation called for the setting aside of 17 percent of seats for women in both the national and provincial assemblies. The women would not be elected by popular vote, but would be nominated for a seat by their political parties.

"If I'm not mistaken," I said, "I believe that for every four and a half general seats, one would go to a woman."

Zia was pleased. "I couldn't have put it better myself," he said. "I was right: You are cut out for this."

"Cut out for what, Zia Sahib?" I said.

"Okay, this is serious," Zia began, pushing a file aside so he could lean forward. "You know that Farooq Leghari has started his own political party, Millat." Millat is Urdu for "unified." I nodded. I had read that in the paper recently.

"From what I've heard," Zia continued, "there are a number of pro-Musharraf political parties planning to form a union, the National Alliance. The Millat party is one of them. I assume you've heard of the Pakistan Muslim League-Quaid?"

I had. The PML-Q—"Quaid" refers to Muhammad Ali Jinnah, the founding father of Pakistan—counted a number of seasoned politicians among its ranks. Many of them were members of other parties. It didn't surprise me at all that Farooq Leghari, once Benazir Bhutto's staunchest ally, was lining up with the new administration. Leghari is from a long line of political pragmatists. After years of corruption under Bhutto and Nawaz Sharif, Pervez Musharraf, for all of his contradictions, represented the promise of accountability, transparency and change. Leghari had been in Pakistani politics long enough to know a promising candidate when he saw one, so he was throwing his lot in with him.

"Well, the PML-Q is widely favored to win the elections," Zia said. "The National Alliance plans to align with them and be part of the ruling coalition, if they win. Do you remember seeing Farooq Leghari last night?"

"I would hardly have forgotten seeing the former President of Pakistan sitting in your lounge, Zia Sahib," I said. Zia ignored my sarcasm.

"Well, Leghari and I discussed a number of things, most of which don't concern you," he said. "One thing does: Leghari wondered if I might want to nominate someone from my family for one of the reserved seats in the provincial assembly. I told him that I would, and I told him that I would propose your name."

I was completely caught off guard. "My name!" I said. "But, Zia Sahib, I know nothing about politics!"

Zia laughed out loud. "That's okay," he said. "Neither do any of this country's politicians." He explained that the intention of the reserved seats wasn't only to have a greater proportion of women in the parliament, but a better class of politician altogether. "They want women who are educated and articulate and who have a sense of purpose to represent their parties in parliament. I think you fit the bill," Zia said.

I thought perhaps he was pulling my leg. "Well, I don't know what to say, Zia Sahib," I said. "This is all a bit of a shock."

"You don't have to say anything just now," he said. "Take your time and think about it. But I believe that you would do a good job, and I'm going to recommend you to Leghari, anyway."

"I'm sorry," I said. "I just don't understand: Why me?"

"Because you are the one," Zia said. "And you have the potential."

As Zia saw it, becoming a Member of the largest and most influential provincial assembly in the country* would be a natural extension of the advocacy work that I had begun at the newspaper. As a legislator, I could tap the same desire for justice that

---

*Fifty-six percent of Pakistan's population resides in the Punjab, the province that feeds the nation, has the highest literacy rate and contributes the largest percentage of tax revenue to the federal government. The three other provincial assemblies are: the Provincial Assembly of Balochistan; the Provincial Assembly of Sindh; and the Khyber Pakhtunkhwa Assembly (formerly North-West Frontier Province). The role of provincial assemblies is threefold: to make laws; to manage the purse of the nation; and to keep checks and balances on the policies and practices of the government. Each assembly governs its own province and legislates on province-specific issues, though some laws passed in the Senate (the Upper House) and the National Assembly (the Lower House) of the federal government apply to the provinces, as well.

drove me as a journalist; I would have an opportunity to influence a legislative agenda that put Pakistan's most vulnerable at its center. Zia anticipated that the power to change laws, not just to write about and speak out against bad ones, would be a very good fit for me.

And what would my fellow Members of the Provincial Assembly make of a journalist in their ranks? My concern wasn't about whether or not I could occupy both worlds, journalism and politics, and keep their business separate. I knew that I could. My concern had to do with how, as a journalist from a newspaper that, since its inception, had been a perennial thorn in the side of whichever government was in power, I would be received—by fellow MPAs, but also by readers. Wouldn't both assume that I had sold out?

Zia had a ready response. Whenever the government, unhappy about *Khabrain*'s reporting, had blocked its subsidies, the newspaper's circulation had gone up. In other words, the people rewarded the paper for the stands it took. They appreciated that its journalists exposed corruption, held politicians accountable and reported their failures to the people. Zia told me that my presence in the parliament would signal to readers and to parliamentarians alike that I was an independent voice. *Khabrain*, in other words, would be my calling card, signaling that I would maintain a critical distance. Secretly, I wondered how I could lay claim to the paper's long-held anti-government stance by becoming a part of it.

I went straight to Ednan's office with this news. "He could have spoken to me first," Ednan said. He was irritated. "He might have asked my opinion about whether or not your name should be proposed." I balked at his presumption that, as my husband, he should hear first about a matter that involved me. Of course, should anything come of Zia's crazy proposition, it would have to be a joint decision, and in truth, I couldn't conceive of making such a move without Ednan's support. Still, Ednan's initial response struck me as a touch patriarchal, and I told him so. Both irked now, we agreed to let the idea sink in and our hackles descend before we discussed it further.

SUMMER WEATHER RUSHES THE CALENDAR in Lahore, arriving in early spring and enveloping the whole of the city in an unrelenting heat. When the rains come in July, the parched earth and all of its people respond like dry coals in a sauna under a fresh water bath: steam rises off of everything and everyone. Whatever relief the monsoons bring is fleeting; for the next two months, life takes on the feel of moving through a carwash. It is one long spell of pelting wet heat. It also becomes impossible to hang anything to dry.

That spring was one of the hottest I could remember. As the mercury rose to a record 113 degrees Fahrenheit in early May, and as the question of my political future hung heavy in the air, it began to feel as stifling inside our air-conditioned home as it was outside. No matter where I went, there seemed to be no escaping smothering heat of one kind or another.

Even my parents lost their typically cool heads when I raised the specter of becoming a politician. My father was still lamenting my departure from teaching, a profession he held in the highest esteem. I come from a family that views politicians as self-serving and pompous sycophants more interested in private gains than public good. Of course, in Pakistan, this opinion has plenty of examples to back it. When I discussed the prospect of joining the provincial parliament with my parents, it was the first time in my life that they told me they wished I would not do something. They feared that I would be compromised by association if I did. They had worked so hard to instill in me the values of honesty and integrity; what would happen to my disposition, they worried, after time spent in corrupt company? What would happen to my reputation?

I understood their unease, but as my frustration over the limits of what I could achieve as a journalist—even one with an activist agenda—mounted, I began to eye the political realm more hopefully. I still possessed enough youthful idealism that I saw it as the responsibility of politicians to improve the conditions of the people they serve. I had also come to believe that a political position might be the only way to achieve real reform. Time and again in my work on the Helpline, I'd encountered the twin obstacles of indifference and injustice; the only way around each, I thought, would be to change minds and laws.

All that being said, I still had reservations of my own. I wondered how I would be treated in the male bastion of the parliament, for one thing. Holding elected office was no guarantee of enlightenment, as my dealings with some male MPAs had taught me. I also worried about adding one more spinning plate to a life that already felt at times like a high-wire circus act.

Ednan expressed apprehension of his own. He anticipated that my independent nature and strong will would clash with the herd mentality required to succeed in the parliament. He worried, too, about what the pressures of the job would do to me. He already complained about my bringing Helpline work home; I didn't always lug the actual files with me, but I was rarely out from under the psychic weight of pending cases. There was also his concern about the spotlight's unsparing glare. Ednan worried that my activism and education would invite a harsh light and bring taunting and disrespect from those who preferred for women to have no voice or will of their own. I would be exposing myself to a potentially dangerous and demoralizing world, he said.

I paid heed to Ednan's caution, because my respect for him was as profound as my love. I saw the worry in his eyes, and I thought, *If he is raising an eyebrow, he must have good cause to do so.* At the same time, for years, I had been living and working inside my husband's four walls, in a manner of speaking, so I understood that a degree of Ednan's anxiety on my behalf had to do with his own fears about letting me go.

ONE AFTERNOON THAT MAY, Ednan and I were sitting in his second-floor office discussing how well my team at the women's pages had incorporated the Helpline content into the newly newsworthy section. I was crowing a bit, and teasing him, too, about his great fortune to have a flesh-and-blood, get-things-done kind of wife, and not, as I said that day, a lump of wax. It was my way of leading up to a request for a new hire.

I wanted Ednan's go-ahead to compile a database of four years' worth of *Khabrain* articles, beginning in the year 2000 and going forward, to 2003, that would provide statistics on violence against women and the law enforcement and judicial responses to that violence. In order to increase the effectiveness of our reporting on and responses to Helpline cases, I wanted to better understand the numbers and types of crimes that had been committed; whether occurrences increased or decreased over time; how often the police filed a First Investigation Report; what kind of investigative follow-up there had been; how many of the cases went to trial; and how many convictions had resulted.

"This sounds like very boring and tedious work, Humaira," Ednan said. "I doubt you will even find somebody willing to do it." I insisted that any ambitious intern keen on a career at *Khabrain* would leap at the chance. At that, he raised his usual objection.

"Why do you always have to focus on violence and crime?" he said, not pausing for a response. "Why do you have so much activism in you? Do you remember what your Vice Chancellor said about you when you were teaching literature at Fatima Jinnah? That if she had the permission she would have made you design an activist course and you would be the best activist teacher they could have!"

"Really! You are mocking me. I taught short stories!"

"Sure! Mary Wollstonecraft. D. H. Lawrence. George Orwell. Ama Ata Aidoo. Margaret Atwood. Kafka. Sartre. And, and, and!"

"They are amazing writers!"

"Yes, but activists also. My wife is obsessed with activists! And Absurdists!" he said, smiling.

"I married you, after all. I suppose that could be a coincidence."

"I will always love you, my firebrand sweet, but thanks to you, all my reporters now behave like activists." I sensed that what was really eating at Ednan that day was this business about the reserved seat. We had avoided the subject with each other since Zia first brought it up with me, but at home, my father-in-law talked of little else.

The phone rang. Huma Sadaf was on the line. Since the women's section had been revamped, she had become one of my most dedicated Helpline staffers, utterly committed to women's issues. In the reception area, she had met a young woman whose haggard appearance had drawn stares from visitors and employees alike. "Please, madame," Huma said. "I have someone here that I think you should see right away. It's a very grim case, and this woman has come asking for you by name."

Even though I had been on the Helpline for less than a year, by that time, I had visited victims of domestic violence, acid attacks and stove burnings in the local hospital often enough to have become known to the medical staff there. An emergency room nurse who had seen the worst of the worst recognized the cruelty to which this woman had been subjected and urged her to come to our Lahore offices and find me.

I asked Huma to bring the woman to me in Ednan's office. When she arrived, I first noticed her gaze, and the mixture of fear and suffering that I saw in it. The memory of her hazel eyes haunts me still. Like so many victims of chronic abuse, trauma had etched itself into her face. The exhaustion that I saw there was literal—I would learn that she had just survived a harrowing ordeal—but it was also existential: "How can this be my life?" her expression seemed to ask. Gaunt, she stood with the posture of one who had lived for too long under the unbearable weight of fear. Had I not been told that she was the young mother of two children, I would have guessed that she was decades older. By virtue of the fact that she stood before me, however, I knew that for all that had been taken from her, something of her spirit remained. It was there in those eyes, which blazed with outrage, and it was there in her voice, which was resolute. "Help me, Bibi," she said, using a term of endearment that startled me for the warmth it conveyed in the midst of a chilling moment.

I will call her Salma, because to use her real name even today, a decade after I met her in 2002, would be to risk endangering her all over again. In Pakistan, to be a victim of sexual violence is to lose one's honor, and to lose one's honor is to invite further abuse.

She wore a simple pale green floral print shalwar kameez and an olive green chador that matched her skin. In spite of what she had just been through, she was clean and well kept; only her hands gave away her social status, their roughness indicating that she worked with them for a living. Her voice was strong, clear and assertive, a fact that I marveled at considering the story she had to tell.

Our son Nofal had just arrived at our offices from school, and Ednan was keen that he not see this woman, whose appearance was upsetting. He made a graceful exit to join our son in my office, and at Salma's request, I locked the door behind him. As I did so, the composure that she had struggled to maintain until that point gave way to an almost wild wailing. She recoiled from my touch when I reached out to put my arms around her to comfort her. I stood back as she began to recount in Punjabi the facts of her ordeal. She had been gang-raped.

In Pakistan, gang rape is used as a punishment, a so-called "honor crime" to avenge other wrongs and to restore honor to a family. It is a very difficult crime to punish, and it is a crime that evades reliable statistics because many cases go unreported by women too frightened to seek help. The Human Rights Commission of Pakistan reported 128 gang rapes for the year 2002 in the Punjab alone (and another 1,421 reported cases of rape in the Punjab).* I imagined that I might know something about what had happened to Salma because of the terrible sameness that characterizes so many instances of that particular crime. As I was about to find out that afternoon in my husband's office, however, I could not have imagined the particular heinousness that defined Salma's case.

When she was still a teenager, Salma told me, her family had married her to a man who was a decade older than she. This detail was happenstance enough; poor families all over rural Pakistan make the same bargain, finding a home for a daughter with no dowry and who is a strain on already meager family resources, and receiving a small sum of money in return. As happens still to so many girls who don't have the benefit of education or other resources, their married lives are ones of indentured servitude at best. Not all girls, however, are also subjected to such base and savage brutality as Salma was.

She struggled through tears as she explained that from her earliest days with her husband, a drug pusher, he beat her. In the past year and a half, Salma said, her husband had been having an affair with an older woman who had ties to a violent criminal gang. During that time, the frequency and ferocity of his beatings increased. Salma suspected that he had been drawn into the gang's mainstay—prostitution—and that the violence he witnessed in that work had inured him to it and made him crueler still.

Salma had had enough. After a decade of marriage and bear-

---

*Human Rights Commission of Pakistan, *State of Human Rights Report 2002* (March 2003), p. 89.

ing two children, who were three and five years old when I met her, and after enduring beatings every other day, Salma told her husband that she wanted a divorce. In Islam, a woman's right to seek a divorce is called khula, and that is what Salma invoked with her husband. Doing so was uncommon and gutsy. In Pakistan, divorce can bring disgrace upon a woman, regardless of her economic status. For a woman like Salma, seeking to end even an abusive union, in spite of her right to do so, was almost unheard of.

Her husband became enraged. "He said he wanted to teach me a lesson," Salma said as she paused to dry her eyes with her chador. "He said this would be a lesson for me and any woman who dared to raise her voice against her husband." Her husband had hired two local thugs to rape her in front of him.

She began to disrobe. Her clothing in a heap around her feet, Salma stood naked, weeping. I wept, too, but with fire in my heart. I wanted to look away; instead, I focused my eyes on hers. Her courage and dignity in that moment overwhelmed me. "This is what they did to me," she said.

It had been ten days since the attack, but deep purple and yellow bruises still covered Salma's thighs and buttocks. The men had kicked her, punched her and gouged her body with lit cigarettes—she had oblong burn marks up and down her torso and across her legs. The men raped her repeatedly, and then her husband joined them. When I heard this, my chest tightened as though all of my body's organs had expanded, making it difficult for me to breathe. I thought with gratitude of my gentle, sweet Ednan. I could not fathom that what happened to Salma had been orchestrated and perpetrated by her husband, the father of her children.

When the men had finished with her, one of them held her down while the other two shoved fresh red chilies inside her. I felt that I might pass out.

When her attackers had done with Salma, they dumped her

into the back seat of a car and drove her miles from her village on the outskirts of Lahore, where they threw her out in the pre-dawn darkness. Left for dead, she was discovered by some neighborhood women who brought her to Mayo Hospital. In my work on the Helpline, I had already come to know the hospital well for the compassion it offered to victims of domestic abuse and other crimes. So many of them were broken, their wills and their spirits done in by their assaults. Salma's defiance set her apart, and her fortitude moved me. She wanted to fight for justice.

"This man I call my husband didn't respect the fact that I am the mother of his children," Salma said. In a country where even gang rapes that receive international outcry have gone unpunished, where law enforcement refuses to take seriously allegations of rape, and where the judicial system is weighted heavily against women and the poor, Salma wanted to fight. She implored me to expose her husband and his accomplices. She had come to the newspaper, she said, because the police had responded with indifference each time she went to the station to report the crime. "They were more interested in the details of how those animals raped me," Salma said. Three times she went to them, and three times they refused to file the First Investigation Report, which would have gotten an investigation underway.

Low-level police officers are among Pakistan's most easily corrupted; the payment of rupees or the promise of retaliation is enough to persuade them to look the other way. Enmeshed in a powerful criminal element, Salma's husband and his mistress had mocked her efforts to report her rape. "He said, 'Go, be my guest,'" Salma recalled of her husband's taunts. "Try all the police stations," he said to her. "See who files a report."

Even though a raped woman in Pakistan is a marked woman, Salma had decided that publicity might be her best recourse. She pleaded with me to help her. "Approach these powerful authorities," she said. "Print my picture in your newspaper. I am not afraid of showing my face to the world. I want people to know what happens in this society where men claim that their women are their honor and then beat them up and rape them."

I believed that Salma's agony was also mine to bear, and that something of her suffering diminished every mother, wife, daughter and sister. In keeping with the Qur'anic ideal that harm to one is harm to all, I was moved by a conviction that when just one woman's body and dignity are degraded, so all of ours are. So when Salma stood naked before me that day, I saw all of humanity denuded, and I felt ashamed.

Helping her, however, would not be straightforward. Even though there was no doubting that Salma had been the victim of terrible violence, I and my staff still needed time—weeks, most likely—to piece together every aspect of her story before we could publish anything about it. A reporter on my team summed up our odds: "Madame," she said to me, "we hardly have the evidence if the police don't cooperate." It was true. We had to build the case in order to solve it, and if the police still refused to investigate the matter, we were sunk.

In the interim, I feared for Salma's safety. I was prepared to send her and, if she wanted, her children, to Dar-ul-Aman— literally, "home for the homeless"—a shelter in Lahore. She chose instead to go with her children, left by her husband with relatives in their village, to the home of a friend.

For hours after Salma's departure, I sat dazed in Ednan's office. This was unlike anything I had ever dealt with in my life. While my uncle's murder had shattered any youthful sense I might once have possessed about the world as a safe place, I had still been fortunate to grow up in a loving, nurturing home with parents who raised us children to think for ourselves, be self-assured and follow our dreams. My good fortune had extended into adulthood with marriage to a kind man who made me feel like his queen.

That night and for many nights after, I could not sleep. I cuddled with Nofal and Fajr, as though in proximity to their innocence I might find an antidote to Salma's desperation and the haunting facts of her story. I found also that I needed prayer and a strong heart to help soothe the ache I felt for Salma. I needed to stay connected to my fundamental belief in Islam as a religion that would never sanction such violence against women.

VIOLENCE PERMEATES NOT ONLY the daily lives of many people, but the structures and institutions that should exist to prevent and punish it, as well. What results is a feedback loop of violence: Institutional complicity protects the perpetrators and violates victims anew. Without it, I believe that would-be abusers would not feel impunity to act, and justice would not seem to be some random, moving target. My efforts to help Salma felt like running an obstacle course with no end in sight.

Salma returned to our offices several times to ask about our progress in pursuing her case. It was very difficult to tell her that we were hard at it, but that we could not yet help her. We had first to verify her account and then to determine who in the police department was squelching the investigation of it, and why. Our guess: The police were being paid to do nothing by the gang that now employed Salma's husband. We were stymied by the fact that she couldn't say which gang it was or where in the city they operated. The location she identified was a den of criminal activity; our reporters could not pinpoint which of the several prostitution rings was the one that involved Salma's husband and his mistress.

We also needed to consult our lawyers and find out which courses of action we could reasonably pursue. As a newspaper and not a law enforcement agency, there were legal restrictions that limited our work. I planned to take her case to the Governor of the Punjab, the region's highest authority, as soon as I had amassed the evidence to do so. In the meantime, I urged Salma to keep a low profile and to return to safety. I feared what her husband might do if he found out that she had sought our help.

Salma could not hide her disappointment. "I won't get justice because I am poor, because I am a woman!" she said. I couldn't tell her that she was wrong, a fact that sickened me. I promised Salma, however, that I would do everything in my power to see that her husband and his accomplices were apprehended. Later, in the dark of another sleepless night, I wondered what justice could possibly mean given a crime such as theirs. That, I decided, would have to be a matter between those men and their God.

A full week after Salma first came to our offices and nearly three weeks since her attack, my team had finally assembled enough evidence to publish an account of what had happened. The article took up three full columns of the back page of the women's section—prominent placement. As I expected, readers responded with outrage to her plight and to the police's lack of action. I was hopeful that I could build on the momentum that the story had generated among our readers to make a case to a senior law enforcement official whose word alone could compel his underlings to act.

I decided to take Salma with me to see him. What feeling person could meet this woman, I thought, and refuse to help her? He could, it turned out. His response to Salma stunned me. "*This* is the rape victim?" he said. "Who would want to rape *her*?" Salma looked down at her feet and clutched her chador tightly around her. Tears fell from her cheeks, but she made no sound. It was a fresh assault. I was disgusted, and I was also angry with myself for having possessed such naïveté. Having faced the indifference and prurience of the junior police officials that I had approached about her attack, how could I have expected the man who led them to be any different? My rage burned. I put my arm around Salma and led her away.

I didn't want to subject Salma to any further insult or

injury, but I couldn't accept that the police would just do nothing. I returned to the police station, this time armed with the follow-up stories that my staff had written, as well as the letters from readers that Salma's story had generated. I presented medical evidence of rape, as well as Salma's identification of her three attackers. I also wielded the promise—threat—of more publicity about the police's lack of action. If for no other reason than to get rid of me, the police relented and filed a First Investigation Report, and with it issued warrants for the arrests of Salma's attackers.

It was too late. Likely tipped off by the very police who half-heartedly filed their report, Salma's husband and accomplices had fled. In fact, I'm certain the police knew where they went. I just could not prove it.

Not long after, Salma disappeared, too. I do not know if she had been intimidated or threatened anew, though I suspect she had been. The last time I saw her, she expressed her fear that her husband or his mistress would try to take her children away. I don't know what prompted her to flee, and I never got the chance to ask her. It would be a month before I received a letter from her written in poorly worded Urdu explaining that, afraid for her safety, she had moved to a village far from her own. There, she hoped, the notoriety of being a rape victim would not dog her or endanger her further. I was relieved to read, at least, that she had her two young children with her.

By going into hiding, Salma had given up on the possibility of getting justice. I could not sit with this. It was the beginning of my education into the state of things for so many women in my country. Could justice for such an open-and-shut case truly be so elusive? What in Pakistan's culture and society made it so? Was this Islam, as some would argue, or was Islam just a scapegoat for a culture in which violence against women is endemic and justified by ignorance?

For days after receiving Salma's letter, I mentioned her to

guests at Zia's table. The details of the crime would have been too much for dinnertime conversation, so I hewed to the broad outlines of her story: young mother, rape victim, unpunished attackers, victim gone into hiding. Guests included newspaper colleagues, government ministers and other politicians. Whenever I pondered aloud the apparent vacuum of justice in Salma's case, I was often met with the rhetorical equivalent of a shrug, regardless of how enlightened or otherwise I considered my interlocutor to be. "But this is the way things are for women in this country!" I was told in so many words, again and again. I found that facile response infuriating.

That sweltering spring of 2002, I had an epiphany: My married name, Shahid, means "one who bears witness." How prophetic, I thought, because when I joined the newspaper, that is what I became. When I was unable to help Salma, however, I felt acutely the limitations of merely witnessing. If the first step was to see, the second, I decided, must be to act.

CHAPTER EIGHT

A Raging Sea

As SPRING TURNED TO SUMMER, I had come to feel like an Ophelia torn between loyalties. I was reluctant to disappoint my family, who remained tilted against the political realm, but I didn't want to let myself down, either. Increasingly, I saw the prospect of becoming a member of the Provincial Assembly as a challenge that I owed it to myself to meet. Even so, I stalled in submitting the necessary papers to establish my candidacy. If I missed the deadline, I told myself, the decision would be made for me. When the government announced a three-day extension of the filing date, I took it to be a second chance to get my application together. I renewed the topic with Ednan, who would be the one to second Zia's official nomination before I could file. Every candidate for a reserved seat requires a nominator and a seconder. In my case, my father-in-law and husband would be mine.

"Okay, Humaira," he said. "Suppose we do file the papers." Ednan was fond of metaphors, and he used one now. "If I nominate you, it will be as if I am throwing you into a raging sea, and you will have to learn to swim back to the shore."

I thought my husband was trying to scare or dissuade me, but what he said next lifted my heart. "It will not be an easy journey," he said, "but the struggle will endow you with powers you never knew you had. I know you will do it."

I knew that it was not easy for Ednan to suppress his protective instinct, but I was grateful to him for not letting it override his ability to see my strength and potential.

"Just imagine," he said, "if you do decide to go for it, and you win, you'll be in an even better position to do something for the people who approach you for help through the Helpline." He expressed how I had been feeling exactly. It seemed that Ednan had come around in his thinking, too.

With my party's nomination and, more important to me, Ednan's blessing, I filed my papers as a member of the National Alliance, on the twenty-sixth of August 2002.

Zia was thrilled. My parents held their breath but rallied to my cause, even as members of their extended families tut-tutted about the disgrace I was soon to bring upon them. What could be worse, their thinking went, than a politician in the family? I could tell that Ednan remained apprehensive, but I appreciated how gamely he cheered me on. I was nervous. I didn't give in to frissons of anticipation, nor did I envision myself striding about the halls of power; I had too much work to do. I returned my attention to the Helpline, which in recent months had been receiving an increasing number of calls about acid attacks.

IN PAKISTAN, you could not attempt to kill someone with a gun or a dagger without going to prison, but you could throw sulfuric or hydrochloric acid on them and walk free. It doesn't take much of the corrosive liquid to have a devastating effect. As soon as it makes contact with the skin, acid begins to eat away at it, destroying the fat underneath. In the worst cases, acid also destroys bone and the underlying facial structure. Most victims live, but endure a life sentence of physical and psychological challenges and pain. Often, survivors are ostracized in a culture that blames the victim. Many attackers, meanwhile, receive no sentence at all.

That summer, as my Helpline team reported a surge in calls

about acid attacks, I asked *Khabrain*'s lawyers to explain the legality of the crime to me so that I would know what actions I could reasonably demand of the police. I was shocked to learn that victims had almost no legal recourse under existing Pakistani law. Acid crimes, I learned, were loosely grouped under the category of "injury," which carried a light sentence, if any at all. In my attempt to understand this, I discovered that acid attackers had been able to exploit the Islamic concept of ijtihad, whereby a crime is up for interpretation. As a relatively new crime, acid attacks were not specifically forbidden; they were likened, then, to the lesser crime of inflicting bodily harm, like a punch in the belly. Given acid attacks' flimsy legal definition, police often didn't bother to pursue any investigation, because they didn't know how to categorize an attack. "How can this be?" I asked. I was incredulous. "These victims nearly die! Many of them do! If their assailants had stabbed them, they'd be locked up for attempted murder! But not for this?"

I discovered another legal loophole: diyat. Attackers could often be persuaded to offer monetary compensation to victims in exchange for a victim's silence. Because many victims were from poor families, the pressure to accept the compensation was great. What was the price, I wondered, of a destroyed life?

I pursued a different line of inquiry. All over Pakistan, acid is plentiful and cheap to procure. A small bottle can be purchased just about anywhere for about 20 rupees—less than 25 cents. "What about the sale of this acid?" I asked. "Is it even legal to own this stuff?" Goldsmiths and tanners use sulfuric and hydrochloric acids in their trades, but there is no licensing or regulation of the use or sale of the acid. Anyone can buy it.

During my first year working on the Helpline, there were instances of children being doused with acid, and of attacks on men, as well. One such was a journalist from Karachi whose reporting exposed a fraudulent real estate scheme. The men whose plot he uncovered retaliated with a bottle of acid. By far the overwhelming majority of acid attack victims, however, are women. In 2002, forty-six acid attacks on women were reported in the Punjab alone. It is impossible to say how many more went unreported. Acid destroys a woman's face, and that is precisely the intent: to rob her of beauty that cannot be possessed by a jilted lover, a jealous suitor or a forsaken husband.

I struggled with how best to help the victims I met. From a medical standpoint, Pakistani hospitals had limited resources and expertise with the kinds of treatments and reconstructive surgeries that many victims required. This was especially so in rural areas, but even in a large city such as Lahore, only one hospital, Mayo, had anything approximating a burn unit, and its facilities were vastly insufficient for the treatment of acid burns. Only one true burn unit existed in the Punjab, at an army hospital in the city of Khariyan in the northeast. Priority there was given to military officers, however, and the equipment dated to the 1950s.

EARLIER THAT SUMMER, while a young acid attack victim named Shaista lay recuperating from her fifth surgery in Nishtar Hospital in Multan, her parents went to *Khabrain*'s bureau in that city to seek help. Helpline reporter Imrana Kookab met them. Sympathetic relatives and friends had collected funds for Shaista's surgeries, they told her, and now those resources were exhausted. So were the young woman's medical options at the hospital that was treating her. Their hope was that the newspaper might be able to collect zakat, a form of Islamic charity, to help pay for the many other operations Shaista would need. They also wondered if Helpline staff knew of another hospital in the Punjab that might better help her.

Shaista's parents explained that because they were older and poor, they had worried from the start about their daughter's future. In order to secure a more stable life for her, they had followed a long-established rural custom and promised her in marriage to the son of a better-off family in their village. At the time, Shaista and her intended were just children.

Years later, another family with still better prospects requested Shaista's hand in marriage for their son. Shaista's parents did what most in their circumstances who wanted the best for their child might do: they agreed. The parents of Shaista's childhood fiancé accepted the news of the broken engagement with disappointment but with equanimity. Their son did not. He cast himself as the spurned lover and vowed to avenge the slight.

Came Shaista's wedding day, the ex-fiancé broke into her home, where the twenty-year-old bride sat dressed in her humble wedding clothes. He pulled her to the ground, held her down and emptied a vial of acid onto her face. If he could not have her, then no one would.

Shaista's assailant was not arrested; in fact, he was going about his business as though nothing had happened. Shaista's parents were desperate to help her.

Imrana Kookab relayed all of this to me later that day. We made arrangements for Kookab to send Shaista to Lahore for a medical evaluation when she had healed enough to travel. It would likely be several more months until that time. As I learned, acid attacks leave victims vulnerable to infection. It is important to allow a seal to form over the wounded skin before risking exposure. I asked Kookab to keep me apprised of Shaista's condition and progress. In the meantime, I would try to secure zakat funds for her surgeries while exploring her options at area hospitals.

BY LATE AUGUST, the question of whether I would bid for a seat on the provincial parliament settled, there was more room on the Shahid family's dinnertime agenda for other matters. One evening, I took advantage of this to talk about the prevalence of acid attacks and the problem of prosecuting them in general, and about Shaista in particular. Zia, whose management approach was very hands-on, already knew that I had been struggling with these issues and with Shaista's case. I told him that if I won a seat in the provincial assembly, I would propose legislation to mandate stiffer sentences for acid crimes.

"I think you should get in touch with Tehmina Durrani," Zia said after hearing me out. "She's been doing a lot of work with acid attack victims, and perhaps she can be helpful to you."

I had met Durrani, a good friend of my in-laws, once before, when she came to lunch at their home sometime that spring. This elegant woman, famous in Pakistan for the exposé she published a decade earlier, *My Feudal Lord*, about her abusive marriage to Ghulam Mustafa Khar, Chief Minister and later Governor of the Punjab, had made an immediate impression on me for her warmth and charisma. Her memoir is not just a retelling of the abuses she suffered at the hands of Khar, but also an examination of the power that feudal landowners like him derive from a culture that distorts Islam and tacitly sanctions violence against women. I found that Durrani and I had much to talk about. I told Zia that I would welcome the chance to see her again.

The following weekend, Zia and I met Durrani in her refined home in the affluent Gulberg suburb of Lahore. As soon as we sat down to tea and a spread of local delicacies, the diminutive and beautiful author and activist came straight to the point.

"So, Humaira, I understand that you've been working with acid attack victims through your newspaper's Helpline," she said.

Yes, I told her, and I outlined the medical and legal limitations that we had run up against in trying to secure help for victims. As I would find out, Durrani was already well versed in these shortcomings.

"The elections are coming up," I said, "and since Zia Sahib has proposed my name for a women's seat, I thought that I might push for a law that calls for harsher sentencing for acid attacks. I'd welcome your advice on how best to proceed, Tehmina Sahiba."

A radiant smile spread across her face. "First, you must call me Tina," she said. "Second, I would be very glad to be of any help."

Durrani was known for her work with one acid attack victim in particular, a young woman named Fakhra Yunus, who, on the fourteenth of May 2000, was attacked with acid by her abusive husband, from whom she had fled to her mother's home in Karachi. Durrani learned that Yunus's husband happened to be her stepson from her previous marriage, Bilal Khar. At the time, Khar was an MPA representing Muzaffargarh, in the southern Punjab. Khar allegedly poured acid on his wife in front of her five-year-old son from a previous relationship, and then used his political connections to evade arrest.

Fakhra Yunus's story made headlines around the world in part because it dispelled the prevalent notion that acid crimes were the domain of the poor. But if Khar, who was wealthy, educated, politically connected and powerful, didn't fit the supposed profile of acid crime perpetrators, Yunus, who was young, beautiful and had transcended her red-light district background to marry into one of Pakistan's most powerful families, was a typical acid attack victim. Durrani told me, "I've worked with several young women who have had their lives destroyed by these attacks, and I have noticed that the victims are usually beautiful women, strong women, independent women. It's as if the men who do this to them resent their beauty and their strength and their independence."

After three months in intensive care, Fakhra Yunus was released to Durrani's care. "There was nothing that could be done for her here in Pakistan," Durrani said. She learned of an Italian NGO called Smile Again that offered reconstructive surgeries and psychological counseling to acid attack victims without charge, but in Italy. Durrani and some friends raised funds to send Yunus to Rome for treatment. In spite of an early effort by the government to block Yunus's visa to leave the country—they feared that her story would bring bad publicity to Pakistan, and they were right—Durrani prevailed. She accompanied Yunus abroad for the first in a long series of operations. After years of personal struggle, physical pain and more than three dozen surgeries, Yunus would jump to her death from the sixth-floor balcony of her Rome apartment on the seventeenth of March 2012. She would be called the woman who died twice.

Tehmina Durrani's work with Fakhra Yunus was a watershed for her. As she told me, it would be impossible to meet one victim of an acid attack without feeling compelled to help others. A survivor of domestic violence herself, Durrani used the celebrity she had gained from her book's success to advocate for other acid crime victims. She worked closely with Smile Again to find others in Pakistan to help. She also joined forces with activists who called for a fourteen-year jail sentence for anyone found guilty of committing an acid crime. Even as a hypothetical, however, that punishment seemed insufficient. In contrast, in 2002, Bangladesh introduced the death penalty for acid attacks, an easy copycat crime that had become rampant across South Asia. Acid crimes initially fell in that country, but they have risen steadily since, in part because of the wide availability of acid, and in part because the law, though harsh, has been scarcely implemented.

"Taking up issues like these in parliament is the only way that women's seats will be useful," Durrani told me. "I'm with you all the way on this."

Her support galvanized me. I told her that I had been thinking about holding a press conference to draw attention to acid attacks and their victims.

"Brilliant idea," Durrani said. "This issue needs to be highlighted as much as possible, and sensitizing the media to the gravity of the problem is the first step. I'll be with you on this. Let's meet again and make a plan."

We agreed that we would wait for the results of the October elections before holding our joint press conference. If I won a reserved seat, I would have that much more clout. If I were not among the new MPAs, I could at least do my best to put this issue on their radar.

In the meantime, Durrani and I decided right away to launch a series of public service announcements in all editions of *Khabrain* calling on acid crime victims and on those aware of them to come forward to seek help. Our thinking was simple: Media pressure might compel the police to take action against perpetrators and inspire hospitals to better allocate limited resources for victims. Durrani also hoped to identify victims who could benefit from Smile Again's services.

The response to the ads was so overwhelming that our Helpline staff alone couldn't handle the volume. I enlisted *Khabrain*'s correspondents across the Punjab to help gather victims' stories so that we could coordinate our reporting and follow-up efforts. We were stunned: Acid crimes appeared to be even more widespread than we realized. As the elections approached, I was more certain than ever that acid crimes would be a cornerstone of my platform as an MPA, should I win a seat.

ANOTHER ISSUE SEEMED to be cropping up with increasing frequency: predatory private moneylending. Ever since *Khabrain* ran the story about Rehana, who sold her kidney to free herself and her husband of debt with menacing lenders, the Helpline had received an influx of calls about the desperate ends to which other borrowers had been pushed. The cases presented variations on a theme: Unscrupulous lenders ensnared poor borrowers in a cycle of debt that, given interest rates that exceeded 100 percent, they were never going to be able to repay. The borrowers, in turn, fearing for their safety, resorted to ever more extreme measures to satisfy lenders' demands.

Another disturbing pattern emerged, as well. Lenders confiscated the borrowers' collateral—jewelry, motorcycles, property;

they even seized harvests, taking with them the only shred of economic security a poor borrower had. Still not satisfied, they returned to pressure the borrowers into handing over their women or girls, some as young as eight and nine years old, as "compensation." I shook with anger reading a letter from a widowed seamstress that described the straits that she had found herself in. When she defaulted on a usurious loan that she took out to pay for her older daughter's wedding, the lender, part of a network of moneylending mafias, sent a gang of toughs to the woman's tiny rented flat in a poor section of Lahore. If they had to come back again, they told her, they'd take her six-year-old daughter with them and sell her to a local pimp.

That case was a turning point for me, a moment when my outrage overrode my despair and feelings of helplessness, and when I refused to accept that I could not alleviate this woman's burden. Ednan saw my conviction. After a meeting with my staff at which I declared that I would never allow "those criminal hyenas" to take a child away from her mother, Ednan seemed proud. "I have never seen you look so determined, Humaira," he said.

My Helpline team informed senior police officials of the mother and daughter's situation and convinced them to offer their protection. Meanwhile, *Khabrain*'s lawyers filed a case against the debtor, and the Helpline raised the funds to pay him off. It would have been preferable to have him locked up without giving him a single rupee, but we knew that even if he were apprehended and jailed for a period, the mother and her child would not be safe so long as their debt was outstanding. As it happens, the lender was never arrested; like so many perpetrators tipped off by media attention and police scrutiny, he vanished. My consolation was that the mother and her daughter were safe. That case would yield the seeds of another bill that I would propose if elected to a reserved seat: one to ban private moneylending.

THE TENTH OF OCTOBER, a Thursday, arrived, and with it, the country's much-anticipated elections. For fully twenty-eight of Pakistan's fifty-five years, military rule had been the order of the day. Now came an opportunity to shift the balance to democracy. The pall that hung over Musharraf since the controversial spring referendum, however, caused many to fear for the legitimacy of the elections. A skeptical people—a skeptical world—watched the voting with caution.

The vote was closely watched for another reason, as well: Since 9/11, Islamist parties in Pakistan had made claims of burgeoning popular support. In siding with the United States in its War on Terror, Musharraf had made himself a party to the demise of the Afghan Taliban, Pakistan's erstwhile ally. Islamist groups claimed that Musharraf had done so at peril to his own standing and that big wins in their favor would prove it.

At the Shahid home, of course, interest in the elections was keen. I was third on a list of women nominated to the National Alliance. Given proportional representation, that meant that the National Alliance would need to win at least twelve seats for me to be elected to a reserved one. It was very exciting, but less for reasons of my personal stake in the outcome than for what I hoped the elections would mean for Pakistan: the formation of a government that paid more than lip service to the ideals of democracy, and the first time that Pakistan had more than a few women, if any at all, in the National and Provincial assemblies. On election day, I was just one of millions of Pakistanis who hoped that Musharraf would be able to deliver on his word.

Ednan and I spent much of the day touring polling stations around Lahore—as journalists, not as a candidate and her spouse. Meanwhile, *Khabrain*'s tightly coordinated election coverage, with bureaus in cities large and small, kept us apprised of developments, from the projected vote count to reports of fraud. Once back at the newspaper, we almost didn't leave Ednan's office, but stayed there monitoring television coverage of the voting.

Ednan's excitement over the elections surprised me. I didn't expect him to become as swept up as he did. As the day wore on, it became clear to me that if he was anxious about anything, it wasn't that I might actually end up in the parliament, but that I might not.

I remained tentative. I still saw no prestige in my possible foray into politics; my family's low opinion of it weighed on me. If a degree of ambivalence muddied my feelings about winning a seat, I was very clear on one thing: the legislative agenda I would take with me into the Assembly.

Ednan and I were up all night watching the returns. It wasn't until morning that it was confirmed that the National Alliance had won enough seats—twelve—for me to win a reserved one in the Provincial Assembly. I had seen Ednan scream with such glee only when his favorite cricket team won a particularly contentious match. As ever, my outward response was the opposite of his. We were both, I realized, glad for the outcome. But Ednan was jubilant. He paced and leapt and clapped his hands. I was quiet. I sat very still and watched my husband's giddy exertions, as though conserving my energy for what I knew instinctively would be a struggle ahead.

Almost as soon as the outcome was announced, I felt as though I were matriculating in a university that taught coursework wholly unfamiliar to me. In a way, I was. So I approached my nascent political career as I had my studies, prioritizing what I needed to know and setting about learning it. I wanted first to know how to translate the bullet points in my head into proposed legislation; next, to understand how best to bring the proposed legislation before my fellow MPAs; and finally, how to persuade them to back my cause without forming unholy alliances or watering down the potency of my proposals. I had no idea how to do any of it, so in the days following the election, I sought the tutelage of a former parliamentarian, Haji Muhammad Saifullah, a white-haired, sharp-eyed éminence grise of Pakistani politics.

In his day, Saifullah was known for his power to transfix

a session when he held the floor. "Teach me rules and procedures," I said to him, unsure of whether or not he would agree to help me. He saw that I was serious—a rarity, it would turn out, among the women who occupied reserved seats—and he said, "I see potential. At least you are interested and you want to know." Saifullah, whose gentle air belied a certain fierceness, taught me all that he could about the rules and procedures and how best to employ them in the House. He also warned me of the tactics that fellow MPAs, even those I might think of as allies, might use against me. His warnings would prove prescient.

WHILE I PREPARED to enter the parliament as a member of the National Alliance, the people of Pakistan would wait for more than a month to find out which party would run the government, because none had won the absolute majority required to do so. A coalition would have to be formed; as is typical of Pakistani politics, forming one wouldn't be straightforward.

One development wasn't up for debate: The United Action Front, Muttahida Majlis-e-Amal (MMA), an alliance of six Islamist parties, won far more seats in the National Assembly than most had anticipated. So many, in fact, that their tally placed them third behind Musharraf's Pakistan Muslim League-Q and Benazir Bhutto's Pakistan People's Party. Now, faced with the prospect of a hung parliament, the religious party alliance had enough seats to help determine which party would form the national government and which way that government would likely lean. Meanwhile, in the North-West Frontier Province, now known as the Khyber Pakhtunkhwa Province (KPK), which shares a border with Afghanistan, the MMA won enough votes to form its own provincial government. As allied offensives continued in Afghanistan, the Islamists' anti-Western, anti-American agenda had found unprecedented traction.

At last, a coalition government, to be led by Musharraf's

PML-Q, was announced in November. According to the particular laws of transitivity that determine Pakistan's political party alliances, that meant that I would take my oath as a member of the ruling coalition. This is how it worked: Farooq Leghari first nominated me as a member of his Millat party, which then joined forces with the National Alliance, which later allied itself with the PML-Q. Bhutto's PPP and Nawaz Sharif's PML-N would sit in opposition, each of their leaders still residing in exile to avoid facing corruption and other charges at home.

THE WAIT FOR THE ELECTION results over, I reached back out to Tehmina Durrani. We had remained in frequent touch since our August meeting, and she had followed the response to the acid attack ads with interest. Bolstered by that response, and with a late November date set for the parliamentary swearing-in, we decided to hold our press conference on acid crimes the first week of November. Durrani, with her passionate advocacy for acid attack victims, was a huge draw; I was amazed by the turnout of journalists that crammed into our room at the Lahore Press Club, no doubt just to see her.

I sat with Durrani on the dais and watched transfixed as she ran the proceedings. She fended off left-field questions, urged a few ramblers to get to the point, and projected unflappable authority and good humor. She inspired me. Her remarks to the gathered journalists were direct but eloquent. "You must highlight how difficult survival is for an acid attack victim," she said, raising her voice just slightly to drown out a reporter who tried to interject. It would be a trick I employed myself in press conferences to come. "And you must raise this issue on as many platforms as you can."

THE PUNJAB ASSEMBLY building's soaring Roman architecture suggests a grandeur not always risen to by those elected to carry out their business inside of it. I would learn that soon enough. But the morning of the twenty-fifth of November, I was sufficiently taken in by the majesty of the place to believe otherwise. I was moved by the magnitude of what I was about to do: promise to help make Pakistan a better place. I wanted to believe that lofty ideals were the freight carried by each of us who had come to take our oath that day.

Across sprawling lawns and manicured walkways, I made my way to the Assembly building, my nerves mounting on the approach. A scrum of journalists jostled for place outside the heavily barricaded entrance. I slalomed my way through a course of popping flashbulbs and jabbing microphones. The age of the independent television channel had just begun in Pakistan, which accounted for a smattering of television cameras from local media outlets. The rest were from the international media. Headlines heralded the return of popular democracy; op-eds sounded a note of doubt; and now, all eyes were on Musharraf and us, his newly elected parliamentarians. I ascended the Assembly building's limestone steps to arrive at last among four graceful columns, perched like watchful sentinels atop them. In the midst of the hubbub around me, I permitted myself a moment of awe.

I was one of sixty-six women who had won reserved seats. Four others had won seats in the general election, and I found them to be an impressive group for their experience and energy, and their youth. Each of them hailed from well-established political families, with fathers who had served in the provincial Assembly at one time or another. At just 30 years old, Syeda Sughra Imam was the eldest of them. Educated at Harvard and having worked for the Council on Foreign Relations, she had the additional distinction of having a mother, Syeda Abida Hussain, who was not just a prominent politician and a longtime member of the Provincial Assembly, but was among the first women in Pakistan to serve in that capacity. Sughra, as I called her, would become one of my closest friends and best allies in the Assembly.

The other three women, Hameeda Waheed-ud-Din, 26; Maria Tariq, 27; and Dr. Nadia Aziz, 29, who was a member of the opposition, made me hope that their example would elevate the standard for all of us on reserved seats.

The rest of the new Punjab Provincial Assembly's new MPAs, 371 in total, were men. Inside the packed Assembly Hall, we would discover that the chamber had the capacity to hold precisely 100 fewer of us. Some of the newly elected would find their seats one level up, in the press gallery. I found mine, number 351, in a cramped section reserved for women.

Collectively, I thought, we seventy must have resembled a gift box of petits fours, the lid lifted to reveal frosted pastels. I was mortified. Next to us, the men were a duochrome legion: some wore black, others white. I was among the few exceptions in my ranks who had not dressed for a fancy affair. My first impression, an unflattering one, of many of my fellow women parliamentarians in their vivid saris and frilled dupattas was that they couldn't possibly be serious. How glad I was that I had worn a simple black shalwar kameez that I might have donned to run errands on any day of the week. Out of respect, I covered my head with a pale peach chador.

"What will you wear?" Ednan had wanted to know that morning. *Don't tell me you're going to try to tell me what to wear!* I wanted to say.

"Something very simple," I said instead. It was a spark that ignited our relationship, and also a particular annoyance of mine, that Ednan so enjoyed telling me what to do. His fondness for giving me instructions was matched only by my mischievous delight in ignoring them. Most of the time, we managed a playful sparring.

"They will overdress," he said, referring to the women MPAs. "It's a beginner's mistake, and you must avoid it. No one will ever take you seriously if you dress like a bauble."

I knew, of course, that he was right. Even so, the imp in me wanted to grab my loudest, most inappropriate outfit and give my husband a fright.

Aside from the sartorial, my next surprise that day was the utter lack of decorum. To my right, women members of the PPP stood and shouted anti-Musharraf slogans. "Leave us alone, dictator!" some cried. Others yelled, "Go, Musharraf, go!" As in, go away. Plenty of men from the opposition jeered, too, some using Urdu epithets that would have been jarring enough to overhear in the streets, let alone in the province's seat of power. Some waved placards while others banged on the benches like caged animals in a zoo. I would never become accustomed to the incongruity of such raucous behavior in so rarefied a space.

When at length the Assembly settled, we stood to read our oaths. The surge of emotion that I felt took me by surprise. Tears welled up in my eyes as I read: "In the name of Allah, the most Beneficent the most Merciful, I do solemnly swear that I will bear true faith and allegiance to Pakistan: That, as a Member of the Provincial Assembly of the Punjab, I will perform my functions honestly to the best of my ability faithfully in accordance with the Constitution of the Islamic Republic of Pakistan, the law and the rules of the assembly, and always in the interest of the sovereignty, integrity, solidarity, well-being and prosperity of Pakistan: That I will strive to preserve the Islamic Ideology, which is the basis for the creation of Pakistan: And that I will preserve, protect and defend the Constitution of the Islamic Republic of Pakistan. May Allah Almighty help and guide me (A'meen)."

To this day, I think of those words when I am successful in my work, and more often when I am not. I feel tied to them; more than once, they have kept me going.

The oath taken, the members, one by one, ascended the dais to sign our names. And with that, I was a Member of the Punjab Provincial Assembly. I felt at once that I would have my work cut out for me, and that I was up to the task. Ednan had likened it to a raging sea. I braced myself to be buffeted, and dove in.

CHAPTER NINE

Taking Flight

SO THIS IS DEMOCRACY, I remember thinking. A President who still wears a military uniform; a parliament that fails to make a quorum just a month after its swearing in; and an Assembly so raucous that the Speaker of the House cannot make himself heard above the din of pro- and anti-government sloganeering. In my first month as an MPA, I learned some other things as well: The opposition has more freedom to express itself than the party in power, which, from its seats on the Treasury benches, is expected to issue hosannas, not criticisms; a number of women on reserved seats are merely extensions of whichever male member of their families nominated them—their opinions are not their own; and the reason no one could hear me when I stood to speak was that my microphone had been switched off.

By then, I had already submitted the language for two resolutions, one to ban the practice of vani and thus strip village councils of having bartering power over the lives of women and girls; and the other to give acid attacks a commensurate punishment while establishing a designated burn unit in the Punjab to treat victims of acid and other burns. I attended every party briefing at which either the Chief Minister of the Punjab, Chaudhry Pervaiz Elahi, or the Law Minister, Raja Basharat, laid out the legislative agendas that we, as members of the ruling coalition, were expected to support. I used every meeting as an opportunity to speak up about my resolutions. The responses ranged from lukewarm to outright hostility—and these were members of my own party.

In the case of vani, MPAs from rural constituencies where the tribal code of honor prevails were especially reluctant to consider my resolution. They made it clear that when it came to long-standing customary practices, politicians had no place interfering. They were content to let clans run their own affairs, regardless of the consequences for women and girls. Rather than support me, the party leadership sided with those MPAs, telling me that if they weren't pressing to ban the practice in their own regions, why should I? In the meantime, I would wait, impatiently, for one or both resolutions to make it onto the Assembly agenda.

I presented my dismal summation to Ednan one evening in December. I had barely just begun, and already I felt demoralized, laid low by a sense that I was out of place amid shouting MPAs and out of step with other women on reserved seats, and already out of favor with members of my own party. "Look," Ednan said, "it's not about shouting or being loud or being prominent or being singled out by the cameras. It's about doing meaningful work. Your work should speak for you, and it will."

I took heart, even as I wondered aloud how my work could possibly speak for me if I literally couldn't make myself heard. Ednan, who even before I had secured a reserved seat had appointed himself as my guide to government dysfunction, reprised that role. He asked what I did at party briefings.

"I listen," I said. "And then I talk about the legislations that I want to propose."

"Right. In other words, you talk about things that highlight deficiencies in the system and in the laws. You signal to them that when you stand to speak in the assembly, what comes out of your mouth isn't going to be pro status quo. They see you as trouble, Humaira."

"So what?" I said, irritated. "The status quo stinks! We have to punish acid crimes and establish a proper burn unit in the Punjab for victims! We need to make bartering women and girls punishable by imprisonment so that these tribal councils stop consigning them to sham marriages of misery and abuse! And we have to stop these moneylending thugs who prey on the poor!" I realized that I was venting my frustration at Ednan. "I'm sorry," I said. "It's just so maddening to finally be in a position to do something, and to be blocked before I even begin."

Ednan smiled at me. "I knew from the moment I met you that you were the woman of my life," he said. The first time Ednan said this to me was shortly after we were married. The declaration had since evolved from romantic testament to gentle ribbing, a sometimes weary husband's way of letting his sometimes fiery wife know he loved her even when she was hard to reach way up there on her high horse. I thought he was teasing me now.

"Don't make fun of me!" I said.

"My darling wife, you ridiculous hot head, I am telling you that I am proud of you! Please, do not make an adversary of me. I am your ally in this, Humaira. No one wants to see you succeed in this more than I do."

I calmed down.

"The thing of it is, they know you don't do servile flattery," Ednan said. "They know that by virtue of the fact that you're a Shahid, you're going to challenge the status quo. Just give it time."

Ednan assured me that things weren't as stark as my first impressions suggested. Where I saw black and white, he saw extenuating circumstances. "You're dealing with MPAs from areas that don't have electricity, irrigation canals or roads," he said. "Their top priorities won't be the same as yours, but it doesn't mean they won't support you." He advised me to speak privately with individual members about my proposed legislations before taking them before the entire House. "Garner support one by one," he said, cupping my face in his hands. "You are very hard to refuse." He kissed my nose, and I gave him a loving shove.

"Condescending man!" I said, feigning insult. "I bet you'd turn my mic off if you could."

"Only some of the time," Ednan said.

BY LATE DECEMBER, my Helpline team had been hard at work on two cases in particular that underscored the urgency I felt to make progress in the parliament. The first was a case of forced marriage that had ensnared two young girls in tribal justice. By month's end, it would form the centerpiece of my proposed legislation to outlaw vani. The second was a follow-up on the acid attack victim, Shaista, from Multan.

With regard to the former, we had received a troubling letter written in a child's untidy hand and rudimentary Urdu. The letter bore a postmark from a remote village in Mianwali, a district in the northwestern Punjab on the eastern bank of the Indus River. The letter, addressed to the Helpline, read:

> I am born in a very poor family, few months before the Ramadan. A girl from a very powerful family has accused my brother of making her pregnant. But my brother works in Karachi and he has no clue about this whole event. The tribal heads of this girl held a jirga [tribal council] on us, where we took a solemn oath on the Holy Qur'an that we don't have anything to do with this whole incident, but they did not believe us. The jirga made this decision which has shook the earth and the sky, the decision they made is that my brother Riaz Akram has done zulm [cruelty and injustice] to that girl, and the compensation is the two sisters of the accused should be given in vani [forced marriage] to the two brothers of this girl. We are too scared to inform the police because they will take away our father.

I am writing this letter in secrecy. After Eid-al-Adha [annual Feast of the Sacrifice] would be our wedding that is our funerals. I have already bought rat poison, and the day me and my sister are forced to send away with these two brothers, we will commit suicide. I know my home is very remote from the big towns, but not that far away that no one can come and save us from this cruelty.

The letter was signed by the sisters, Afshan, aged seventeen, and Faiza, aged eight.

The older girl's courage in acting so boldly in her and her sister's defense struck me. So did the fact that it should be considered a fair trade to offer two young virgins in exchange for dropping apparently false charges against their brother. I was deeply disturbed by the scenario spelled out in the girls' letter. I was determined that the paper's response be swift so that we could free them from the marriages. I knew that once one of my reporters was seen in the area, word would spread and with it, fear. Often, just sending a correspondent was enough to create a stir. I sent a reporter that day.

It took my correspondent little time to verify the girls' account. It seemed that their entire village had witnessed the nikkah, the wedding ceremony at which the marriage contract was signed, in April. Afshan was married to twenty-year-old Ghulam Murtaza, and her younger sister was married to ten-year-old Imtiaz Tariq. The girls' rukhsati, or their departure from their parent's home, was delayed, as is often the custom, until after Eid, the feast that marks the end of Ramadan, in the fall. There was still time to save them.

The marriage of minors is a violation of Pakistani civil law as well as the teachings of Islam. Vani, the practice of offering a girl as compensation or in reparation, and often in marriage, also lacks either a legal or a religious basis. As I was coming to learn, however, tribal justice dwells in that gray area between civil and

Islamic laws. It sufficed that vani was a long-standing customary practice, if not a legal one, for the tribal elders to settle on it as a solution.

With Zia's go-ahead, I sent three more of *Khabrain*'s investigative reporters up to the girls' village in Mianwali. Once there, they located the imam who had conducted the wedding ceremony. He denied that it had taken place, so the reporters returned the following day with relatives of the girls who had witnessed the wedding and contradicted the imam to his face. This time, the imam changed his story. Yes, he had performed the ceremony, he admitted, but only because he had been ordered to do so by the tribal council. The council of elders, in turn, deflected their responsibility. According to them, the parents of both the girls and the boys had sanctioned the wedding. When a relative of the girls contradicted them, two members of the panchayat changed their stories, while another two ran away, literally. The remaining members said they had ordered the wedding to avoid a blood feud between the two families. No one, it seemed, wanted to acknowledge their role in forcing the girls into marriage.

Our team brought the police into the matter. Traditional law enforcement is virtually impotent in tribal areas, but with the press pursuing the matter, the local police had traction. They informed all involved that if the wedding ceremony had taken place, it had been in violation of the law. In response, the imam, the village council and even the parents of the young people who were married denied that there had ever been a wedding. The mosque's records of the event vanished. It seemed that there was little more that our reporters could do if everyone involved conspired to lie. I summoned our team back to Lahore, and I felt defeated.

Back at home that night, I picked up my daughter Fajr, soon to turn two, and held her close. I tried to fathom what it would be to consign her to a life of misery, as Afshan and Faiza's parents

had done. The thing about becoming a mother is that it immu-
nizes you from feeling indifference to the plight of any child. I
mourned for those girls as I held my precious own.

About a week later, welcome news made it to our Lahore
office: The panchayat in the village had reconvened both families to negotiate a different settlement. The press exposure, it
seemed, had influenced their thinking, after all. The council
determined that a diyat, monetary compensation, could replace
the girls as capital. The girls were returned to their family, and
a sum of money was handed over in their stead. The matter was
considered settled.

While my Helpline team rejoiced at this unexpected development, I remained deeply unsettled. What if the sisters hadn't had
the wherewithal, the daring or the literacy to appeal for help?
If no one had known of their plight beyond a tiny village that
seems to have colluded in their fate, what shape would their lives
have taken? What kind of lives would they yet live, if their own
parents had been prepared to send them away once already? And
what of other tribal councils striking similar bargains with the
lives of women and girls, but doing so away from media scrutiny? What would compel them to reverse their judgments? The
practice of vani was widespread in tribal regions. Women and
children offered in vani often faced lives of indentured servitude and abuse; traded as chattel, they were treated as such. I
was relieved that the paper had been able to help Afshan and
Faiza, however indirectly, but I was bothered by the thought of
the countless others like them that wouldn't be so lucky. Who
would protect them?

IF, AS EDNAN HAD SUGGESTED, one by one was the only way
to build consensus or garner the majority of votes I needed, I
would do it. And I would start at the top. As head of the provincial government, Chaudhry Pervaiz Elahi would be well placed,

I thought, to convince the Assembly to support my vani resolution. Elahi listened patiently as I made my case against the practice, and then he passed the buck.

"I would recommend," he said, "that you should discuss this with Law Minister Raja Basharat. I think he will be able to tell you how best to proceed."

A few days later, I approached Basharat, a career politician with a canny knack for smiling warmly and wielding the charms of a seasoned diplomat without ever budging an inch if he didn't want to. He summed up my push for a vani resolution thus: "The purpose of resolutions that are passed in the Assembly is merely to indicate that such a problem exists. Even if you manage to get the resolution passed, it will be of very little consequence."

I understood what Basharat was saying, even if I couldn't share his defeatist, why-bother attitude. Moving a resolution as a private member required time, perseverance and patience. Because so much of the business of the Assembly was taken up with proposals put forward by an entire party—and with a fair amount of political posturing, too—only one day a week, Tuesday, was allotted to business proposed by private members. If a resolution didn't make it onto the agenda on a given Tuesday, it was incumbent upon the member to resubmit it, and to continue doing so, until it made the agenda. If Basharat or another highly placed official didn't support a private member's resolution, it might never find its way out of the queue and onto the agenda. For that reason, many MPAs didn't bother submitting resolutions at all. Others became fed up with the process and abandoned their efforts. I understood the deterrent effect this had on individual members, but I assured Basharat that it would not have such an effect on me. He seemed unmoved.

Over my five-year term in the provincial assembly, I would deal many times with Raja Basharat. Always, I would think back to this first meeting with him, when he offered his personal opinion in the place of actual legal insight into what I might do to further my cause, and thus established a pattern. Dismissive and complacent, Basharat's advice offered an early glimpse into the epidemic apathy that I would come to learn was widespread in provincial government, where the path of least resistance, especially for cabinet ministers, was never to rile the ruling party.

Having approached, without success, two men at the top, I decided next to approach individual MPAs about my vani resolution. Over the course of several weeks, in the cafeteria and the corridors of the Assembly building, I sought out members of both the ruling coalition and the opposition from rural areas where the practice of vani was prevalent. I spoke with landlords whose stakes in vast landholdings made them reluctant to risk alienating their base by supporting an initiative that went against age-old tribal customs. I persisted, seeking out MPAs from opposing clans and trying to persuade them in part by demonstrating that I understood their predicament vis-à-vis their constituencies, and arguing that that was no reason to look the other way when it came to the basic human rights of women and girls living in their regions. "We are devaluing human beings and sanctioning their abuse," I said. I also appealed to MPAs on religious grounds. I was encouraged when conservative religious members responded favorably to my argument that vani, as a violation of Islamic law, undermines the teachings of the Prophet, praise be upon him; the Qur'an forbids forced marriage.

After several weeks, I began to receive responses that weren't dismissive or rude, but they weren't openly supportive, either. The implication was that if I pursued the resolution, I would have support, but I could not count on any fellow MPAs to co-sign it. That was good enough for me. Perhaps Ednan had been correct, I thought, when he told me that things were more nuanced than my first impression suggested. The extent to which listening to my colleagues in the parliament helped me make my case and persuade certain among them to offer their support made an impression on me. Understanding context was everything.

Whether tacit support would translate into passage of my resolution, of course, would remain to be seen.

AROUND THE SAME TIME that my Helpline team was working on Afshan and Faiza's case, Imrana Kookab from our Multan bureau called to tell me that Shaista, the young woman doused with acid on her wedding day, was at last medically stable enough to travel to Lahore for doctors at Mayo Hospital to assess her condition. If they determined that they could help her, her surgeries would be paid for by the zakat funds that I had been able to secure for her. If, in the more likely event that the doctors at Mayo determined that Shaista's needs were beyond the scope of what they could do, Tehmina Durrani would involve Smile Again to help her. "Steel yourself, madame," Kookab told me. "The poor woman remains badly disfigured."

A few days later, Shaista and her parents arrived at the paper's Lahore headquarters. Shaista wore a burqa, which covered her from head to toe. Only her father spoke. "Look at what that heartless fiend did to our daughter," he said, fighting tears. Shaista sat absolutely still as her father lifted the burqa. Next to me, Imtiaz Ghumman, the reporter who had accompanied Shaista and her parents from Multan, inhaled sharply. I strained not to flinch and tried to betray no response whatsoever, lest I cause the young woman further humiliation.

What I beheld shocked me. The acid had totally melted Shaista's features, claiming her right eye, her nose, her chin and both of her lips. Holes remained where her nose had been. Surgeries had pulled her burned skin tight in places, so that it bore an unsettling sheen, and left it deformed and lumpy in others, so that she almost did not look human. I would learn later that the acid had also claimed her breasts and eroded bone in her face and sternum.

I could not reconcile the intelligent-eyed, round-faced girl in the photograph that Shaista's parents showed me with the mutilated remains of a face that I saw before me. They were the worst acid attack injuries I had ever seen.

That night, as I tried to describe Shaista's condition to Ednan, I broke down. What evil could possess someone to do this to another human being? What future was there for this girl? And what help could I possibly offer her that would make a difference to her life? I could not get past the details of her story, and I could not unsee her destroyed face.

"Ednan, I can't do this," I said. "I don't even know where to begin. They won't even hear me on this in the Assembly."

"Like it or not, Humaira, you have been put in a position where you can help this woman, and I know that you will. As for the Assembly, you'll find a way," he said.

I passed the first of what would be many restless nights thinking about Shaista. One morning, I awoke with an epiphany: I couldn't bring Shaista herself to the parliament—I would never use her in that way. But I could use the newspaper to bring her story, and the stories of others like her, to my fellow MPAs. With press coverage pushing this issue, I would defy them to keep it off the agenda. I decided to submit an article about Shaista's ordeal to *Khabrain*'s front-page editors, who ran it alongside another that I had edited about all of the acid attack cases that the Helpline had fielded in the past year. In only one of them had a perpetrator been apprehended, and in that case, he was arrested and sentenced to death for a separate crime, not the acid attack.

I used the articles as leverage to pressure Raja Basharat to pledge to have Shaista's ex-fiancé arrested and brought to trial. His weak promise to do so was never tested; as had happened with Salma's husband and his accomplices in her rape—likely a tip-off from the very officials who should have taken them into custody—Shaista's attacker, the man who destroyed her face and, in the process, her life, fled and was never found.

That defeat was predictable given the way the current system worked. Rather than give in to my disappointment about it, however, I kept my eyes on the bigger picture: changing the legal definition of acid crimes and their prosecution. As a follow-up to the articles, I addressed an open letter to the Punjab Provincial Assembly and published it in *Khabrain*. In it, I stressed the imperative of passing a resolution that would force the National Assembly to take up the question, at the level of federal law, of acid attack sentencing. My hope was that the one-two punch of the articles and the open letter would compel my colleagues in the parliament to back my resolution when and if it finally made it onto the House agenda.

My letter, published in *Khabrain* on the thirtieth of January 2003, highlighted the growing number of acid crimes, the pain and suffering that victims face, and the utter lack of justice for them. I wrote about the loopholes that make it possible for perpetrators to evade meaningful consequences for their actions, and I urged that acid crimes be exempt from such options as offering monetary compensation to a victim in lieu of serving time. I urged the formation at the federal level of a new law that categorizes acid crimes as attempted murder, punishable by life imprisonment or, in the event of a victim's death, the death penalty. I called for accelerated trials for perpetrators, so that victims would not have to endure protracted proceedings; free legal aid for victims, who were often destitute; and the creation of treatment centers specialized in treating acid burns. I also called for the new law to restrict the production, importation, transportation, storage and sale of acid in Pakistan. Finally, I outlined the need for a designated burn unit in which victims of acid burns, as well as victims of other kinds of deliberate burnings, could receive specialized, subsidized, care.

I couldn't help but roll my eyes when, the same day that my open letter on acid attacks appeared in the newspaper, my fellow MPAs passed the Punjab Marriage Functions Act, which banned ostentation and wasteful spending on weddings. According to the language of the bill, wedding celebrants could not decorate any public space with lights, celebrate with fireworks, or serve more than one dish at their ceremony. *Well at least that menace is taken care of!* I thought.

Recovered from my bout of cynicism, I began a person-to-person campaign in the Assembly. If I could not reach a fellow MPA on human rights grounds, I would argue a different case: What did a country, and by extension, its legislators, look like in the eyes of the world that did nothing about so barbaric a crime?

I WAS PUSHING both resolutions simultaneously, waiting to see which, if either, would make it onto the House agenda on a Private Members' Day. Acid attacks came first, on the fourth of February, just days after my open letter decrying the difficulty of prosecuting the crime appeared in *Khabrain*. I didn't think it was a coincidence. Unfortunately, the Speaker was never able to present it for a vote, and I did not have the chance to speak on its behalf: Some, though not all, members of the opposition staged a walkout to protest another resolution, this one to praise Chief Minister Elahi's role in restoring democracy and developing the farm sector. The house adopted that resolution with a majority vote, and then adjourned.

After that, my vani resolution twice appeared on the agenda. The first time, the session was adjourned before a vote. Adjournment was a common tactic used to squelch a resolution. Or perhaps on that day it was simply inertia, or lack of will, as was often the case when a session adjourned before the day's business had been completed. Either way, the outcome was the same: back to the drawing board. I pleaded with Raja Basharat to readmit my resolution for balloting, the random process by which private members' proposals are added to the agenda, pending the approval of the House Secretariat.

Finally, on the twenty-fifth of February 2003, my vani resolution came up for a second time. I stood to speak on its behalf. "Women and girls across our country are bartered, like chattel, to settle debts, or handed over to men of another tribe to atone for the crime of a brother or a father. Women and girls given in vani have no rights. Captives in a society where tribal customs trump Islam's teachings, they disappear into lives of sexual, physical, and emotional abuse. Speaking out can be a death sentence," I said. I called for making vani punishable by a minimum of five years' imprisonment.

When I finished speaking, I realized that not only had my microphone been left on, there had been pin-drop silence as I addressed the usually cacophonous House. My resolution passed unanimously. That was just the first step. The next would be the time-consuming and politically fraught business of drafting it into a law, and that would entail a saga all its own. Nevertheless, the resolution to ban vani was my first victory.

IT IS THE RARE TRIUMPH that comes without exacting a toll, and this was true with my modest gain in the parliament. In the months that I had been working toward it, I had become, to the chagrin of my husband, something of a spectral presence at home. By March, Ednan, who had been so keen to help me advance and conquer, had grown bothered by my absorption in my work. Fellow MPAs met me in my office at the newspaper, crowding out the time that Ednan and I often shared in the middle of a workday. They came to our home for dinner, dominating the conversation with the kind of political shop talk that had never bored my husband, until now.

It didn't help that once our guests had gone and the children were tucked into their beds, I would make another cup of coffee and settle in at the kitchen table with thick legal tomes I had borrowed from the newspaper's legal office or the parliament's

library. If at the outset I had missed or bungled some bureaucratic procedures and technicalities, I had decided that my
safeguard against further flubs was assiduous study. I could do
nothing about the MPAs who would make sport of tripping me
up, or those that would use my outsider status as a journalist or
my gender against me. I could, however, make it harder for them
to fault my work by mastering parliamentary procedure. Ednan's
help was invaluable, of course, but I had to learn by doing.

Ednan relished his role helping me understand the parliament—the players, their tactics, the stakes. There was something protective about this, and endearing. I didn't have political
exposure, and Ednan wanted to shield me; he knew how ugly
things could get. As I got my bearings, however, and as I became
more assured of the soundness of my proposed legislations and
more confident about my ability to see them through, I needed
and sought his input less. This hurt him. When I was drafting
my vani resolution, for example, I wanted to discuss questions I
had with the Law Secretary of the parliament's secretariat. That
morning, Ednan said, "I'll go with you. I'll accompany you to
the secretariat." I assured him that I would be fine. I was by that
point fluent enough in the parlance of parliamentary matters
that I didn't feel I needed an interpreter to speak for me. I told
him so, and he looked wounded. What I didn't express, but what
must have been resoundingly clear from my tone that day, was
that I really didn't want my husband to run interference for me. I
learned later that Ednan had called the law secretary in advance
of my arrival to tell him that I had some questions. "Then why
doesn't she call us herself?" the Law Secretary reportedly said to
a duly admonished Ednan. Other times, Ednan wanted to coach
me about what to say. "This is ridiculous," I said one evening to
him, shutting down his well-meaning attempt to test my ability
to field hostile challenges to my vani resolution. "I have to be able
to think on my own!"

It didn't help matters that, almost overnight, I had gone from covering the news to being covered in it. Part of this was the novelty of a woman on a reserved seat actually getting something done; expectations had been set very low for us, and here the first significant resolution passed by the new Provincial Assembly was mine. For the first time since I had known him, Ednan's insecurities began to show. He feared that all of the attention would take me away from him. "Just don't fly away from me!" he had said in Multan, and here I was, taking flight. When he warned me against letting the attention or the privileges of being an MPA go to my head, I was insulted.

He became a very demanding husband. Ednan had never before questioned my commitment to him or to our children, but he did so now. When I had extra parliamentary sessions and legislative work, he made a point of noting my absences. "We're not on your mind, anymore," he said to me one evening when I returned, exhausted, from a grueling day. I was floored, hurt and angry. His insinuation that I was neglecting our children cut especially deep. For all of the guilt he placed on me during that time, nothing compared to the guilt I placed on myself. It was the beginning of the first period of protracted strain on our marriage. Neither of us in those days was in ready command of our old standby, a sense of humor.

The tension abated somewhat when my friend and fellow MPA, Sughra Imam, paid us a visit. Her charm and warmth absolutely dissolved my husband. "You don't have to tell me a single thing about you, Ednan Sahib," she said warmly. "Your wife has told me everything about you!" Ednan was flattered. *So that was what he needed,* I told myself: Assurance that even when I was away from him, he was so much on my mind that I talked about him with female colleagues. I imagined he thought we huddled together like a couple of schoolgirls dissecting the fever of a crush. I marveled at the fragility of the male ego and at the fact that not even Ednan, my rock, was spared the condition. The next day, Sughra and I had a good laugh when I thanked her for managing to do what I hadn't done in weeks: bring a smile to my husband's face.

After that, Ednan appeared to relax a bit. A short while later, when the leaders of the opposition parties, Syed Ihsan Ullah Waqas from MMA and Rana Sanaullah Khan from PML-N came to our newspaper office for interviews, I was surprised to learn that they had complimented me to Ednan. "We have so much respect for the work your wife is doing and the way she carries herself in the parliament," Waqas reportedly told Ednan. Khan, who would emerge as one of my most steadfast, if stealth, allies in the parliament, reportedly said, "We take your wife very seriously. She speaks about the right issues." It is high praise in Punjabi culture to be likened to a family member, so when Khan told Ednan that he considered me like a daughter, it went a long way toward assuaging Ednan's worries about how I might be perceived in the Assembly. Though I wasn't seeking any-one's huzzahs for my comportment, if their assessment allayed my husband's concerns about all of the press fuss turning me into a raging egotist, I was glad. I was struck, too, by the diver-gence between the opinion of me expressed by members of my own party and that shared in private by these members of the opposition.

WITH LATE SPRING came a medical imperative to slow down: I had suffered a miscarriage. I lost the pregnancy in its very early stages, but the loss shook my body and my heart. Unlike with my stillborn son, there was no tiny face to haunt my dreams, still and lifeless and blue. But that didn't prevent me from feeling a deep sorrow. I had never quite recovered from the fear that my body was unfit, somehow, for the business of nurturing another life. Not even two healthy children were testament enough to convince me or assuage my lingering guilt over the death in my womb of one of my twin boys.

If Ednan and I had spent the previous month or two waging something of a cold war over the competing demands of our life together, after the miscarriage we found our way back to peace. Where tragedy can turn the fissures in the surface of some relationships into crevasses that engulf them, it had the opposite effect on us. We pulled more closely together in the face of it. Never once did Ednan suggest that my relentless pace might be to blame for losing the pregnancy; it was a heartache that befell us both. I spent the rest of that spring in a decelerated mode, looking ahead to moving my third piece of legislation, a bill to outlaw private moneylending, and plotting my strategy to see my vani resolution passed into law. I also thought about how best to ensure that my acid attacks resolution would be brought to the House. Beyond that, it became a time to pause and reflect and count my blessings. The miscarriage would have the curious effect not of throwing me off balance, but of forcing me to find it again.

CHAPTER TEN

Let Us Do Our Job

SMALL BREAKTHROUGHS. Unexpected cooperation. A resolution passed. If my early progress in the Provincial Assembly defied certain of my low expectations, another aspect of parliamentary business reinforced them: the treatment of women on reserved seats. Some male MPAs resented proportional representation. As they saw it, by virtue of not having submitted to the rigors of the electoral process, women on reserved seats had been handed a free pass. We hadn't had to campaign, glad-hand, deliver stump speeches or court constituencies. Our reputations had not been assaulted by opponents; our private lives not scrutinized by the media; our personal wealth not depleted by the expense of running for office. Why should we have it so easy? Reserved seats struck some as filling a need that didn't exist.

In the summer of 2003, as I juggled three legislative goals—an amendment to Pakistan's penal code to outlaw and punish vani nationwide, a resolution criminalizing acid attacks, which had yet to be put to a vote, and a bill to ban private moneylending—there were male colleagues who said to me, "Why don't you just enjoy the perks and privileges of your seat, like all the other women do?" In other words: Sit pretty and leave the matter of legislating to them. I was incensed. Men in the House began referring to female MPAs as dessert. It had the effect of making even the most substantive among us feel that our presence was merely ornamental.

It was easy—and, for the most part, accurate—to write off male members' criticism of proportional representation as craven sexism. At the same time, I began quietly to harbor misgivings of my own regarding whether setting aside seats for women truly advanced our—or democracy's—causes. The intention of the reserved seats was to enrich the parliament with women who would bring the diversity of their experiences, educations and backgrounds to bear on legislative matters. With so many of the seats more or less handed to the most powerful families, who had no stake in shaking up the status quo, I wondered: *What diversity?* That I had been able to vie for my own seat because of the well-connected family that I had married into only exacerbated the conflict I felt within myself about reserved seats. Whither democracy if only a tiny fraction of the nation's women, by virtue of their connections or their birth, could ascend to a seat in the first place? And what did it matter to the cause of women across the country if so many of their representatives in the parliament were unable or unwilling, by virtue of their parties' politics or vested interests, to help them? I took comfort in knowing that, success or no, I would use my position in the Provincial Assembly to fight for the common good.

I discerned three general groupings among the sixty-six of us who held reserved seats: professional women, i.e., those holding other day jobs in fields such as law, medicine, journalism and business; women affiliated with grassroots politics and district-level local governance; and the wives and daughters of powerful landowners and industrialists, as well as those coming from Pakistan's feudal elite, of which some one hundred families were represented in the Punjab parliament.

This last group of industrialists and feudal lords' wives and daughters was the cause of my greatest skepticism about reserved seats. Many of the women were Begum, meaning that they were from families of social rank. It is an honorific, Begum, but it is also a term that can imply a certain lack of gravitas among a group better known for its displays of wealth. From the start, the Begum in the provincial assembly advanced little beyond their own media profiles. Seemingly possessed of no voice of their own, no personal convictions, they voted with their families, never spoke before the Assembly unless in the role of pro-establishment toady, and dressed lavishly to the point of the absurd. At best, they were obliging puppets; at worst, spoiled and preening. They played right into the hands of the most dismissive critics of reserved seats by seeking the spotlight but having nothing to say. When disparaging male members shouted "Sweet dish!" and "Dessert!"—put-downs that carry with them a lurid double entendre in Urdu—I thought guiltily of my first impression the day of our swearing in: petits fours.

I had far more respect for the women MPAs with backgrounds in grassroots organizing and local government. Indeed, their impressive work in development and district-level politics led me to anticipate that they would be sympathetic to my proposed legislations. This was true only to a certain point, however. I learned that these MPAs were first and foremost beholden to their groups' leadership and specific legislative goals. They were in the parliament to serve specific constituencies' needs, such as building roads, hospitals and sewer systems; worthy projects all. But an epidemic of political myopia afflicted their ranks; by focusing exclusively on their own agendas, many missed the chance to back other causes that would have benefited from their attention and support. While I forged several strong relationships with MPAs from this group, I noted with chagrin that in the aggregate, these women did not feel free to act or to speak without a directive to do so. Nor did they join forces so that they might harness the strength of numbers. It seemed to me that they lacked an understanding of their own power. I came to think of their presence on reserved seats as a lost opportunity, because this group—far more than the women from powerful families—was poised to effect change. I was frustrated by their inability to maximize their potential in the parliament, and I felt sorry to see so many interesting, smart, committed and eloquent women allow themselves to be hamstrung, politically speaking.

The professional women parliamentarians, of whom I was one, hewed to no one's agenda but the one dictated by their own consciences. Not everyone spoke before the Assembly or waved high the banner for democracy or women's rights, but when reserved-seat voices rose up, they came, by and large, from these women who had professional experience outside of politics. Because of this, many of the male MPAs who resented the reserved seats took particular aim at us. If on the floor of the House they at first derided the Begum, whose frivolity made them easy targets, behind the scenes, they wasted no energy on low-hanging fruit: We were the threats. Certain male MPAs attempted to hinder our progress by canceling workshops and training for legislative processes, lest we learn the procedures and mobilize. I hadn't realized what an advantage I had claimed for myself by turning, early on, to Haji Muhammad Saifullah for private mentoring in parliamentary procedures. He had warned me of the hurdles and roadblocks that I would face, but I didn't anticipate that such obstacles would boil down to dirty tricks and officious bureaucracy by the small of mind and faint of heart in the parliament. That summer, I would encounter all manner of hindrances as I pursued each of my legislative goals, starting with my vani legislation.

ONCE APPROVED, A RESOLUTION has no legal bearing beyond the Assembly, but it places an obligation on the Assembly to act. Passage of my vani resolution, then, did not yet ban the practice but set in motion the legislative process that, if successful, would do so. While the Assembly was required to act, the onus was on me to push for its adoption into law. My goal was especially ambitious: Not only did I want to outlaw vani in the Punjab; I sought to make it illegal across Pakistan. As a member of a provincial assembly, however, I could not create or amend national law. I therefore had two options: I could hope that a member of the National Assembly would pick up my vani bill, take the considerable time to draft it into law and then push for its adoption, or I could draft the law myself, send it on to the federal Law Department, and campaign for President Musharraf and other influential government ministers to support it. Rather than risk seeing my vani bill stall somewhere between the Provincial and National assemblies, I opted for the latter. I wrote private letters and published public appeals in *Khabrain* to President Musharraf, calling on him to acknowledge vani as an evil custom with no place in civilized society and asking him to support an amendment to the Pakistan Penal Code to outlaw the practice. I also appealed to Nilofer Bakhtiar, an adviser to the federal government on women's affairs, and a dynamo, to keep up the pressure on Musharraf to back women's issues. A longtime advocate of women's rights, Bakhtiar promised to do so.

It would be my Sisyphean summer, inching a draft of my vani law ever forward, only to be sent several steps backward by some senior Law Department official, and starting all over again. Between June and September, the Law Department would reject every draft of my vani law on the basis of technical errors or incorrect phrasing. It seemed that no amount of studying the minutiae of drafting legislation had helped me. I was caught in a thicket of legalese and arcana; no matter which way I moved, I became more deeply ensnared. Someone, it seemed, was determined that I should fail.

In fact, members of my own party had begun telling me that I was becoming an embarrassment to them. There is an expectation on members of the ruling coalition, which sits on the Treasury benches in the House chamber, to toe the line. For this reason, it is often members of the opposition that have the most success in putting forward new legislation; their role is to challenge the order of things. I considered that my role as well, however; hence the irritation I caused certain members of my party who wished I'd kindly shut up, and said so.

During all of the time that I was pushing for my three main legislative objectives on vani, acid attacks and moneylending, I was also standing to speak out against cases of rape, stove burnings and other crimes against women. When a particularly horrible case came in to the Helpline, for example, I would move an adjournment motion during the next session of the parliament. By doing so, I was requesting that the business of the day end a half hour early so that the House could take up discussion of the case in question and expedite a legal remedy for the victim. More often than not, however, a House staffer, responding to a barely perceptible nod from the Speaker, would switch off my microphone, and I would never get to speak. That was what happened when, over the course of nearly four weeks, I tried to call attention to the case of a nine-year-old girl who had been raped and left unconscious. The Helpline had published her story, but law enforcement in the region, Sahiwal, had not acted on the girl's behalf. I sought to compel the police there to act by securing a parliamentary order for the perpetrator's arrest. I never managed to do so. By highlighting such appalling crimes, I was putting fellow MPAs from the regions where the crimes were committed on the spot to act, which they resented. Some considered my attempts meddlesome; what gave me the right to demand that their constituencies respond in a certain way? I also learned that some MPAs had given the guilty party protection; money might have changed hands, for example, or the perpetrator might have other connections that helped him evade arrest. I was beginning to realize that the only reason my vani resolution had passed was because it didn't take aim at a specific region in the Punjab, but sought a change in federal law. Even so, the provincial Law Department appeared to be doing all it could to prevent my law from making it to the federal Law Department by rejecting each of my drafts and by refusing to give me data, statistics and other research that I was well within my rights to request.

Growing desperate and feeling demoralized, I decided that if the provincial Law Department's administration could tell me what was wrong with my drafts, it must also be able to tell me how to fix them. I sought their help on these grounds; predictably, they didn't care for my reasoning. I learned that it was extremely rare for a private member from a provincial assembly to draft a law for sending to the federal Law Department. Worse, no woman had ever done it; senior law officials, I gathered, weren't fans of "firsts." Some officials were openly dismissive of my effort, others outright condescending. "Why do you want to stress yourself out by trying to accomplish something that can never be achieved?" one MPA asked the moment I took a seat in his office. I hadn't even asked him for help yet, and I didn't bother doing so.

While my legislation languished, cases of vani appeared to be on the rise. Almost daily, *Khabrain* and other leading newspapers carried stories of young girls and women whose lives were being ruined by the rulings of panchayats that traded them like commodities. Unable for the moment to finalize my law, I sent op-eds to every major newspaper in Pakistan condemning vani and questioning the jurisdiction of panchayats to issue such rulings. In an article entitled "The Journey of My First Legislation" and published on the twenty-fifth of July, I reprised the story of Afshan and Faiza, the underage sisters who had sought *Khabrain*'s help in getting out of a forced marriage. I was determined to keep the issue of vani on the front burner.

Back in the parliament, a junior Law Department official who had witnessed my rebuffing at the hands of senior officials in his department offered me his support. He assured me that he and a few of his junior colleagues would help me draft the law, but they would do so discreetly; their help would come as a personal favor, not official business. This was in part because I was pursuing a law that fell beyond the scope of their jurisdiction; it was neither their responsibility nor their bailiwick to help a member draft legislation for the federal Law Department. They also feared ramifications to their own standing in the Law Department if senior colleagues found them out. This wasn't only because the work was beyond their scope, but because it was for me: The junior Law Department staffers' efforts on my behalf could be construed as insubordination. In all, it would take nearly seven months of constant reworking to come up with a draft that would not fall prey to the Law Department's officious niggling. I didn't know that, though, and so I continued to hope for more immediate progress.

"THE TASK NOW is for civil society to keep their advocacy going and for the media to keep on highlighting what a major social evil vani is," I said to Ednan as we drove to dinner one evening in late July. "We can't allow this to drop below the radar. You know how fickle our government departments can be. If they feel the heat has died down a bit, they might just dawdle and delay the process—if it ever starts. God knows how many young girls and women will continue to suffer because of this awful practice."

Ednan waited until we were stopped at a traffic light before he replied. "Humaira," he said, his glasses reflecting the red glow of the taillights ahead of us, "it'll all work itself out eventually. All you can do is to keep your end going as strongly as you've made it go."

He smiled at me as the light changed. "Now, do you think we might discuss something else over dinner?"

I gave Ednan a playful poke in the ribs. He laughed and

Already headstrong: me, four years old, in Kuwait in 1975.

The young Bhatti family in 1975. My father, Abdul Hamid; my mother, Musarat; my brother, Samir, at age eight; and me at age four in Kuwait.

A quiet moment in the Lawrence Garden in Lahore just a month before our wedding, as captured by Ednan in November 1996.

In prayer: My father-in-law, Zia Shahid; my father, Abdul Hamid Bhatti; and my Nana ji, my maternal grandfather Muhammad Nazir; the day of my and Ednan's Nikkah, or the singing of our marriage vows, the eighteenth of December 1996.

With my younger sister, Aisha, and my older brother, Samir, on my wedding day, the twentieth of December 1996.

Radiant and happy the day after our wedding at the Walima, the reception given by the groom's family, on the twenty-first of December 1996.

Taking in the Kite Festival with Ednan from the rooftop of the home we shared with his parents in Model Town, Lahore, in 1997.

Our young family: With Ednan and our first child, Nofal, the summer of 1998 in Islamabad.

Our growing family: Celebrating Nofal's fourth birthday with ten-month-old Fajr and Ednan in September 2001 at our home in Model Town, Lahore.

Attending Ednan's cousin's wedding in Lahore in December 2003.

With one-year-old Hafsa watching Ednan's cricket match in Lahore in 2005.

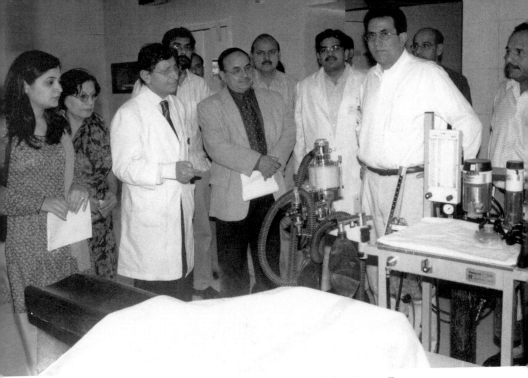

The ribbon-cutting marking the official opening of the Ganga Ram Hospital Burn Unit, with Dr. Akbar Chaudhry and Health Minister Dr. Tahir Ali Javed in Lahore in February 2, 2006.

Celebrating Fajr's sixth birthday, her last with her father, on the twenty-first of December 2006, the day after our tenth wedding anniversary.

The view of the Lawrence Road and St. Anthony's Church from the penthouse I shared with Ednan atop *Khabrain*'s headquarters in Lahore. We used to watch the most remarkable sunsets from these windows.

Silly business: Nofal, age twelve, Fajr, age nine, and Hafsa, age five, playing outside at my cousin's home in North Carolina in 2009.

Addressing an assembly of students for the graduate course "Women and Security" at Harvard in January 2010.

Speaking at the reintroduction of the International Violence Against Women Act on the fourth of February 2010 in Washington, DC. © *Women Thrive Worldwide*

Addressing the Punjab Assembly after taking my oath to serve a second term in October 2010. *Photographer: Shahzad Qamar. Copyright Provincial Assembly Punjab*

Missing Ednan: With fourteen-year-old Nofal, seven-year-old Hafsa and eleven-year old Fajr on a hill above Islamabad in July 2012.

sighed at once. I knew that I talked a great deal, probably even too much, about my work. I did not share Ednan's gift for leaving the office at the office. As each of us had stepped out of the protective cocoon that we had swaddled ourselves in following my miscarriage, and as the pace of our lives had regained its usual clip, Ednan's complaint that there wasn't enough of me left over for him and the children became a refrain. Sometimes, I felt sad to hear it. Other times, I fumed. Always, it underscored my fear that the double standard, a pillar of Pakistan's gender politics and societal dysfunction, had taken root in my own home. After all, for all of the times when Ednan's work had hampered his ability to be present for the children and me, I had never complained or made him feel guilty. I knew that he would be home with us if he could. He had always afforded me the same support and benefit of the doubt—until now. I didn't imagine that any of my male colleagues in the Provincial Assembly were cleaved in two by the opposing demands of their home and work lives. Were they also running themselves ragged trying to be all things to all people— spouse, parent, colleague? Couldn't Ednan see how hard I was trying? In the midst of another torrid Pakistan summer, a touch of cold war lingered in the air.

At the heart of our chilly contretemps, I believed, was Ednan's insecurity about being left behind. Whereas he had joined and mentored me in my newspaper work and been the first to celebrate my successes, his exclusion from the ins and outs of my daily life as a parliamentarian bothered him. My reluctance to let him smooth the way for me in the Assembly made him feel irrelevant. I vowed with myself to solicit more of his input and advice and to balance out my talking with more listening. That evening, however, I resolved not to say a single word more about anything having to do with legislation, crime or injustice over dinner.

It was a rare night out without the children or colleagues or other family members in tow. We had dropped Nofal and Fajr off at my parents' house, so the night was ours. It was, in fact, a "date night," that special contrivance of overworked couples everywhere who at least have the good sense to pause long enough from the swirl of their lives to notice that the home fires need fanning. I never would have dreamed that Ednan and I would have had to resort to such a measure, but there we were, all dressed up and on our way to an evening of meaningful eye contact over dinner and candlelight. We hadn't had a date since well before my miscarriage. I tried to shake off my low opinion of the entire enterprise of an evening of forced romance. It had been months, after all, since Ednan and I had just sat across a table and looked at each other. Perhaps meaningful eye contact was exactly what we needed.

"Thank you for a lovely evening, Mrs. Shahid," Ednan said when we reached my parents' home to pick up the kids.

"Thank you, Mr. Shahid," I said and smiled. I looked up and recognized a look in his eyes that I knew well but hadn't seen of late—adoration, contentment, a mixture of both. My long-suffering husband, I thought, regretting the irritation I had been feeling with him. Samir had asked him all those years ago if he had any idea what he would be getting himself into if he married me. "A woman you can never convince," Samir had said. I wondered in that moment if Ednan, knowing what he knew now about his workaholic bride, would still propose to me. I thought of putting the question to him, but instead I said, "I had forgotten you could be such charming company." We both laughed. I decided that he would still ask me to marry him, and I would still say yes.

Once back home, the children tucked in for the night, Ednan flopped himself onto the sofa and settled into the highlights package of a World Cup cricket match between Pakistan and India. The game was months old, but Ednan didn't tire of watching its best moments. I worked until the wee hours of the morning, and Ednan didn't complain.

THROUGHOUT THE SUMMER, as I worked on redrafting the vani law, I waged two other campaigns, as well. One was to see that my acid attack resolution made it back onto the House agenda—it had languished since February. The other was to see that my bill to ban private moneylending did the same. I was having difficulty drafting the moneylending bill; the vani struggle had shaken my confidence in my ability to draft legislation that would pass muster with the Law Department. For all of the truculence I encountered from MPAs and others in the House bureaucracy, however, there were angels in disguise who guided me when I was at a loss for where to turn and what to do. A man named Maqsood Malik was one of them. A career bureaucrat in the Assembly secretariat whose title at the time was Legislative Deputy Secretary, Malik quite readily offered me help with redrafting the bill. Malik is a soft-spoken man, with a broad forehead and eyes that shine with kindness and a keen intelligence. He exudes a generosity of spirit that makes him the rarest of Pakistani bureaucrats. Malik's interest in moneylending was personal: He hails from a neglected region of the Punjab, Rajanpur, where moneylenders troll with ease for new prey. He had seen the ravages firsthand that poverty and desperation wrought on a poor population, and he wanted to help me do something about it. He also anticipated the problems I would have in drafting a version that would not be rejected outright by the Law Department. Over the course of my term in the parliament, Malik would prove to be one of my staunchest allies. In the shorter term, he helped me to invaluable effect, rewriting and reformatting my entire bill, thus ensuring that the Prohibition of Private Money Lending Bill 2003 that I submitted to the Assembly on the thirteenth of June was technically unimpeachable. Now we had only to wait for it to appear on a Private Members' Day. If it was not opposed, it would be referred to the relevant committee for further examination before being sent back to the Assembly for a vote on whether to make it law.

That summer, a surge of correspondence about moneylending arrived at Helpline bureaus all over the country. As we had done with acid attacks, the Helpline had placed public service announcements in *Khabrain* editions nationwide soliciting victims of predatory lending to come forward with their stories. The response was overwhelming and suggested that predatory lenders were becoming more brazen, their tactics more destructive. The practice had metastasized into a societal cancer. What I had assumed to be a shadowy gray market enterprise turned out to be a thriving industry of business conducted openly, in plain sight of law enforcement, and often in cahoots with them.

Letters sent to the Helpline detailed a host of abuses. In July, the NGO Welfare of Humanity, or Anjuman e Tahafaze Insaan, sent a detailed account of the moneylenders of Multan, who had ties to drug mafias and called themselves the Kings of Multan because of their seemingly unassailable power over a populace that had no recourse against them. As a condition of receiving funds, the Kings of Multan required borrowers to hand over the titles to their properties as collateral. Most borrowers, illiterate, used their thumbprints to stamp contracts that specified interest rates of between 75 and 300 percent. When borrowers defaulted, gangsters held them in dairas, rural compounds, of sorts, and subjected them to psychological and physical abuse while other thugs ransacked their homes, tossed out their possessions and destroyed what remained of their property. The letter identified marketplaces across Multan where moneylenders operated out of offices thinly disguised as other businesses. The letter also alleged police collaboration with the lenders and offered eyewitness accounts of police getting drunk with lenders in the dairas while terrified borrowers looked on, powerless. According to this letter, these gangs were known to have killed borrowers whose last and only assets to give were their lives.

Another letter arrived from Khushab, in the central Punjab.

It was written by a private citizen named Hafizullah, who documented instances of women caught in a cycle of indebtedness that landed them in brothels. Unable to repay one lender, these women would take out a loan from another, and then another, until they were in debt to several lenders at once. Hafizullah offered to help our Helpline staff find the brothels where the women were held until they had worked off their debts. He knew of several who had become chronically ill and others, desperate, who had committed suicide.

Other letters identified major hubs of moneylending in Lahore, or instances of lenders seizing agricultural lands and leaving borrowers without any means to support their families. The examples were myriad and transcended class lines. One borrower, a man named Sarfraz Butt, traveled from Gujranwala, about an hour's drive north of Lahore, to meet with me personally about his predicament. He had borrowed 12 lacs, or 1.2 million rupees—almost $20,000 at the time—for a business venture. In present-day Pakistan, where rural areas lack brick-and-mortar bank branches, basic banking services are out of reach for local populations. (Mobile banking is only a recent, and not widespread, development.) Because of this, even comparatively well-off people like Butt who do not have access to banks are forced to turn to the informal economy to acquire the sums they need. Private moneylenders know this and exploit it. Butt explained to me that he had repaid more than he owed, a sum of nearly 20 lacs. His moneylender insisted that he hand over another 11 lacs in order to get back the title to his home. Butt didn't have it, and now he feared for his safety and his life.

With each letter that I became aware of, I better understood why God forbids usury. It is not about economics; it is about human rights. I had come increasingly to understand that poverty is a human rights issue. Private moneylenders effectively bought the power to suppress, oppress and abuse the poor, to disenfranchise them by commandeering law enforcement, and to devalue their lives by persecuting them for not having economic security. With ever more urgency, I pressed the Provincial Assembly's secretariat to put my moneylending prohibition bill on the agenda.

On the twenty-eighth of July, I published an article in *Khabrain* that chronicled how widespread the problem of private moneylending had become: In towns and villages across the Punjab, as many as 70 percent of households were in debt to two or three moneylenders at a time. I cited the Helpline letters that revealed the presence of moneylending networks operating out of busy commercial centers, and I laid the blame for lack of enforcement squarely on the police. I also reminded readers that usury is fundamentally anti-Islam; the Qur'an puts usury, also known as riba, which means excess, on a par with incest with one's mother as offenses against God. I expected to return to the House the next day and continue the moneylending push, but on the twenty-ninth and thirtieth of July, the treatment of women on reserved seats reached a new low, making it impossible to accomplish anything meaningful in the Assembly.

The misogynist chorus that had been the soundtrack to every session during my first year in the Punjab Provincial Assembly reached a fever pitch that July. All of us on reserved seats were jeered by our male colleagues, shouted down, told that we were burdens to the taxpayers of Pakistan, and laughed at for rising to speak in our own defense. If at the start of my year in the parliament I discerned groupings among us, and if my own assessment of some of my fellow MPAs on reserved seats had been less than flattering, by midsummer, we had no choice but to stand together: We staged a walkout to protest our treatment and to force the House proceedings to a halt.

If the intention of our en masse display of solidarity was to force the men in the Assembly to reflect on their boorish, demeaning and counterproductive behavior, we fell short of our goal. Once returned to the House chamber, we were jeered at some more. I had had enough. Disgusted, I returned home and spent the afternoon writing an angry op-ed that ran in the next day's *Khabrain*, on the thirty-first of July. In "Let Us Do Our Job," I demanded a call to order and exposed my male colleagues' antics and behavior. I revealed that they derided women MPAs on reserved seats as undeserving and unworthy of being in the parliament, and that they referred to us as eye candy but not legislators. I insisted that we be allowed to pass the resolutions we put forth, to work on behalf of women's rights and other issues, and to peacefully coexist in the Assembly without having to justify our presence. I made a direct appeal in my op-ed to President Musharraf. As the man who put the system of proportional representation in place, I thought that he of all people should be concerned about the joke it was becoming. "If he or his administration will not support their own decisions," I wrote, "who else will?" I closed with a simple entreaty: "All we ask is to let us do our job."

Remarkably, two of the MPAs who had been the most vocal opponents of women on reserved seats apologized to me in the wake of my editorial's publication. Like a couple of naughty lads caught tattling, they insisted that they hadn't been talking about me. I suggested they pick up a mantle more constructive than the persecution of their female colleagues, whichever ones they felt so free to assail. Other male colleagues in the parliament scolded me. "Humaira Bibi, you have gone too far," they said. The women on reserved seats roundly thanked me.

The thirty-first of July happened also to be the day that the Assembly at last moved my moneylending bill, which sought an outright ban on all private moneylending and a prison sentence of up to ten years and a fine of up to a half-million rupees for violators. The bill, unopposed, was referred to the Revenue Committee for further discussion. The Revenue Committee, however, lacked a chairperson, so before there could be discussion of anything, one would have to be selected. Even so, I considered the bill's referral to the relevant committee progress.

The following week, in order to underscore the long and troubled history of private moneylending in Pakistan, I published an article in *Khabrain* about the history of attempts to outlaw it. Sir Chhotu Ram, an Indian politician and pre-partition Member of the Punjab Provincial Assembly, authored the Punjab Relief of Indebtedness Act of 1934 and the Punjab Debtor's Protection Act of 1936, each of which aimed to give poor farmers respite from moneylenders who sought to mortgage their lands. Those protections were scrapped following partition, in 1947.

The issue wasn't taken up again until 1960, when the Punjab Money-Lenders Ordinance attempted anew to curb and regulate private moneylending by requiring private lenders to register with their local commissioner and secure licenses to operate. Because of the complexity of the regulatory and licensing systems proposed, however, the ordinance was never implemented. Since then, the mechanism of local governance had changed so many times that the 1960 law, which was based on the British colonial commissioner system, was obsolete. My bill sought to remove the 1960 law from the books and replace it with one that was relevant to the circumstances and governance of twenty-first-century Pakistan.

After my Prohibition of Private Money Lending Bill was referred to the Revenue Committee, I was hopeful that, for the first time since Sir Chhotu Ram's successful but short-lived efforts to protect the poor from the predations of unscrupulous lenders, private moneylending's days would at last be numbered. Had I known then what I would come to learn about the capacity of my colleagues on the committee for stalling and subterfuge, I might not have harbored such optimism.

I would come to learn that there were those in the provincial parliament who were determined to see my bill die in committee. The reasons for this are various, but two stand out among the rest: First, I sought to ban a practice that would cut into a sideline of many of my fellow MPAs. While it would take years before I would fully comprehend the magnitude of the problem—as well as the degree of some of my colleagues' duplicity—it was clear to me even early in my term as an MPA that private moneylenders weren't just thugs fronting sham businesses in bustling city markets; they were also elected officials and high-level parliamentary bureaucrats whose own stakes in exploiting Pakistan's dysfunctional economy made my bill a terrible threat. Anyone with wealth or connections could secure an easy bank loan of, say, 5 percent interest, and turn around and loan that money to poor families and farmers at 14 to 17 percent interest. I would also learn that some of my fellow politicians were in even deeper, working with or offering protection to moneylending mafias and sharing in a cut of their ill-gotten gains.

The second reason that my moneylending bill was so unpopular is that it took aim at usury, which, as a cornerstone of a capitalist monetary system, depends on credit. I sought only to ban the impossible-to-regulate, highly exploitative business of private persons or companies lending sums to individuals, but I knew that my bill would be construed as a threat to Pakistan's entire banking system.

It might seem like an improbable leap—that outlawing small-scale credit could imperil institutionalized lending—but context is everything: The Qur'an forbids usury, or riba. A riba-based economy in an Islamic country such as Pakistan, then, uncomfortably straddles what is and is not permitted in Islam. For decades, Islamists and scholars of Islamic finance had argued in favor of doing away with riba altogether and establishing an alternative economic system based on mutual profit and loss.

Their cause received a terrific boost from the Federal Shariat Court on the fourteenth of November 1991. Its jurisdiction no longer restricted from adjudicating fiscal matters,* the FSC issued a landmark ruling in a case that brought together 115 separate petitions against riba. In *Mahmood ur Rahman Faisal v. Secretary of the Ministry of Law*, the FSC ruled that modern interest banking constituted riba, or the augmented profit from loans as proscribed by the Holy Prophet, praise be upon him, and it declared interest-based banking completely forbidden. The federal government and various financial institutions filed sixty-seven appeals with the Supreme Court of Pakistan's Shariat Appellate Bench. The governments of Benazir Bhutto and Nawaz Sharif were content to let the Supreme Court sit on the appeals, lest a ruling upholding the FSC's verdict mean undertaking a grounds-up overhaul of Pakistan's economic system.

The appeals pended until 1999, when the Shariat Appellate Bench of the Supreme Court, in *Dr. Mohammad Aslam Khaki v. Syed Mohammad Hashim*, upheld the FSC's judgment against riba and mandated the end of interest-based banking by the year 2000. In its extensive ruling, the court called for the establishment of an economic system based on the injunctions of Islam. The Musharraf government and banks immediately appealed, if only to stay implementation of the judgment. In 2002, the Shariat Appellate Branch reviewed its judgment and remanded the case to the Federal Shariat Court for fresh examination, and that is where the matter remained in 2003, when I introduced my Prohibition of Private Money Lending Bill.† My bill no doubt struck many in the ruling alliance as having the potential to force open that troublesome can of worms. At the same time, it

---

*Established by General Zia-ul-Haq to challenge any law or regulation deemed repugnant to Islam. While vested with extraordinary jurisdiction over Islamic matters, the court's power did not extend to Muslim personal law, the Constitution or, for a time, fiscal matters. Nor did the FSC have the jurisdiction to overturn the martial law that Zia-ul-Haq himself imposed. He would risk no challenge to his power, not even from Islam itself.
†As of this writing in 2013, the Federal Shariat Court, under sustained pressure from the government, banks and other financial institutions protecting their interests in maintaining a credit-based economy, has yet to rule definitively on the matter.

risked exposing the hypocrisy of colleagues, Muslims all, who were protecting—if not also practicing—a system forbidden by their holy book.

WHILE PURSUING MY MONEYLENDING BILL, I also spent months pushing to have my acid attack resolution included in a Private Members' Day agenda. I went so far as to beseech the Law Minister, Raja Basharat, to suspend the rules and add it himself, which he had the power to do. "Look," I had said to him toward the end of July. "Twice my acid attack resolution has been on the agenda, and twice the session has adjourned before a vote. I have earned this." He was disinclined to help me, but never would have had to deliver; luck intervened on the fifth of August, when my acid attack resolution made it through the random process of balloting and onto that day's agenda. It happened to be the last day of parliamentary sessions before a break of more than two months. This time, there was a vote on my acid attack resolution, and as with my vani resolution, the count was unanimous in its favor. I might have taken this as a victory, but by then I knew better than to count on my resolution making it out of the federal Law Department. I had grown weary and pessimistic. By that point in my first year on the Provincial Assembly, I knew well that good intentions and diligence did not always add up to progress. I also realized that for every two or three MPAs I might convince to support my measures, there would always be another one against me, willing to use deceit, if necessary, to deter me.

Helpful colleagues had begun to urge me to focus on just one measure; in their opinion, I would have the most success with moneylending, because it fell within the purview of the Provincial Assembly. I wasn't sure what to think. I returned home the day of the vote on my acid attack resolution looking as dejected as I felt.

"You need to snap out of it, Humaira," Ednan said the next morning when he saw that my disposition hadn't changed. "Most people would regard this as some sort of victory. Why not you?"

"Because," I said, "nothing is going to come of it until the federal government takes notice and acts. A resolution isn't going to achieve anything until a law is created." Ednan listened as he tucked into an enormous breakfast of buttered parathas and eggs; built like a reed, he ate like a heavyweight. At length, he said, "It seems to me that the only way to bring it to the attention of the federal government, other than writing about it in the paper, is to bring it up personally with President Musharraf when he next meets with your party." As he spoke, bits of egg flew from his mouth and landed on the table. I shot him my best look of revulsion—talking with one's mouth full was a particular peeve of mine—and we both burst out laughing.

"But seriously," he said, composing himself and setting down his fork to let me know that he got the message, "if you speak with the President, you won't be out of your place to do so. You're not requesting favors, just drawing his attention to another critical issue. Your articles have alerted him to the work you're doing on vani, so my guess is that he'll listen to you on this, as well."

Ednan's notion was a good one, and not at all far-fetched. I had heard from the Governor of the Punjab, Lieutenant General Khalid Maqbool, that the President was aware and supportive of my work. Maqbool, himself an advocate of women's rights and protections, had also expressed his personal encouragement for my efforts. I knew that he had Musharraf's ear. Now I had to get it, too. That opportunity would come sooner than I would have hoped.

Whenever Musharraf came to Lahore, the provincial ruling alliance turned out to hear him speak, most often at Khalid Maqbool's official residence, the Governor's House, a mansion built in 1851 along the Mall Road in Lahore. It is a splendid, if curious, building, a sprawling amalgam of Mughal, Sikh, British colonial and Italianate architecture, and going there always felt like an event.

One afternoon in August, as the monsoons pummeled Lahore's parched greenbelt and cloudbursts drenched one neighborhood after the other across the city, I watched as Nofal and Fajr stomped, weather-possessed, in puddles outside. I made a note to myself to remember their joyful spectacle when, fighting to get them bathed and into dry clothes later, they would be transformed into wailing, protesting savages.

The phone rang. A parliamentary colleague told me that Musharraf would be at the Governor's House the following weekend, and we were expected to attend. I hung up and turned to tell Ednan, who was just heading out, soccer ball tucked under his arm. He was on his way to my mother's house to join my brother Muhammad and cousins Ziad and Zain in a match in her waterlogged garden. For a reason that I will never understand, whenever the rains were heaviest, that is when my husband most loved to play soccer. "You don't get it, and you never will, my love!" Ednan called to me as he took the stairs two at a time out the door. "But that's okay, more fun for me!" *Great*, I thought. *My biggest child has just left, and now I get to spend the next hour corralling the other two into the bath.*

The following weekend at the Governor's House, I found Musharraf relaxed, amiable and engaging. At these more intimate gatherings, he was so unlike his otherwise stiff and unduly humorless public self, the demeanor he perhaps considered most befitting an army chief and president. Musharraf had established a reputation for forthrightness in his dealings with people and for his ability to be inclusive. That evening, I appreciated the way he made the discussion interactive, inviting feedback from all of us, especially the newer and younger parliamentarians.

When it was my turn to greet the President after the meeting, I was surprised when he turned to Governor Maqbool, who stood by his side, and said, "Isn't this the young lady who's responsible for the recent resolutions passed by the Punjab assembly on human rights issues?" Maqbool said yes. "Mr. President, Humaira has been doing a lot of work on human rights since even before she entered parliament. I have met her and her husband, Ednan Shahid, on a number of occasions in connection with the splendid work she has done over the past couple of years."

I took that introduction as my cue to engage Musharraf in more than the customary hello. "President Sahib," I said, "having women on reserved seats in the parliament will serve no purpose if we are not allowed to speak or legislate. And if we cannot do that, what else are we supposed to do? You need to help us. When I, or my female colleagues, try to speak, our mics are shut off. We need support and encouragement from you. We need to better understand the government's stances on human rights and social policies so that we can be more effective when we are finally given the chance to do our work."

Musharraf smiled. "You'll see a difference very soon," he said. "This was exactly my vision: to have young, educated people like you in parliament to bring diversity into the parliamentary set-up."

I used my remaining moments with the President to talk about the need to outlaw acid attacks and the practice of vani. Regarding the latter, I referenced the horrific gang rape of a woman named Mukhtaran Mai. While many details of her case remain in dispute, what was known in the summer of 2003, when I had my audience with Musharraf, was that a year earlier, in June of 2002, a tribal council in the Punjab district of Meerwala had ordered the young woman's gang rape as recompense for a crime allegedly committed by her brother—a case of vani in the extreme. Her attackers had not been brought to justice; the panchayat had not been held accountable. *Khabrain* was the first newspaper in the world to report Mukhtaran Mai's story, which sparked outrage across the globe. The international press and human rights groups seized on Mukhtaran Mai's story as evidence that Pakistan is a backward and uncivilized country. Tremendous pressure from the world over bore down on President Musharraf and his government to prove otherwise by bringing Mai's rapists to justice. I put that pressure to work in appealing directly to Musharraf about my vani resolution, his support of which could make or break it in the National Assembly.

Musharraf was incredulous that the world blamed him for Mukhtaran Mai's ordeal. "Rapes happen in the United States, and no one blames the President," he said to me. He also explained his predicament, politically speaking: Poverty and lawlessness breed religious extremism and hatred of the Paksitani government, and nowhere more so than in tribal regions. Musharraf knew that he could ill afford to upset tribal regions by attempting to question or curb the jurisdiction of panchayats and still remain in power; extremists from those regions had come to pose an increasing security threat since the start of the War on Terror.

I understood the stakes and the challenges that Musharraf faced, but I rejected them as excuses for inaction, and I urged his support in spite of them. As I told him, women and girls shouldn't pay the price of a domestic policy held hostage by religious extremism. It was an intense few moments with the President.

We moved on to discuss briefly the efforts by women MPAs from other provincial assemblies to outlaw other forms of crime against women, such as honor killings. Musharraf turned to shake someone's hand. When he turned back to me, he said, "I agree with you, Humaira, about the need for a human rights policy. The work you are doing is very commendable, and we are following it very keenly. You will see that we shall soon come up with something positive: a comprehensive plan to deal with the human rights situation."

An aide to Musharraf appeared and whispered in his ear. My time was up. I thanked the President and bid him goodbye. As I walked away, I felt buoyed up, more so than I had in a very long time. I couldn't be certain that he had really heard me, but I appreciated that he let me have my say.

Back home, Ednan saw that I was satisfied with the evening's outcome. "So, you managed to get a word in with the President, did you?" he said. I told him about our exchange, and Ednan smacked his hand on the magazine he was holding. "Good stuff! If he says something will be done, something is bound to be done! Now, tell me, what did he have to say about your private moneylending bill?" I felt a pang—would I regret the omission? I told Ednan that I hadn't had time to bring it up. "There were too many people swirling about us," I said, "and I had used up my time."

My brief exchange with Musharraf left me feeling hopeful, not only about the ultimate fate of my legislative proposals, but about the future of Pakistan. I published an editorial to that effect in *Khabrain* not long after that meeting. In "An Encounter with a Reformist," published on the sixth of September, I wrote that I had come to view Musharraf as sincere in his desire to reform Pakistan; it would, of course, remain to be seen whether he, unlike his predecessors, would be successful. I could not agree with all of his policies or approaches, I wrote, but I appreciated his transparency, as well as his stated commitment to human rights and to the advancement of women. I also wrote about what I called the "red tapism" that hindered the work of the parliament, and I appealed directly to Musharraf to make good on his stated commitment to see progress through, especially when it came to Pakistan's most vulnerable populations. Time would tell.

THE REVENUE COMMITTEE was scheduled to meet for the first time the thirteenth of August to select its chairperson. In addition to the chair, the committee consisted of nine MPAs, plus several non-voting members of the secretariat bureaucracy whose job it was to oversee the collection of meeting minutes and the execution of rules and procedures. Revenue Committee meetings would also be attended by representatives from the Law, Parliament and Revenue departments, who might be asked for research or documentation relevant to my bill. As the mover of the moneylending bill, I was not a member of the committee and did not, therefore, count toward the quorum or have a vote.

I arrived at the appointed hour to find Maqsood Malik, who by a turn of good fortune was one of the secretariat staff assigned to committee. We were the only two there. "Don't worry, Humaira Bibi," Malik said. "I'm sure the others will arrive soon. After all, they have to elect the chairman, too, you know. I will remind them, in case they've forgotten." Malik left to place calls to the nominated members; he didn't reach a single one of them.

Three hours passed. I drank so many cups of coffee that I might have had the sensation of floating if I weren't so furious; nobody else came. "I think it's fairly obvious, Malik Sahib, that no one's going to show up today," I said. "I'll just go home now. My children will be getting restless."

"I'm sorry, Humaira Bibi," Malik replied. "I'm sure something important must have come up."

"Yes, I'm sure something important must be keeping all the others away at once," I said and laughed.

The day of the second scheduled session, the twenty-eighth of August, the farce was repeated: Maqsood Malik and I were the only ones in attendance. This time, I did not make the mistake of waiting for three hours, and left after two.

"You are pursuing a good cause, Humaira Bibi," Malik said as I gathered my things to leave. "Don't let these little bumps get in your way. I'm sure they will turn up in the next meeting." I smiled with appreciation for his kindness and walked out the door.

Once home, Ednan saw that I was upset. Trying—and failing— to persuade me to adopt his optimistic viewpoint that it would all work out in the end, he took a different tack: diversion. He initiated an indoor round of cricket with Nofal. Almost six, Nofal had inherited his father's passion for the game. He took wild swings at Ednan's soft, underhand tosses, and Fajr, almost three, and I clapped and hooted when his bat made contact.

Fajr wanted to watch her favorite *Tom & Jerry* cartoon, so we left the game in progress and sat together in front of the television. I had probably seen the episode a few hundred times by then, but that day, smarting with disappointment, I watched and recognized the universal dynamic of cat and mouse. When it came to parliamentary affairs, I wondered, which was I: Hapless cat? Hunted mouse? Fajr's giggles snapped me out of my dreary musings. I cuddled her, inhaled the sweet fragrance of her just-washed hair, and found myself laughing, too. Hearing us, Ednan and Nofal joined us on the couch. Ednan raised an eyebrow at me over Nofal's head, and I whacked him softly with a cushion. "All is well," he said, thumping me back. Nofal, thinking that we had started a pillow fight, got very excited and grabbed a cushion, only to hesitate; he couldn't decide which side, Mama's or Baba's, to join. Instead, he took advantage of our collective good humor to ask if we could all go out for ice cream. *Cunning little operator*, I thought. *That's exactly what I would have done at his age.* And so that's what we did, heading off in the car to our favorite ice-cream parlor.

From the driver's seat, Ednan looked over at me and said, "Didn't I tell you?"

"Tell me what?" I asked, knowing full well what he meant.

"That there is no point in fretting about things all the time, Humaira. Take things as they come, and live in the moment, my love. Isn't this better than sulking upstairs about things you can't control? That's my philosophy. It should be yours, too." I aimed an elbow at his side, but he was too quick and blocked me. We both laughed. That was Ednan: always living in the moment, blessed with a perspective that didn't come naturally to me, pulling me out of the dark and into the light. He was right, of course, though I never would have told him so. *Darn him*, I thought, and loved him so much.

CHAPTER ELEVEN

Waiting for Happy

SEPTEMBER BROUGHT WITH IT much-needed rest. With the Assembly adjourned and Ednan preparing for a journalism exchange in the United States in October, we decided the time was right for a family holiday. We had a standing invitation to stay with Ednan's maternal uncle, Sarmad Qureishi, and with Ednan's cousin Sohaib and his family in Ilford, in northeast London, and so off we went with the children and Ednan's mother, Yasmine, in tow.

If somewhere in the diagnostic manuals of psychology there is a listing for that particular disorder that afflicts those who most need vacations but rarely take them, Ednan and I exhibited all the symptoms. An almost giddy disbelief gripped us as we reacquainted ourselves with the unfamiliar satisfaction of doing nothing but enjoy ourselves. We fawned like honeymooners, ate like gluttons and reveled in the relief of trading the heat and pressures of home for the freshness and freedom of a waning English summer. We indulged our jet lag and slept for more hours in a night than we sometimes did over the course of several days. Nofal and Fajr found instant chums in Hamza and Naziha, Sohaib's son and daughter, who were close in age and possessed the additional charm of sounding like tiny English people. We played at being tourists, visiting Lord's Cricket Ground and

Charing Cross, Madame Tussauds and the Tate galleries, the Sea
Life London Aquarium and the British Museum. We soared to a
height of 441 feet on the London Eye Ferris Wheel, taking in the
magnificent view of the glittering city at night. And when we'd
had enough of comparing London curries and dosas to the ones
back home, we ate steaming, vinegary fish and chips out of newspaper pouches and chased them with cotton candy, which I love.

What had initially struck me as excessive—three weeks
away—turned out to be just right; restoration takes time. There
was no lingering trace of the frost that had chilled my marriage
at various points in the preceding year. The children luxuriated
in having both of their parents so near at hand, and, with our
edges worn soft by good times, so malleable to their requests for
sweets and relaxed bedtimes. And I had time to think of matters
other than the cretins blocking my progress back in Lahore.

I had succeeded in not talking about my work too much when
an old friend of Ednan's, a journalist named Aamir Ghauri,
called to invite me to discuss it in a televised interview. I couldn't
resist. Ghauri worked for Prime TV, a Pakistani news channel
based in London. For thirty minutes, I spoke with him about the
role of women in Pakistani politics, the effectiveness of reserved
seats, crimes against women, and apathy. After the segment
aired in the U.K., Ghauri called to tell me that the response had
been so positive that he wanted to do another, this one an hour
long and for international broadcast. I agreed, and the response
overwhelmed me. Just as I hadn't realized how acutely I needed a
break from life as I knew it, it wasn't until my email's inbox was
flooded with notes of support for my work that I understood how
much I needed the encouragement. The previous year's travails
in the Provincial Assembly had steadily depleted my stores of
optimism. On the eve of my return to Lahore, I felt renewed and
hopeful, fortified and in fighting form.

BUSINESS WAS SLOW when the Assembly reconvened on the seventeenth of October, a Friday. It remained so until the twenty-second of the month, when the first bill of the new session was introduced: an amendment to the Punjab Privileges Act, 1972, that called for official license plates bearing the letters MPA to be given to all members of the House, for all of their vehicles, at government expense. Unopposed, the bill went straight to committee. The requisite report was prepared, and the bill reappeared before the assembly on the twenty-ninth of October, where the yeas took it by a landslide. I was aghast. A perk to spend government money on license plates to herald the status of the driver—and to signal to traffic police to look the other way—passed in the course of just three workdays.

My moneylending bill was not so lucky. Time had nearly lapsed for the committee to discuss the bill and prepare the requisite report on it. It was, therefore, incumbent upon any member of the committee other than me, the mover of the bill, to stand during a House session and request an extension from the Speaker of the House, Muhammad Afzal Sahi. Such a request was an admission, of sorts, of a lack of action on the committee's part. The Speaker, in turn, asks the House why such an extension should be granted. In the case of this first extension, the answer was simple: the Revenue Committee had yet to meet at all. Extensions exist as a protection for a bill; in theory, a bill cannot die because of a committee's inertia or apathy. At the same time, extensions are not guaranteed. But on the same day that the MPA license plates were approved, the twenty-ninth of October, my bill received its first extension.

The special MPA license plates created a furor in the press. Back from his tour of newsrooms in Washington, D.C., New York and Seattle in early November, Ednan joined the fray with an editorial lambasting the Provincial Assembly for allocating Treasury funds to the scheme while ignoring other critical legislative issues. He reserved his harshest judgment for members of the Standing Committee on Law and Parliamentary Affairs, who had moved with such haste to approve the bill. He noted that, to attend committee meetings, members receive a Travel and Daily Allowance (TADA) stipend of 12,500 rupees, approximately $210, or just under half the amount earned by a typical Pakistani household in a year. (According to World Bank estimates, the gross national income per capita in Pakistan for 2003 was $540, or 29,831 rupees, given the exchange rate for October 2003.)

At home, the license plate fracas served as marvelous blackmail. Ednan had forbid my putting it on our car. Recognizing the symbolic value of threatening to make him look like a hypocrite, I kept the license plate on a side table and brandished it whenever I felt it time to tease Ednan about not paying enough attention to me—payback for all of his whining in the past year. "I think you should buy your wife a bouquet," I would say, "or it goes on the car!" He would shake his head in a display of tremendous if feigned sadness and reply that a year in the parliament had turned me wily and wicked.

THE ELEVENTH OF NOVEMBER, the Revenue Committee was again to meet to elect our chairperson. I wondered if it would just be another tea party for Maqsood Malik and me. I arrived early and went to Malik's office. "You are the first to arrive, Humaira Bibi," he said. "But today you won't be the only one. I have received confirmations from all the nominated members that they will be present."

"I'll believe it when I see them," I said. We sat together and I showed him a brief that I had prepared for the meeting.

"It is extremely well put together," Malik said. "But I must tell you: This won't be required today."

"Why not?" I asked.

Malik smiled sympathetically. "You'll see," he said. "I'm just telling you this now so that you don't get disappointed." His cellphone interrupted; the caller announced that the other committee members were arriving, and so we left for the meeting room.

Samina Naveed, the only other MPA from a reserved seat on the committee and formerly a member of her district council in Bahawalnagar, was the first to arrive after us. I would learn that Naveed, who had worked at the grassroots level in her district, was aware of and sympathetic to the plight of moneylending victims in her constituency. She would tell me that she supported my bill, but she would attend very few of the committee meetings.

Mian Majid Nawaz, a landlord from Vehari in the southern Punjab, entered next. We already knew that Nawaz had been put forward as the committee chairman, an impending appointment he bore with pride—arrogance even. As he maneuvered his beefy frame around the lavishly appointed room, I noted that his mustache, the most voluminous I had ever seen, marked him as a man from the country. Facial hair was not out of fashion in the city, exactly, but such a great pouf of it was. Nawaz was obsequious with me, flirtatious and condescending at once. It would not be long, however, before his disposition toward me would curdle into outright hostility.

The Punjab Minister for Revenue, Gul Hameed Khan Rokhri, a veteran politician, was next to arrive. As an ex-officio member of the committee, Rokhri did not have voting power. He did, however, have influence. I was glad to learn that in his work in the transportation business, Rokhri had been forced to deal with moneylending mafias. He could not cast a vote that would help me, but I hoped that he would be a good person to have on my side.

We had full attendance: nine MPAs, each with voting power, plus our chairman, as well as Minister Rokhri and Deputy Secretary Malik, who announced the start of proceedings. I put my brief about moneylending on the table and readied myself to discuss it. A show of hands confirmed Nawaz as committee chair. Next, Nawaz ordered tea for everyone, and fifteen minutes of polite sipping and small talk followed. Then, in his first official move as chairperson, Nawaz adjourned the meeting, setting the next one for the first of December. *That's it?* I thought. I was stupefied.

I sat down after everyone left; a wave of nausea had hit me. "Humaira Bibi," Malik said, his tone all apology, "this is the way things are done in this Assembly. You are pursuing a good cause, a noble cause, so all you have to do is be patient and persevere." He left the room, and I sat there for a long while, feeling as disoriented and far from home as Alice down the rabbit hole.

Ednan laughed so hard when I told him about the meeting that tears filled his eyes. I wanted to see the humor in it, to appreciate its absurdity, but I couldn't. "Is there even a point to what I'm trying to do?" I said. "Was it really too much to hope for a conversation, let alone an actual debate on the substance of my bill?" Ednan dried his eyes. "Don't worry," he said. "Stay with it. Next meeting, assert yourself. As the mover of the bill, you would be within your rights to demand their attention."

I felt queasy again. "I need to lie down for a bit," I said. "This is too much. I've felt nauseous all day."

Ednan brought me a sandwich and a cup of coffee. "I'm sorry I laughed," he said, putting his palm on my forehead to check for fever. "You're going to do this. I know you'll see this through." I sighed and sipped my coffee. "And when you do," he said, "I'm going to be even more proud of you than I am now." I teased that if he didn't stop, he risked making my nausea worse. In truth, it was exactly what I needed to hear.

When several more days of nausea and dizziness followed, I knew that my condition was something other than acute disappointment in provincial governance. A trip to the gynecologist confirmed my suspicion: I was pregnant. Ednan was ebullient. "I hope it's a girl," he said as he drove me home from the doctor's office. "Nofal and Fajr would love to have a baby sister, wouldn't they?" I held my breath; I just wanted a healthy baby and an uneventful pregnancy.

Ednan launched into fussing mode as soon as we were home, treating me like a fragile, delicate thing, fluffing the cushions on the sofa and bidding me to sit. When I protested that I was pregnant, not a Fabergé egg, he became uncharacteristically serious, his voice unusually soft. "Humaira, what happened when Nofal was about to be born—I never want anything like that to happen to you again. So please, let me look after you."

WITH A COUPLE OF WEEKS yet until the next Revenue Committee meeting, I had time to attend to other priorities. One was a survey of crimes against women that I had been overseeing at *Khabrain* since 2002. We were nearly ready to publish our findings. It was by no means comprehensive: The report would cover only crimes reported in our paper and by the Helpline between 2000 and 2003. The objective of the study was twofold. First, to offer readers a wide-angle perspective on the prevalence of crimes targeting females in Pakistani society. In a twenty-four-hour news cycle, it was all too easy to move from one terrible crime story to the next, to discard yesterday's paper, and with it, the memory of yesterday's victims. I wanted readers to remember, and I wanted them to see how the numbers added up and what the tallies revealed about our culture.

A second objective of the study was to trace the line from crime to punishment. For every crime committed, how many First Investigation Reports were filed? Meaning: How many investigations were launched? How many arrests were made? How many of those arrests were brought to judgment? In that regard, the study was as much about documenting law enforcement responses as about charting the incidences of violence against women.

My other priority during that time was my acid attack resolution. Nothing was happening with it in the federal Law Department. Rather than submit wholly to the glacial, uncertain legislative process, I had come up with a way to tackle at least one aspect of what I proposed: the establishment of a designated burn unit with subsidized care in at least one of the Punjab's government-run hospitals. With funds for community welfare available through Temeer-e-Pakistan, the Project Development of Pakistan, I decided that I didn't have to wait for the Law Department to act on this aspect of my resolution; I would pursue it myself.

There was just one hitch: Early on in my tenure as an MPA, Ednan had urged me to steer clear of seeking funds for anything at all; corruption was rampant, and he didn't want me to be tainted by association. "There's no accountability," he had said. "Massive amounts of money always end up in someone's pocket rather than going to the intended purpose." For this reason, I expected him to try to dissuade me from my scheme to secure funds for a burn unit, but to my surprise, he was very supportive. One burn victim's case in particular had revealed to both of us the extent to which care in the Punjab was wanting. It was in great part because of her that I included victims of stove burnings in the language of my resolution.

Her name was Naila, and I met her not long after I joined the newspaper in 2001. Zia had asked me to go with a *Khabrain* reporter named Faisal Durrani to the emergency room of Lahore's Mayo Hospital, where a woman had been admitted with third-degree burns all over her body. A doctor there had alerted the newspaper of his suspicion that Naila, a mother in her early thirties with two young children, had been set on fire by her husband and in-laws. I had yet to meet victims of domestic violence in my work at the paper, and what I knew of stove burnings, acid attacks and other such crimes was anecdotal, lacking the life-changing grit of meeting a victim. Naila's case would prove a harsh but important initiation.

It took me a while to find Naila. Hospital staff had seques-tered her from view behind a makeshift partition because she was shocking to see. Her flesh was a melted, mottled, bright pink. She writhed; contact from the bedclothes caused her searing pain. Her doctor told me that her injuries exceeded what he was equipped or trained to treat. He predicted that she would be dead within forty-eight hours.

Naila's husband, mother-in-law and sister-in-law were at the hospital, and they were agitated. To my mind, theirs was not the agitation of worry for a loved one who had been hurt, but the edginess of guilt. When Faisal Durrani questioned them about what had happened to Naila, the mother-in-law railed against his "intrusion from the press." As her son attempted a feeble explanation for his wife's injuries, his mother broke in, yelling, "Her clothing caught fire when the gas stove she was cooking on exploded!" All over Pakistan, exploding gas canisters are blamed for deliberate stove burnings. I was overcome from the sight of Naila and her pain, and I challenged the mother-in-law's account. "Is this true?" I asked.

"You are interfering in a private family matter!" she shouted. Her daughter demanded that we leave, letting loose a torrent of expletives in the coarsest Punjabi. I insisted that we would stay.

I thought I saw Naila's hand move. I returned to her bedside and saw her eyelids, fused shut, move, and her lips part. She was trying to speak. I leaned in close. "Did these people set you on fire, Naila?" I asked. "Don't try to speak, but if these people set you on fire, try to raise your index finger. I will understand that to be a yes."

For a few tense seconds, as her in-laws hovered and each of us held our breath, there was no response from Naila. Her chest heaved and her burned lips moved. Then I saw what everyone did: Her hand moved ever so slightly, its index finger trembling upward. The gesture must have required all of her remaining strength.

I leaned in closer still and whispered that she could trust me, and that I was there to help her. "Your husband and his family can't hurt you anymore," I said.

Tears emerged from the corners of Naila's closed eyes. I thought I heard her whisper something, so I moved my ear in close to her mouth. In the faintest rasp, I heard her. "My children," she said. "I am dead. But my children . . . help them . . . these people . . . "

Her mother-in-law, incensed that Naila was communicating with me, pushed me aside. "I want you to leave!" she screamed.

Back at *Khabrain*'s headquarters, my heart pounding and straining to keep my composure as I passed colleagues in the elevator and hallways, I ran to Ednan's office. Before I was able even to express what I had just seen, I broke down in tears in his doorway.

The next day, Faisal Durrani traveled to Dharampura, a middle-class neighborhood in Lahore's Old City, and found the run-down house where Naila lived with her husband, their children and his family. Neighbors were forthcoming. They told Durrani that Naila had long endured cruelty at the hands of her husband and in-laws, who felt justified in punishing her for bringing an insufficient dowry. No one, however, had witnessed Naila being burned deliberately, or burned at all. Regarding the mother-in-law's story about a cooker's gas canister exploding, no one reported hearing an explosion, either.

I returned to the hospital. Naila's family barred my entry until a senior doctor on the hospital staff, to whom I appealed for help in gaining access, escorted me to Naila's bedside. I wasn't prepared for the overnight change in her condition. Naila's skin had turned black like coal, and her breathing had grown rapid and shallow. I was witnessing the final moments of her life.

Khabrain's legal team dispelled my hope for justice for Naila or safety for her children; hearsay testimony about previous beatings did not amount to a case against her family, they said, nor did a doctor's suspicions. Without Naila's testimony, and in the absence of an eyewitness who could testify that she had been set on fire, we could not insist that the police make arrests. Nor could we have Naila's children removed from the home. I felt helpless. It would be weeks before I slept through the night without waking with a start to the image of Naila's blackened corpse. I remain haunted by the dying mother's last request to help her children, and by the fact that I was never able to do so.

Since then, I had thought often of Naila and of the other women whose deaths might have been prevented had there existed more than a makeshift burn unit to care for them. In November, I went to see Raja Basharat. The Law Minister who had tried to dissuade me from bothering with my vani resolution, the man who had refused to put my acid attack resolution on the House agenda when he had the power to do so, also oversaw funding for district development projects in the Punjab. I had also met with Basharat many times seeking his support of my moneylending bill, never with any progress. Basharat was a gifted politician, an artful dodger as adept at avoiding me as at telling me what I wanted to hear without ever intending to follow through on a reassurance. I didn't dislike Basharat, but I didn't relish the thought of another meeting with him, either. He was the man who could help me, however, and so I went to see him.

I explained to Basharat that there was not a single designated burn unit in all of the Punjab. The need for one was dire, I said. I made the case that the burn unit should be housed at a provincial hospital, not a district one. The distinction is important: District hospitals are small and lack the staff with expertise in treating burn injuries and performing reconstructive surgeries, whereas provincial hospitals are larger and better funded, staffed and equipped.

The distinction also presented a bureaucratic hitch: Development money is allocated through the district, so my desire to fund a provincial project would require a series of Steering Committee meetings to authorize the transfer of the money from the district to the province. More bureaucracy.

I had already identified where I wanted to build the burn unit: Sir Ganga Ram Hospital. One of the oldest and best-known hospitals in Lahore, Sir Ganga Ram was named for the pre-partition engineer and philanthropist who built it. At a time of uneasy coexistence between Indians and the British, Ganga Ram was almost universally admired.

In the pause between my committee meetings on private moneylending, I had worked with Dr. Akbar Chaudhry, a professor of medicine at Fatima Jinnah Medical College, and with his hospital management team at Sir Ganga Ram Hospital, to come up with a feasibility study that examined the expense of a treatment unit with six deep-flotation beds, which spare the victims of severe burns the agony of skin contact with an unyielding solid surface. They knew even better than I the magnitude of the problem of treating burn victims, many of whom had died in their overburdened emergency ward for lack of proper treatment. They responded favorably to my proposal.

I shared all of this with Basharat, and I presented him with the feasibility study's figures. "The hospital is ready to offer the space as well as the dedicated staff. We lack only the funds," I said. Basharat agreed to help me.

Red tape loves nothing more than paperwork, however, and I was charged with providing reams of it to the local government. Over the next several weeks, I worked on the requisite documents: An outline demonstrating the need for the burn unit; a projected expenditure of building, equipping and staffing it; and the length of time, from start to finish, that it would take to build. And then I waited.

THE DAYS GROWING SHORTER, the foliage gone gold, and my craving for the salty sweet warmth of Kashmiri chai were all signs: winter was coming to Lahore. Thus far in my pregnancy, I was feeling well and hopeful. It was a time of great contentment at home. Nofal and Fajr were excited about the arrival of a little one; Fajr gathered up a bag of her favorite small things—a sweater, some toys, tiny clothes—and declared it all for the new baby.

The morning of the first of December, a Monday, Ednan drove me to the Assembly for the next committee meeting on my private moneylending bill. I was anxious. "It'll be fine, Humaira," Ednan said, seeing the look on my face. "It's the system. This is how things work. Just go in there and give it your all."

The ever-reliable Maqsood Malik was waiting for me. Within fifteen minutes, we had a quorum—nine in all. I was heartened. (I didn't know that I would never see so many committee members assembled in that room again.) Chairman Nawaz called the meeting to order, and Malik gave me a nod. The floor was mine to seize.

I stood to speak without delay. "Chairman Sahib, if I may speak on my bill's behalf." The time granted, I explained that the Punjab Money-Lenders Ordinance of 1960 had called for regulatory and licensing systems that were beyond the scope of Pakistan's government to enforce and, thus, never set in motion. Criminals had taken advantage of this to operate with impunity. I therefore sought to repeal that regulatory law and to replace it with one that called for the outright prohibition of private moneylending, so that no private individual or company could act in place of a bank.

Chairman Nawaz shifted his ample frame and waved a dimpled hand in my direction. "Humaira Bibi," he said in rural-tinged Urdu, his booming voice almost startling for its contrast to mine, "talking about repealing a law and creating a new one is all fine. But this committee needs to understand exactly what it entails."

I began to explain when Nawaz interrupted to ask if everyone wanted tea. I waited, gritting my teeth, while a bearer was called in and asked to deliver tea and spicy chicken patties for all of us.

"You may begin now," Nawaz said when the tea bearer had served everyone and left. I tried to ignore the sipping and chewing. I cited the widespread abuses, the exploitation and the violence endemic to private moneylending. I explained why the 1960 law was obsolete and unenforceable. I reminded my colleagues that Pakistan's Constitution holds that it is the responsibility of the state to enable its citizens to live according to the tenets of Islam; therefore, I argued, it is a failure of the state to permit its people to be drawn into a practice that is expressly forbidden by the Qur'an. I also cited a 1995 ordinance that declared that only the State Bank of Pakistan and those financial institutions authorized by it can offer financial assistance to those who need it, not public or private companies functioning as high-interest banks. I argued that if an ordinance forbids companies from operating as banks, how, then, could private citizens be allowed to do so?

I had barely finished speaking when the Secretary of the Board of Revenue, Nasrullah Khan Chattha, spoke up. "I would like to voice my opposition to this proposed legislation," he said, his tone as cool as his demeanor. "The complete prohibition of private moneylending will go against the interests of the general public." Chattha appeared to have decided the issue even before hearing me out.

With that, others offered their points of view, which echoed Chattha's. After thirty minutes of unmoderated chatter, Chairman Nawaz interjected with a summation of the committee's opinion: There was no need for a new law, and the committee instead would recommend that private moneylending be regulated by implementing the existing law, which fell in part under Chattha's department's jurisdiction.

Either I had not done a sufficient job of explaining that the 1960 law was not enforceable, or the committee knew full well that by throwing in with the old law, they could pay lip service to the problem of private moneylending while really doing nothing at all. The committee resolved to ask Chattha's Department of Provincial Revenue to explain why the 1960 law was not implemented, and the meeting was adjourned until the next day.

In the Revenue Committee meeting the following day, the second of December, Nasrullah Khan Chattha reported that, owing to various codes in Pakistani law, implementation had been attempted many times but delayed. He demurred when asked to provide evidence to back up his assertion, saying that he would provide the documentation at the next meeting.

Chairman Nawaz, on behalf of the committee, then asked the provincial Department of Revenue to draft the pros and cons of regulation versus prohibition. Frustrated that regulation was still being considered, I asked that the committee members return to their constituencies and find out for themselves what destruction the local moneylending mafia had wrought on their people. I urged them to meet with victims so that they could hear their stories firsthand. I was certain that prohibition would hold more appeal if the MPAs better understood how intractable and widespread a problem moneylending had become. Chairman Nawaz set the date for the next meeting for the end of December, and with that, he adjourned the meeting.

"It won't work," I told Ednan that evening. "They reject my push for a new law. Either they don't understand the logic behind it, or they understand too well and need to prevent it."

Ednan didn't laugh this time. He asked me to recount everything that had transpired in the previous two days. When I finished, he said: "Listen, Humaira, if they wanted to do away with your bill, they would have recommended that straightaway. They didn't, so there is still hope. Stop thinking about it now. You need to rest."

Ednan was like a mother hen, constantly reminding me to slow down. It wasn't enough that I physically stop; he also wanted me to deactivate that part of my brain that obsessed over work. I did my best, because I knew he was right, and because it was so endearing to me that he cared so much. Unfortunately for me, Ednan's idea of pure indulgence involved watching the third installment of *The Lord of the Rings*. It had just come out on DVD, but already the movie had gotten serious play in the Shahid home. Ednan could recite entire stretches of dialogue by heart. To my chagrin, so could I. I gave in to Ednan's fussing, as well as to my fatigue, and within fifteen minutes, I was sound asleep, my head on his shoulder.

In the days that followed, I felt troubled by the fact that nothing in my first year in the parliament had inspired me. From the vitriol hurled at women on reserved seats to what I perceived to be the Revenue Committee's stalling tactics, I was fed up, let down, put off. I wanted to blow the whistle on the Provincial Assembly's institutionalized dysfunction, and I wanted to make as big a splash as possible. Jugnu Mohsin, a friend of mine and the publisher of Pakistan's leading English-language weekly the *Friday Times*, had often asked me to be a guest contributor. Hers was the paper of choice for the government ranks; everyone in Islamabad read it, and I knew that my colleagues in the Provincial Assembly did, too. I asked Mohsin if I could contribute an op-ed about the character failings, as I saw them, that plagued the Punjab Provincial Assembly. She agreed at once.

In "Seven Deadly Sins of Politics," published on the fifth of December, I offered a scathing look at the many ways that provincial parliamentarians used and abused their positions and each other and failed their constituencies. I referenced William Golding's *Lord of the Flies* and Sartre's *No Exit* as parallels in fiction to the realities in the Assembly. The seven sins: regality; politics without principles (this I borrowed from Mahatma Gandhi); indifference; wealth without work; opportunism; publicity-mongering; and sycophancy. The editorial did not endear me to my colleagues. By that point, I was beyond caring. I thought that if I couldn't make headway, I might as well expose the reasons why. Ednan was thrilled with the piece and proud of me for taking a stand. An Urdu translation of it, minus the Western literary references that would have meant nothing to many readers, ran in *Khabrain* a couple of weeks later.

With two weeks yet until the next Revenue Committee meeting, I had a brainstorm for a way to keep the moneylending conversation going without being the only one wielding the megaphone: a seminar that invited experts and borrowers alike to offer their views, both academic and personal, on moneylending. The objective would be to discuss Pakistan's informal economy and private moneylending's growing place in it. I took the idea to Zia, who was all for it. I then invited Khalid Maqbool, Governor of the Punjab, to join us as a guest of honor. He readily agreed. We set the seminar's date for the seventeenth of February.

Meanwhile, I received the news that my vani resolution had at last survived months of redrafting and was en route to the federal Law Department. In an effort to keep its momentum going, I wrote another personal appeal to President Musharraf. He had assured me that human rights were a priority; I felt it time to give him the opportunity to prove it. "Your attention to this issue can change the lives of thousands who are bartered for the crimes of others," I wrote. "They are not animals to be used for settlements, not commodities to be bartered in disputes; they are humans." The open letter was slated for publication the sixteenth of December.

I submitted my open letter to Musharraf to *Khabrain's* editors on the fourteenth of December. The same day, the President escaped an assassination attempt when a bomb exploded as his armored convoy crossed a bridge in Rawalpindi. Given this frightening development, when my letter appeared in the paper two days later, I hardly expected Musharraf to take notice.

Eleven days after the first attack, two suicide bombers exploded their cars as Musharraf's convoy passed, killing sixteen innocent bystanders but sparing the President any injury.

Both assassination attempts had been the work of Islamist militants and served as reminders that extremist factions within Pakistan were still bent on avenging Musharraf's cooperation with the War on Terror.

To my astonishment, I received a letter from the President's office not long thereafter. In it, a deputy to Musharraf acknowledged my open letter. He assured me that recommendations and clauses from the draft of my vani law were, at that very moment, under consideration for inclusion in a comprehensive law against various customary practices that was being prepared by the federal Law Department. I was thrilled by this most unexpected development.

IN RESPONSE TO THE TERRORIST attacks on the President, security was increased at government buildings across the country. It took twice as long for me to gain entry into the Punjab Assembly building on the twenty-sixth of December, the date of our next Revenue Committee meeting. Once inside, I learned that the meeting was postponed until the next day; not enough members had shown up. I exited through the gauntlet of policemen and guards bearing machine guns, quietly seething over my wasted time.

The next day, there was a quorum.

Chairman Nawaz called the meeting to order. When my moneylending bill, which was third on the day's agenda, came up, the committee members asked that I provide them with more cases of moneylending victims. Though I had provided them with many examples, already, I agreed. *Anything to further my cause*, I thought, even as I knew that their request was likely a ploy to further delay progress on my bill. The next meeting date was set for late February 2004, and the meeting was adjourned.

On my way out, I noticed that on the sign-in form for that day's meeting there were nearly twice as many signatures as there were attendees. Because members are paid to attend these meetings, I immediately suspected shenanigans. I pointed out the discrepancy to Chairman Nawaz; it was his responsibility to confirm participants' attendance. "These people are signed in," I said, "but where are they?" Nawaz was dismissive. He responded with a huff that they had signed in before the meeting, and that they were on their way. That made no sense, I told him, since the meeting was adjourned. I pressed. Why had he signed the form to indicate that more members had been present? And that was the precise moment when the chairman's treacly condescension toward me turned into outright animosity. He refused to answer my question. "Do I look like eye candy to you?" I said, furious. "I am here to do business!" He walked past me and out the door.

On the ninth of January, my Prohibition of Private Money Lending Bill received its second extension. Though aggravated that the committee's willful lassitude had again necessitated an extension, in truth, I didn't mind having the extra time to focus on the upcoming moneylending seminar. I was hopeful that the gathering's conclusions, as well as public opinion, would bolster my case for outright prohibition when the Revenue Committee next met.

MY PREGNANCY HAD BEEN PROGRESSING normally when, at the end of January, a nuchal transparency screening, a prenatal blood test that assesses the possibility that a baby will be born with Down syndrome and other chromosomal abnormalities, came back with worrisome results. My obstetrician urged me to consider having an amniocentesis, which could offer a more conclusive result. I didn't want to do that. I knew that the risk of miscarriage was higher with amniocentesis, and I did not want to lose my baby.

Around that time, I began to feel bothered by something that I had always taken in stride previously. An aunt of Ednan's, the widow of Zia's older brother, lived next door to Zia and Yasmine's home with the now teenaged son that she and her late husband had adopted. Born with a neurological disorder, the boy howled for long stretches on end, and we could hear his wailing in our home. I had always felt sorry for the child and his mother, but for the first time, I found his cries even more anguishing. I prayed to Allah to spare the child that I was carrying such agony, and I told Him that I would leave everything to Him. No matter what, I already loved my baby. Ednan and I were in agreement: I would submit to no further tests beyond routine ultrasounds.

In an effort to push worry from my mind, I threw myself back into work. The next item on my agenda was writing the final draft of *Khabrain*'s report on violent crimes against women and girls, which went to press on the fifteenth of February. As a survey of murders, rapes, acid attacks, stove burnings and kidnappings, the study painted a picture of a culture inured to violence against women and girls. Crucially, it exposed the extent of police indifference to victims and of law enforcement's susceptibility to bribery and other forms of corruption. On average, only one investigation was launched for every 2.4 crimes committed over a four-year period. The arrest rate—192 arrests for 1,485 reported crimes over four years—was made only more abysmal by evidence of bribery to spring culprits free, as well as police pressure on victims not to seek charges or to drop them.

I was proud of the study, sickened by it, too. I took it to local police units: Weren't they shamed by our findings? What did they plan to do about them? I took the report to local NGOs, as well, suggesting that the study might help them to solicit additional support for their work. And I took it to the Violence Against Women Committee, an ad-hoc group of MPAs that met during its own time and had no official parliamentary function beyond our own good intentions. I thought surely evidence such as what had been compiled would move the entire Assembly, and not just our little group, to pass my acid attack resolution and other proposed protections for women. But I was wrong. There was goodwill on the committee, and there was goodwill to be found among some in the Assembly at large. What was lacking was the political will to go to the mat to protect women. After meeting only a handful of times, the Violence Against Women Committee disbanded, and I resumed my solitary fight.

THE MONEYLENDING SEMINAR on the seventeenth of February was a success beyond my expectations. Held at the Pearl Continental Hotel in Lahore and sponsored by *Khabrain*, the seminar included some of Pakistan's foremost minds in Islamic finance and law, poverty alleviation and banking. To my surprise, the Punjab's ministers of Law, Revenue and Finance, Raja Basharat, Gul Hameed Rokhri, and Hasnain Bahadur Dareshak, respectively, also took part. I had been lobbying them personally for days to attend. I hoped that what they heard at the seminar might persuade them to support my bill. I had an ulterior motive in inviting them, as well: to force them to speak on the record about private moneylending. I had a feeling that, facing an audience of borrowers who had fallen prey to unscrupulous lenders, they would speak rather differently about the issue than they did in the protective cloister of a committee meeting. At that time, none of the ministers opposed me openly. They were perfect politicians—polite, but promising nothing. Rokhri had privately expressed his support for what I was doing, but never on the record; he made it clear that, however he might feel personally, he could not go against party leadership. Only one minister, the National Alliance's parliamentary leader and the Minister of Food, Hussain Jahania Gardezi, spoke openly in support of my bill.

As panelists examined the moneylending issue from the various vantage points of their expertise, a clear consensus emerged: Private moneylending imperiled the moral, social and economic fabrics of Pakistan; the practice needed to be replaced by constructive alternatives; and it was up to the government not only to ban it, but to provide those alternate sources of funding. Attendees also urged expansion in the banking sector, with a focus on small loans—microcredit—to divert business from the moneylending mafias.

Khabrain devoted a special full-page color feature about the seminar in the next day's paper. In addition, every newspaper, as well as the smattering of independent television news channels that had begun to operate in Pakistan, also covered it. *There*, I thought. I had successfully passed the megaphone. Everyone, it seemed, was talking about the problem of private moneylending. I felt certain that it wouldn't be long before the Revenue Committee was similarly persuaded. Mine was no longer the sole voice calling for prohibition, and far more influential advocates than I had joined the cause.

I WAS UNCHARACTERISTICALLY CHIRPY the morning of the twenty-first of February, when the Revenue Committee was set to meet. I had compiled a file of news clippings about the seminar, complete with testimonials from some of the key panelists who urged the provincial government to take action against predatory lending. I felt certain that I could at last mount an unassailable case on my bill's behalf. "You're all fizzy," Ednan said, looking up from a spread of newspapers laid out with his breakfast. He started each day by scanning the competition for stories *Khabrain* might have missed.

I smiled. "This is the day I convince them," I said, shaking a defiant fist. I had become so used to defeat. On that day, I swore I could almost taste victory.

"Don't take anything for granted, Humaira. You know how these things go," he said.

"Yes, well, I don't see how anyone, even my greatest opponent, could take in all this evidence and come to a different conclusion," I said. "And anyway, don't rain on my parade!" I didn't want to let any of Ednan's caution, which I read as doubt, dilute my confidence. I wanted only to charge into the Assembly building, make my case to the committee, and watch their resistance crumble.

It was not to be. I presented the seminar's conclusions, as planned, only to be informed by Nasrullah Khan Chattha, the Board of Revenue Secretary, that representatives from the Law and Parliamentary Affairs departments had been sent to work with me to establish what he called "amicable proposals" before the next meeting in March. In other words, I was becoming a nuisance. The media was abuzz over the moneylending seminar, and the Revenue Committee was uncomfortable in the spotlight's glare. To give the appearance of proactivity, the party leadership had come up with a new strategy: water down my bill with compromises they could live with, then send the report to the House. I refused.

Because of all of this palaver, my bill had again nearly exhausted the term of its extension. The Speaker of the House weighed the unusual prospect of giving it a third one. After two extensions, most bills are acted upon in the proper manner. When Muhammad Afzal Sahi asked the House if an extension should be granted, I stood to respond. "Why not ask why these extensions are needed? Why not demand of the Revenue Committee that it fulfill its obligation to write a report on the bill, and not some watered-down version of it, rather than forever delay it in committee!" By then, I knew that Sahi saw me as a troublemaker. I might have hoped for impartiality on the part of the white-bearded stoic, but on the twenty-fifth of February, Sahi, unmoved by my protest, issued my bill its third extension.

INTO MY SECOND TRIMESTER, I had begun to feel weak, though I did not say so to Ednan. At home, in fact, I found myself engaged in a bit of acting, trying to appear more robust than I felt, lest my hovering, worried husband order me to bed. I wasn't feeling in top form, but there was no question that I would attend the next Revenue Committee meeting on the thirteenth of March. There was much to discuss, including the Federal Shariat Court's landmark ruling against riba in 1999 in *Mahmood ur Rahman Faisal* v. *Secretary of the Ministry of Law*. That ruling had been appealed and sent on to the Supreme Court, which sent it back to the FSC for review, and a definitive ruling had yet to be made. But my bill was exactly in keeping with the argument put forward by the original petition against riba, and I wanted to use it to further my case. Chairman Nawaz denied my request. He alleged that I could not cite the case because it remained under review. I suspected that it was a specious argument. I didn't have proof of that, however, so I had to let it go for the time being.

Before adjourning the meeting, Nawaz requested anew that Nasrullah Khan Chattha from Revenue, Mehmood Haroon from Law and Parliamentary Affairs, and Farooq Altaf from the Law Department provide documentation of their departments' efforts to implement the 1960 law. Each, in turn, replied that they would need considerably more time to do so. By then, they were all in cahoots; Nawaz didn't expect them to deliver, and they didn't plan to. It was the ninth Revenue Committee meeting, and still my bill had nothing to show for it.

RESIGNED TO FURTHER DELAYS in committee and hoping to gather more fodder for my cannon, I sent a letter on the sixteenth of March to the Governor of the State Bank, Dr. Ishrat Hussain. In it, I outlined my moneylending bill, my religious argument against predatory lending, and the shortcomings of the 1960

Ordinance. I argued that the elimination of private moneylending would be a boon to microinvestment, freeing customers from illegitimate transactions and sending them in droves to above-board businesses—banks. I also expressed my belief that it is the responsibility of the State Bank to eliminate the exploitative middleman and to work with the State of Pakistan to provide interest-free loans directly to individuals.

I attached copies of my proposed bill and the 1960 Ordinance, as well as the Banking Ordinance of 1995, which states that no public or private company may function as a bank. I concluded by asking the State Bank to join me in bringing an end to private moneylending. I figured it was worth a shot.

THE NEXT REVENUE COMMITTEE MEETING, the thirtieth of March, lacked a quorum, but the sign-in sheet bore two phantom signatures. I complained on the floor of the House, thus obligating the members in question to explain themselves. The fraud outraged me, and the stress of it undid me. By that evening, I felt on the verge of fainting. Ednan was alarmed. "I am taking you to see Dr. Farooqui tomorrow," he said. "If he says that you need rest, then that is what you must do, Humaira!"

I was nearly five months pregnant, and a visit to my gynecologist the next day revealed that I was extremely anemic. Thalassemia minor, which had caused me to lose consciousness and collapse during my first pregnancy, was again the culprit. My doctor urged me to slow down.

"That's it, Humaira!" Ednan said, after I suggested in the car on the drive home that the doctor was overreacting. "You're going to stay at home, and you're going to rest!" I rarely saw Ednan so furious. "You're more important to me than any piece of legislation, and I am not going to allow this to continue!"

I pleaded to attend just a few more committee meetings, but

Ednan wouldn't hear of it. "No, Humaira," he said. He had calmed down. "Please. My love. You *need to rest.*" We sat in silence for a few minutes.

"I tell you what I'll do," Ednan said. "I'm supposed to go with my father to Islamabad to interview President Musharraf. I promise that I'll take your file along and discuss this whole issue with him in detail. I'll tell him what you've been going through—the stalling, the obstruction, all of it. I'll find out where he stands."

Ednan was nothing if not a man of his word. Later that month, he found a moment before an official interview with the President to discuss my moneylending bill off the record. He called me from his cellphone the moment he stepped out of Musharraf's residence. "The President understands, Humaira," Ednan said. "But his stance, which I agree with, is that your bill needs to be passed by the Provincial Assembly, according to procedure. There's no way for him to intervene directly." The temptation to cynicism was great: the self-appointed President begging off in the name of democracy. But I resisted. If Musharraf supported my initiative, that was something. At least he hadn't dismissed the topic outright.

A few days later, I collapsed and required a blood transfusion. My doctor ordered bed rest. I called Maqsood Malik and told him that I feared that I would be unable to attend any more meetings until delivering my baby, due in early August. I pled with him to keep watch over my bill. "Please, Maqsood Sahib," I said. "Please ensure that the committee doesn't let this bill die."

Malik gave me his assurance. "You just take care of yourself, Humaira Bibi," he replied. "We'll take care of things while you are gone."

THE SECOND WEEK OF MAY, I received from the Senior Joint Director of the State Bank of Pakistan a brief, one-page response to the letter I had sent in March. In it, Muhammad Ashraf Khan expressed his agreement with my assessment of private money-lending as exploitative and predatory. He applauded my initiative and urged the legislature to bring the force of the law to bear on private moneylenders, but he did not offer the State Bank's help. My hope that support from the central bank of Pakistan might catapult my bill to success was not to be.

Later that month, the National Alliance and PML-Q parties announced their intention to merge to form one party, PML, the united Pakistan Muslim League. Musharraf held a meeting at Camp House, his official army residence in Rawalpindi, to welcome members of both parties to discuss the merger. I was desperate to attend, not because of the party politics, but because of the opportunity it presented to get an audience with the President. I had regretted not bringing up my moneylending bill at the Governor's House the previous August, and here was my chance.

I anticipated that I would have more difficulty convincing Ednan that I was well enough to make the trip than I would securing a few moments of the President's time. I was right. Ednan put up a valiant fight. In the end, even he had to concede that my going could bolster my cause. In any case, he didn't want to contend with me if I didn't go.

"Humaira, I am with you completely on this," the President said when I managed to speak with him privately. "Your husband has told me what you are going through. He laid out your case very well," he said. "I think the cause you are campaigning for has every reason to be supported by everyone. However, you must remember that, as the President of Pakistan, I am merely the head of state. I cannot do anything myself beyond instructing the right people to look into this. The ones who are in the best position to decide this are the elected representatives. But you have my support, I assure you."

I wasn't sure what to make of this exchange, which landed on my ears—merely the head of state?—as an artful passing of the buck. Perhaps I simply couldn't face the fact that there was no way around the Revenue Committee. I resolved anew to convince them.

ON THE TWENTY-SIXTH OF JUNE, my moneylending bill received its fourth extension. By then, I had become so vocal on the House floor about what was happening in the committee meetings that I had begun to win the sympathy of some MPAs. I knew this was so because when I stood to protest another extension, to the usual chorus of boos were added loud cries of "Let her speak!"

In spite of the fact that just moving about our home had become an effort for me by then—I felt like a dirigible that was fast losing altitude—I insisted to Ednan that I had to attend the next committee meeting, the seventh of July. If I were not there, I argued, then there would be no hope of seeing the moneylending bill through before the baby came. A second blood transfusion stabilized me; much to the surprise of the Revenue Committee, on the seventh of July, I was there.

It would prove to be a crucial meeting. I had noticed that the minutes of previous meetings, transcribed by staffers in the House Secretariat of Audio Recordings of our sessions, were missing many of the key points that I had made. I suspected that the chairman had put pressure on the minutes transcribers to focus on the broad outlines of the meetings while leaving out descriptions of the Revenue Department's shortcomings and failures, as highlighted by my complaints against it. The impression of anyone reading the minutes was that I had not tried very hard to make my case. This incensed me. So did another omission from the minutes: Nasrullah Khan Chattha's ongoing failure on behalf of the Revenue Department to produce evidence that it had ever implemented the 1960 law. Without that documentation, Chairman Nawaz had claimed, the Revenue Committee could not possibly file a report on my bill. This suited him just fine, of course. Both he and Chattha clearly intended to let my bill die for want of this information. I didn't expect the official record to reflect that deception, but I did expect it to show Chattha's continued promises to deliver.

At the start of the meeting on the seventh of July, I was defiant. "I am putting this committee on notice that if the minutes do not reflect each and every one of the points I make, if they do not reflect Chattha Sahib's claim to have evidence that he nevertheless refuses to produce, I will expose this to the House," I said. The committee members knew that anything aired on the House floor was likely to make it onto the evening news. Addressing Chattha directly, I said, "If you have this evidence, hand it over, or let this committee move on to conduct actual business!"

In fact, Chattha would be forced to admit that day that he had never produced the evidence demanded of his department because it did not, in fact, exist. One staff member from the Revenue Department would subsequently admit that he wasn't even aware of the 1960 law. It was as I feared: My bill was being held hostage by liars. It was my last Revenue Committee meeting before I gave birth, and I felt that it was a watershed. That meeting's minutes reflected all that took place.

ON THE SECOND OF AUGUST, Ednan and I welcomed a healthy, perfect baby girl. The scare from the early genetic screen had been unwarranted. My only child born full-term, our daughter startled me for her big, clear voice and for the features she possessed that Nofal and Fajr, my premature darlings, hadn't: a wild mane of jet black curls, long dark lashes and lush eyebrows. She was also my only baby born while I was conscious; what a miracle it was to see her on my belly, post–Caesarean section, so giant at seven pounds compared to her siblings. I had decided to forgo general anesthesia, lest it plunge me back into the trauma and confusion of Nofal's birth, as it had when Fajr was born.

Ednan took immediately to calling her his "Greek goddess." Officially, we named her Hafsa. My cousin Ziad and another friend had repeatedly donated blood for the many transfusions that I required to keep my hemoglobin levels up so that the baby would not be in distress during delivery. Hafsa is a name that they favored, and I wanted to name her in their honor. Hafsa was the wife of the Prophet Muhammad, praise be upon him. After his death, she became the keeper of the first Qur'an. The name has come to mean one who protects, and it has proved just right for my daughter, who is fearless and strong. My mother likes to say, "Apart from you, Humaira, I fear only that little girl."

These days, we call Hafsa "Happy," a nickname unintentionally bestowed by her cousin, Abdul Wasay. The son of my sister Aisha and Ednan's brother Imtinan, Abdul Wasay was born just two months before Hafsa, on the sixth of June. When they were very small, they were as close as twins. And when Abdul Wasay, unable to pronounce the letter *f*, began saying Hafsa's name, it sounded like Happy. It seemed a good fit, and it stuck.

CHAPTER TWELVE

Looking for Mr. Pakistan

POSTPARTUM DEPRESSION STEALS in like a burglar on day three after I give birth, snatching away jubilation and relief and leaving in their place lethargy and fear. Of a sudden, it becomes almost unbearable to be in the same room as this beautiful, innocent, helpless creature, lest she come to harm in my care. Drained of energy and verve, in pain from the incision in my belly, I get by on a combination of the forbearance of others and my knowledge that, by week three, the shadowy interloper will begin to slink away and, slowly, the world will return to color. The trick is to get through those three weeks.

My recovery plan for my first month at home with my new daughter was to let my mother take care of me at her home. It is a lovely tradition in the Punjab that mothers care for their daughters for the first forty days after they give birth. For the lucky, and I was one, our mothers are our night nurses, our dispensers of wisdom, our original and best caretakers all in one. My mother hadn't left my side in the first month after Nofal was born, and she made all the difference when I was in Lahore after Fajr's birth while Ednan had to be in Islamabad. I looked forward to being back in her embrace, and I was grateful for the reprieve my being away would offer Ednan and my still young children from having to contend with my inevitable, if temporary, decline.

When, just a few days into my stay at my mother's house, news came from Karachi that a beloved cousin, just twenty years old, had died of cardiac arrest, we were all shocked. Bilal was healthy and vital; we couldn't fathom that his heart would just stop, that he might drop dead, the way a bird falls out of the sky. But there was no question that my mother would stay in Lahore with me. I insisted that she go to Karachi to be with her younger brother, whose grief over his lost son would need tending more than I did. After all, I had Ednan, who had long since proved his valor in the night-nursing and caretaking departments. So while Ednan got Nofal and Fajr ready for school each morning and did a million things besides, and while I counted the days until I could welcome my spirit back into my body, our little family managed, and we managed well. I missed my mother, but how fortunate I was to have Ednan in her stead. I could not have gotten through without him.

I spent the first several weeks in bed, weak with anemia and too sore to move with ease. As my strength returned, so did my ability to focus on more than one thing at a time. One of the most troubling side effects of giving birth, I found, besides feeling flattened by it all, was the sense that my brain had suffered permanent atrophy. After finding Hafsa's umbilical cord in the bedclothes, I joked that the desiccated little raisin of a thing might actually be my brain, fallen out of my ear. Ednan noted with hope the return of my sense of humor. It was true: I was beginning to feel like myself again.

WE HAD A NEW BABY, and Pakistan had a new leader: Shaukat Aziz. On the twentieth of August 2004, the suave, well-spoken economist and financier became Prime Minister, replacing an interim PM who had taken over when Zafarullah Jamali, Pakistan's first Prime Minister from Balochistan, resigned in June.

Ednan and I had a special interest in Aziz's new post, because he was a longtime acquaintance of Zia's and had become a particular friend of Ednan's. Aziz had been the executive vice president of Citibank in the United States when he left that post to take over the Finance Ministry at Musharraf's behest following the 1999 coup. Ever since, Aziz had been an occasional presence in our home.

Most recently, Ednan and I had spent an evening with Aziz and his wife, Rukhsana, in Islamabad, all of us guests of Zia, who was now courting his old friend, the country's new PM, hoping to secure an interview at some point in the future for *Khabrain*. Even charm offensives were a Shahid family affair. I was in the last days of my pregnancy with Hafsa, and we had a jolly dinner followed by a performance of ghazals, classical Urdu verse, set to music.

Ednan and Aziz shared a remarkable affinity. Aziz was generous about Ednan's editorials in *Khabrain*, and the two men joked and teased the way friends do. My relationship with Aziz was more formal but always friendly. I took in news of his election as PM with particular interest: Might a career banker, and now a man doing double duty as Prime Minister and Finance Minister, be favorably disposed to my drive to ban usurious private lending? Time would tell.

Meanwhile, news came on the sixteenth of September that the House had granted yet another extension—the fifth—to my moneylending bill. In my absence over the summer, the Revenue Committee hadn't met again. While Ednan urged me to continue to rest and to focus on family, I began lobbying for my return to work. Maqsood Malik had been in touch: The Revenue Committee would next meet on the fourteenth of October. I was determined to be there. "Alright, Humaira," Ednan said, waving his arms as if in surrender. "If you feel well enough, of course you should go. I know what this means to you." I knew that Ednan wanted me to take more time off, but I didn't think I had it to spare.

I needn't have rushed. When the fourteenth of the month arrived, only two MPAs showed up for the meeting. We needed three, excluding me, for a quorum. The sign-in form, however, bore four signatures. I couldn't believe it. On the floor of the House during the next parliamentary session, I stood to demand that the members who had falsely signed in explain their absences. By doing so, I signaled to the Revenue Committee that I would hold intransigent members to account, and I made their deception a part of the official record. I also gave the press corps a story. As time went on, my open condemnation in the House of breaches of parliamentary rules and procedures by committee members would make headlines; the papers loved stories about ineffective governance, and here was one of the ruling party's own crying foul. Before the year was out, my bill would receive its sixth extension, and I would be back in the papers, the MPA who wouldn't back down.

IN NOVEMBER, PRESIDENT MUSHARRAF hosted a convention of women members of the PML-Q at Camp House in Rawalpindi. The gathering convened women MPAs from the Provincial and National Assemblies, as well as high-profile party members who held posts in academia, business and local governance. Musharraf sought our feedback on reserved seats and encouraged us to discuss legislative initiatives. He laid out his vision for the reserved seats and recruited us as ambassadors, of sorts, for that vision.

During one session, Musharraf invited reserved-seat MPAs to speak about legislative hurdles we were encountering in the Provincial Assemblies. I was amazed when he cited my money-lending bill as an example of an initiative he supported, and also as indicative of the kinds of challenges women MPAs were facing in Assemblies across the country. One does not raise one's hand at such a gathering, but that is what I did. Musharraf gave me the floor. I thanked him for discussing my bill, and I laid out in detail the obstructionism it had thus far been subjected to from members of my own party. Musharraf nodded as he listened and thanked me for speaking.

An informal tea followed the session, and there, I spoke with Musharraf privately. We talked about the work of Muhammad Yunus, the Bangladeshi banker and economist, and the father of microcredit. We discussed microfinance and its prospects for helping to alleviate poverty. It was an engaging exchange. Musharraf looked at me through intense eyes; I believe he had thought quite a lot about poverty, economic exploitation and predatory lending and was genuinely interested in seeing Pakistan rid of all three. Once again, I bid him to support a federal law to ban private moneylending, and once again, he promised to look into doing so. It was time to go; we gathered for a group photograph with the President, who was in noticeably high spirits.

While at the Camp House convention, I also met again with Nilofer Bakhtiar, who told me that the ruling party was considering a comprehensive law that would outlaw various customary practices, including vani. Bakhtiar told me that she wanted to include recommendations from my vani bill in one section of that law. I found this reassuring; I wasn't wed to my law specifically but to the imperative that the practice be banned. It had been months since I'd heard anything about either my vani bill or my acid resolution, and I feared that both would languish indefinitely in the federal Law Department. News that vani was on the ruling party's legislative agenda, at least, was good news indeed.

WITH NO REVENUE COMMITTEE MEETINGS on the agenda for the rest of the year and the House adjourned, I was glad to return my focus to life at home. At four and a half months old, Hafsa was well into the smiling, cooing stage. The so-called "fourth trimester" was behind us, and what a relief. My hormones had ended their siege on my equilibrium, permitting me to enjoy Hafsa in all her fast-developing, wriggling wonder. I always fared a little better when my babies got bigger. With Nofal and Fajr, I learned that something magic happens after the first ninety days: interactivity. Hallelujah for that. Hafsa was very expressive as a baby, the most prone of my children to peals of easy laughter, and also the quickest to shed the most tragic of tears. She made adoring slaves of us all, and I sensed that even in her preverbal, vaguely larval state, she knew it. Nofal and Fajr delighted in their little sister, fussed over her. Fajr doted like a little mother, singing poems to her and tying fluffy bows in her curls. She wanted desperately to do useful and helpful things for her. From the start, Nofal poked her chubby cheeks and was profligate with his kisses. Ednan, for his part, was never happier than when the five of us were together.

We were five. I marveled at this. As our eighth wedding anniversary approached, I took in the measure of my life with Ednan and thought with wonderment of all of it—our children, our jobs, the ebbs and flows and evolution of our marriage. Where do eight years go? Where do any of them? They are the river's current, rushing here over rocks and around bends, slowing there in the shallows of the dry season. I had moved beyond that stage in my life when eight years seemed like a long time to do anything. If at the start of our marriage an anniversary such as this seemed a distant peak, some considerable distance to climb, I knew in December of 2004 that eight years was not so great a height at all, but it was a reassuring lookout on the way to the summit. It had passed in a flash. Setting out from a new elevation, I felt that eight years was still just the beginning. Regardless, we had so much cause for gratitude, and that was reason to celebrate.

On the twentieth of December, my brother Muhammad—Momi—who had become like a brother to Ednan, and a dear friend, Ali Jafar, surprised us by taking us out to celebrate our anniversary at a restaurant with a cowboy theme. It was absurd: four Pakistanis donning cowboy hats and fringe jackets, adopting the worst John Wayne drawls. But we had a jolly time, laughing, cheering, eating and talking of the old days, before Ednan and I were parents, before we were anything, just young people finding their way and banking on good intentions and a surfeit of energy to see them through. For an evening, we were our younger selves again: carefree, hopeful, with all of life yet stretched out to the horizon. It was wonderful.

Back home, Momi and Ali had another surprise for us: candlelight, rose petals and a cake festooned with plump, ripe cherries. It must have taken Nofal and Fajr all the willpower in the world not to sink their fingers into it before we got home.

It is stirring to celebrate a wedding anniversary with one's children, to wonder, as each year passes, if the realization is coming to them that once upon a time, their parents existed for a purpose other than to love and care for their children. It had never occurred to me when I was a girl that my parents might have had lives of their own, once. I knew that for Nofal and Fajr, a cake with cherries was excuse enough for a party. *Do they wonder who we used to be?* I asked myself, still awash in memories kicked up over dinner. *Do they understand what occasion we are marking?* I looked at my two oldest children, their eyes shining with the novelty of a Monday night celebration, and I ached for the love of them, and for my yearning, too, that one day, they should know that the reason *they* existed is that I loved their father first.

My reverie was interrupted; Momi and Ali had encouraged the children to give us a serenade to John Denver's "Annie's Song," Ednan's favorite. Ednan grabbed his guitar, and we all sang along. Later, when Momi and Ali had gone home and the children were in their beds, I sat on the couch with Ednan and asked him how he felt about our eight years together. "It is like a dream," he said. "It is like a beautiful dream."

THE NEW YEAR, 2005, began with triumphant news: On the fourth of January, the National Assembly and the Senate passed a comprehensive law that included recommendations from my resolution to ban the customary practice of vani. The new law was part of an amendment to the Pakistan Penal Code of 1860, and it passed alongside other resolutions put forward by MPAs on reserved seats from the Sindh Provincial Assembly and the National Assembly to ban honor killings and other forms of forced marriage. My victory was also theirs, and the new law was a resounding affirmation, I believed, of the potential, once realized, of reserved seats. It was also a shining moment for Musharraf, who had proved, by signing the amendments into law, that his word was good. He had stated his commitment to human rights, and as far as these protections were concerned, he had come through. So had the marvelous Nilofer Bakhtiar, to whom I owed a debt of gratitude. I knew that she had the President's ear on vani all along; she had promised to make it a priority on his agenda, and she had.

Word of the new law reached Ednan and me at the newspaper. What jubilation! We celebrated with cheers and hugs, and I nearly wept for knowing that, after all, progress was attainable in what seemed to me at times to be the most dysfunctional parliament in the world. More than once I had thought of John Kennedy Toole's hilarious, tragic novel *A Confederacy of Dunces* when I took in a bird's-eye view of my colleagues in the Assembly; the title seemed such a sad but accurate way to sum so many of them up. This news brought me hope that it wasn't as bad as that, after all. It was also an affirmation of all of my work to date. I thought of the quote that is often, some say erroneously, attributed to Mahatma Gandhi: "First they ignore you, then they laugh at you, then they fight you, and then you win." No matter who said it, or whether it was ever spoken at all, I thought of these words and felt their resonance. I just had to keep going.

Our moment of private celebration was brief. Ednan and I

hastened to summon our editorial staff to plan the next day's coverage of the law's passage and its significance. A feature of our reporting would be a survey of the role of women legislators and the importance of letting them, as I had once pled, do their job.

One of the arguments that had been mounted in opposition to such a proposed law was that public outcry would result if bans on customary practices were mandated. In fact, public response to news of the laws was joyous. At the newspaper, congratulatory calls poured in from friends who knew of my role in the vani piece of the legislation, as well as from readers among the general public who wanted to celebrate what they considered a victory for women all over Pakistan. It was an auspicious start to the New Year, replenishing my optimism that my acid resolution, still stalled in the federal Law Department, might yet see the light of day, and that my moneylending bill would be the next to become law. How desperately I needed to believe so.

THE NEW YEAR also brought with it a major project for Ednan and me: the launch of an English-language newspaper. In Pakistan, no newspaper empire is complete without an English edition to reach the political elite and policy-makers. The Urdu broadsheet, which has more of a tabloid feel, is aimed at a vast population and has something for everyone, including more than a touch of the sensational. An English paper, on the other hand, aims more precisely for the nation's decision-makers. The emphasis is on analysis and commentary, and the overall presentation is more refined.

Zia had talked for years about his desire to add an English daily to his portfolio, and it had become Ednan's dream to build it. He longed for a project that was distinct from *Khabrain* and its umbrella of newspapers, something that he could create from scratch, imbue with his sensibility and call his own.

The time had finally come: Zia tapped Ednan to launch the paper, and Ednan, in turn, recruited me. I would leave *Khabrain*'s Helpline and women's pages, but I would take my awareness-building agenda with me. It was an exciting prospect; if done well, the new paper would have the potential to reach more people in more positions of power. Officially, I would be editor of the newspaper's weekly magazine, *Vista*, for which I would commission and edit long-format articles that delved into issues concerning women, children, current affairs and the poor. Unofficially, I would be an extension of Ednan's hands and brain. Anything he couldn't get to, I would take on. I would also be his shoulder, there to be leaned on in moments of uncertainty and doubt. Ednan would seek my input on every single decision, from designing the masthead, right down to the font, to determining the motto, "The truth and nothing but," to recruiting, hiring and mentoring each and every staff member. It would prove to be exhausting, absorbing, wholly rewarding work.

I looked forward to working so closely with Ednan again. If our working on parallel but separate tracks in the previous two years had brought strain to our marriage, I hoped that being back to testing the limits of each other's patience by spending hours on end in each other's company would have the old paradoxical effect of bringing us closer still. In early January, we moved our offices from the second to the fourth floors of *Khabrain*'s headquarters, and we began the process of searching for new hires and establishing the new paper's editorial identity. From a field of a dozen or so contenders, Ednan chose the name *The Post* for the new paper.

It was a good time for me to have a brand-new venture: It would not be the most productive year in the parliament. For one thing, the Punjab Provincial Assembly would manage only forty-nine days of actual work out of the seventy days that the parliament was in session. It was a House divided; walkouts by the opposition were the main culprit. Members of Benazir

Bhutto's PPP and Nawaz Sharif's PML-N opposed Shaukat Aziz as Prime Minister, saying that his was an in-house appointment by Musharraf, who had already recruited him to be Pakistan's Finance Minister. The opposition called Musharraf a dictator and stormed out of the Assembly, which had the effect most of all of ensuring that very little of significance was achieved. Eying a return to public life in Pakistan from their stations in exile, both Bhutto and Sharif encouraged their parties' rowdy displays; anything to undermine the ruling party.

When the opposition wasn't hooting anti-Musharraf slogans or staging a walkout, things were relatively quiet in the Assembly. Increasingly, however, I was not. As my moneylending bill was shunted further down the track, I grew even more vocal in my condemnation of the Revenue Committee. On the thirteenth of January, Speaker Sahi again asked the Assembly if my bill should receive another extension, its seventh. I stood to urge him instead to demand action from the Revenue Committee. "Why not insist on a report so that this House can finally put my bill to a vote?" I said. As much as the opposition, I was becoming a thorn in the side of the ruling party. By then, Sahi knew that the reporters in the press gallery above were already scribbling the next day's story about that troublesome MPA on the reserved seat who nevertheless made a good point: Why *not* just demand that the Revenue Committee act on her bill? He moved quickly to shut me down, having my microphone cut off just a few seconds after I began speaking. Then he granted my bill its seventh extension and quickly gaveled the session to a close.

It was the age of the twenty-four-hour news channel in Pakistan. Musharraf's success in liberalizing the media had opened the way for independent stations; since 2002, the stodgy, state-operated PTV was no longer the only game in town. With an influx of new channels came a demand for new content, and that created an opportunity for me. My years at the newspaper had taught me nothing if not the elements of a good story. In my battle to repeal an old moneylending law and pass a new one, and as the only woman MPA to have ever attempted such a thing, I knew that I had a story to tell. With increasing frequency, I appeared on television news programs and talk shows to discuss why, in my third year in the Provincial Punjab Assembly, I could report no progress to speak of regarding my moneylending bill. The popular rap on legislators is that they get so little done. When this came up in interviews, I enumerated the ways my progress had been hindered my members of my own party. I also spoke about the reserved seats for women and pointed to the good and important work that my female colleagues in Provincial Assemblies all over the country were trying to achieve. I held up the recently passed laws outlawing vani and honor killings as examples of what we could accomplish when enlightenment prevailed over misogyny and action prevailed over listlessness in the halls of power.

I started to receive fan emails from viewers within and beyond Pakistan's borders who urged me to continue my fight. I was touched when strangers, particularly women, approached to tell me that they had saved all of the articles I had written, as well as all of the articles written about me, and bid me their blessings and prayers. I also had support among members of the press, who expressed pride that one of their own was taking on the system from within it. Newspaper editorials about me and about my moneylending bill began appearing in papers all over the country; I was being held up as an exception to the rule of do-nothing politicians. None of which served me among the members of the Revenue Committee, who seemed only to dig in harder as popular support of my initiative grew.

While my moneylending bill remained locked in a monotonous pattern of inquorate meetings, refusals by the Revenue Department to provide documentation, and extensions that winter, there was one item of unexpected good news: Raja Basharat, the Law Minister to whom I had appealed for help in securing funding for a designated burn unit at Sir Ganga Ram Hospital one year earlier, wrote to tell me that the funding had come through. The hospital could break ground on a new burn unit, the first of its kind in Pakistan.

BY SPRING, CHAIRMAN NAWAZ had long since dropped any pretense of civility toward me in Revenue Committee meetings. Not even his woolly mammoth of a mustache could mask his sneer. His fealty lay with the committee and to the government; they did not want my bill to go for a vote, so Nawaz would see to it that it did not.

In the past year, Nawaz had built his resistance to my bill on two flimsy claims. The first hinged on his assertion that because the 1999 petition on riba was still pending before the Federal Shariat Court, I could not seek to legislate on the same issue. His second claim was that the cabinet of ministers must weigh in on my bill before the committee could do so. It had never been protocol for the cabinet to judge the viability of a bill; that was the job of the designated committee. But a cabinet ruling against my bill would give Nawaz cover. Both claims were delay tactics.

I defied Nawaz to take my bill to the cabinet. "Go ahead," I said. "And while you do that, I will take this bill to the House for a vote with or without the committee support!" I was calling Nawaz's bluff, but he was also calling mine. He knew that I was powerless to do anything without allies, and as far as he could tell, I didn't have any. That was the view from where I stood, as well.

When the Revenue Committee next met on the second of May, my bill was on its eighth extension. I had little reason to expect that this meeting would go any differently than the others, but I would have a glorious surprise. Zahid Ghaznavi, a section officer from the Law and Parliamentary Affairs Department, presented a letter that he had written to the Revenue Department. In it,

Ghaznavi refuted Chairman Nawaz's claim that a member of the House could not legislate on a matter that was pending before the Federal Shariat Court. The bottom line, Ghaznavi reported, was that the Revenue Committee had no basis on which to bar my pursuit of a new law on the private moneylending issue. I strained to betray no response at all while inwardly, I cartwheeled. In one fell swoop, Ghaznavi left the chairman with just one wobbly leg to stand on, his insistence on first seeking the opinion of the cabinet of ministers before moving on my bill.

Emboldened, I stood to demand that the Senior Member of the Revenue Board, Safdar Javaid Syed, who was Nasrullah Khan Chattha's direct superior, attend our next meeting and explain for himself why his department hadn't yet sought the opinion of the cabinet, if indeed the committee needed it to go forward on my bill. Making such a request is akin to summoning a citizen to jury duty; showing up is not optional. I wanted to hear from the senior-most member of the Revenue Department why his department was stalling. I intended that Syed should be put on the spot.

If the meeting of May second was important because it removed one of the obstacles in my path, it was pivotal for another reason, as well: It was the day I learned that a quiet coalition of supporters had emerged among my colleagues in the House and among members of the bureaucracy. That knowledge shored me up immeasurably. Since 2003, Ghaznavi and other colleagues from his department who had sat in on our meetings had witnessed my treatment at the hands of the committee chair and members. Gradually, he and others had come around to my corner. I learned that the minutes recorder, who listened to tapes of our sessions in producing written records of them, thought it awful what I was being subjected to. Even the waiter who delivered our tea and patties had overheard portions of our meetings and told me, sotto voce, to carry on, that I was doing work on behalf of the poor, and that I must keep going because it was work that mattered. When they held the doors for me in the lobby, the men and women who performed menial tasks around the parliament building would, with kind eyes and words, tell me that I was their hero for fighting for poor people like them. Thus began a trickle of expressions of support for my work on the moneylending bill. It was a most welcome development.

EDNAN AND I were spending long hours together at *The Post*'s offices, and I was working on far more than what fell under my official purview. Evenings around eight o'clock, I returned home to take care of the children, while Ednan worked until one, two, three o'clock in the morning. There was scant time to interact as a married couple, but we were happy. We were building something together, and knowledge of that sustained us. But the pressure was intense. For Ednan, it was nothing new—he had worked with his father on the launch of four different newspapers—but for me, the constant deadlines were nearly stroke-inducing. For months leading up to the newspaper's launch, we produced daily dummies—full versions of the newspaper that were not distributed, but that were meant to train our team to interact as a well-oiled machine. There were deadlines every half hour or fifteen minutes, and Ednan and I fielded all of them. All of this, plus three children at home—Hafsa was only nine months old at the time—and an ongoing push to break through loggerheads in the parliament. My hair started to fall out in clumps.

I had developed a stress-induced case of alopecia areata. My immune system was attacking itself, my doctor told me, and the result was bald patches all over my scalp. I wasn't in the habit of wearing a headscarf outside of the parliament building back then, but I began to cover my head with more frequency. I confess to having felt too vain to let others see what havoc the stress was wreaking on me.

When I wasn't at the newspaper, I continued to attend House meetings. Emboldened by the success at the start of the year of the vani law and also by the expressions of support, both allusive and overt, for my moneylending bill from within and beyond the parliamentary ranks, I continued to agitate for action on the floor of the House. When they cut my mic, I shouted. When I raised my voice, a chorus of boos rose up. Remarkably, they were loudest coming from the Treasury benches, members of my own party. Behind the scenes, I sought out members of the opposition, as well as tribal leaders and landowners in the parliament, members from rural areas where moneylending was a particular bane. I was willing to talk to anyone, to hear anyone out, if it meant securing even just one vote in favor of my moneylending bill. One day in early June, back from another dispiriting session in the House, I found Ednan pacing his office. He looked upset.

"Humaira, word's just come from the provincial government that they're going to cut off all advertising," he said. "They haven't said why, but they implied that it was because of your 'activism.' "

I was stunned. In Pakistan, the government is the largest source of advertising revenue for newspapers. The ads trumpet government initiatives and serve as paid publicity for an institution that needs all the good PR it can get, even PR it has to place in papers on its own behalf. The ads create a particular journalistic conundrum, of course. With the threat of withheld or diminished ad revenues, some newspapers go easy on the government. When the government withdraws ads, the message is clear: Toe the line, or else. It's one of the reasons I was all the more proud to have worked for *Khabrain*. Over the years, ad revenues had been hastily withdrawn in the wake of critical reporting, but always, the paper kept going. Eventually, the revenues returned.

News that my actions in the parliament might imperil my husband's fledgling newspaper, however, upset me deeply. I had to sit down. *How could my own party do this to me?* I thought. Ednan saw the look on my face and tried for a reassuring tone, in spite of his own evident alarm. "These things happen all the time," he said, sitting and putting an arm around me. "Try not to worry." I had the feeling that he was trying to convince himself as well as me.

"But, Ednan," I said, "we're launching a newspaper in a couple of months. With fewer government ads, there's less money coming in. What will we do? What's going to happen to your dream?"

Ednan stood up. "Nothing's going to happen to *The Post*. It'll come out on schedule, don't you worry. And nothing will happen to the Khabrain Group. It's weathered worse droughts than this. You just concentrate on doing what you think is right. You're pursuing a good cause, and I don't want you to be deterred by this. I just thought you should know." After a pause, he added, "Look on the bright side: You're really pissing them off!"

We both laughed, but I knew that Ednan was worried, too. As scare tactics on the part of the provincial government go, this one worked. No wonder my hair was falling out.

What happened next should have rendered me as bald as the Buddha. A few days before the House was to meet to vote on the budget for a new fiscal year, I received a sinister call on my cellphone. "You are being warned," a man's distorted voice said. "Resign from the Punjab Assembly by tomorrow, or face grave consequences."

I demanded to know who was calling.

"You will see your honor flouted before the whole world," the caller said in response before hanging up.

Ednan threw a fit when I told him about the call. "I'm going to trace the number!" he said. "I'll give hell to this creep!"

The calls continued over the next several days. It wasn't just one person; the voices were different every time. Each call was more profane and threatening than the last. We traced them to various public phone booths around Lahore.

Then came an influx of letters, addressed to me and signed by a "Mr. Pakistan," at the *Khabrain* office. The message in each was the same: Resign, or else. Ednan reached out to every contact he had in order to trace the sender.

"Mr. Pakistan" next brought the assault to my email inbox. I logged on at the office one morning in June to find a mass email with the subject line: "Be careful from following professional and corrupt ladies." It had been distributed to the entire provincial government, bureaucracy and media. In it, "Mr. Pakistan" slandered six of us in the Punjab Provincial Assembly and one minister—all women. Betraying himself to be possessed of the fevered imagination of an overwrought schoolboy with the base sensibilities of a pornographer, he labeled us "sex workers" and "whores," alleged that some of us were HIV-positive, named long lists of high-profile men as our alleged sex partners, and purported to have photographs of some of us in the nude or in flagrante delicto. He attributed to each of us a particular sexual fetish. The entry about me began, "Kindly find enclosed herewith some story of your colleague MPA famous sexy lady," and went on to give my personal phone numbers before delineating my alleged perversions.

Other emails, addressed solely to me, promised "severe punishment" if I failed to resign. "We will teach you a lesson," one email read. "We will circulate pornographic videos of you around the country. You will be exposed for the loose woman you are."

I felt on the verge of vomiting and called for Ednan, who was in his office. He came running when he heard panic in my voice. Though livid—I could see the vein throbbing at his temple—Ednan tried first to calm me. "There is a cost of doing something against the system," he said. "This is an acknowledgment that what you are doing is hitting someone hard. Whoever is doing this wouldn't go to these despicable lengths if they weren't terribly threatened." He urged me to remain strong. "No one who knows you will be swayed to change their high opinion of you by a slanderous email. Your character has long been on display for all to see, and the proof of it is in your actions," he said.

"Continue with your noble work, and you will beat them. You will beat them!" Ednan continued. "They want you to be intimidated and to resign, but in this battle of nerves, you will win. I believe in you, my darling, and I stand with you. I am your witness, and that alone matters." Ednan added that he hoped to find "Mr. Pakistan" so that he could break his nose.

I thought about what Ednan said. His determination and clarity helped restore my own. *Yes,* I thought, *my bill must really have touched a nerve to warrant this.* It was oddly satisfying to think so.

As suddenly as they had begun, the correspondence and the calls stopped. We would never know who was behind them; the email had been untraceable. Feeling a mixture of trepidation and rebelliousness, I returned to the Assembly when it was called into session in late June. While sitting in the cafeteria with a group of my female colleagues from the parliament, one of them mentioned a filthy, threatening email she had received. "I received one too," another said. At least a dozen of us, it turned out, had been targeted. Not surprisingly, we were the ones who tended to speak out and speak up the most often in the Assembly. From the start, there had been a direct correlation between our outspokenness and the disdain and catcalling aimed at us in the House. Now there appeared to be a direct link between the most vocal women MPAs and these menacing calls and correspondence. While this reflected most poorly of all on whoever was behind so craven a scare campaign, the tactic had a silencing effect on some of us, but not on me. When, on the seventeenth of June, my moneylending bill received its ninth extension, I once again rose to speak in protest. By then, it was all-out war between Chairman Nawaz and me. He refused even to call a meeting to discuss my moneylending bill, which meant that I would have to wait to find out if the Speaker of the House would grant its tenth extension.

WITH JUST TWO WEEKS to go until launching *The Post* in the summer of 2005, Prime Minister Shaukat Aziz had at last agreed to a panel interview with *Khabrain*. Zia's delighted satisfaction in delivering this news to Ednan and me revealed something of the heat-seeking missile of a journalist he had been; Aziz was a tough get, and Zia relished getting him. I hadn't seen my father-in-law so energized in a long time. He told us that he had given both of our names as interviewers; the following week, the three of us would travel to meet with the Prime Minister in Islamabad.

"This is my chance to bring the private moneylending bill up with the PM," I said, excited by the prospect that my bill might receive a fillip from Aziz's support. "Perhaps he will send some sort of directive to the Punjab government to pass the bill as soon as possible." I indulged in the possibility that Aziz's backing would make all the difference.

I carried the same optimistic air on our short flight to Islamabad, much to Ednan's amusement. We were scheduled to meet Aziz at the Prime Minister's residence, and as we settled into our hotel room, I took out the file I had made on the private moneylending bill and began to read through it. Ednan lounged on the bed and laughed as he flipped through the TV channels. "Give it a rest, my darling," he said, smiling at me. "You don't even know if you'll get a chance to speak to him about the bill."

"Oh, but I will, my darling," I said, straining for flippancy but betraying my irritation instead. "I have to. He's a banker. He'll understand inherently the importance of ridding Pakistan of these parasites and shutting down this informal economy."

In the morning, I was so eager that I was up and dressed before Ednan was out of bed. Later, in the hotel lobby, Zia waited with *Khabrain*'s Islamabad resident editor, and the four of us set off for the Prime Minister's residence. We passed through a security gauntlet before being permitted entry to Aziz's office.

Aziz was a bit of a puzzle. He managed to keep his distance

from the press and so was cast as something of an enigma. In private, he was self-possessed and confident, a good combination for a man whose job included not just projecting Pakistan's image abroad, but embodying it, even if that image was partly aspirational. Our interview ranged from domestic topics, including the state of Pakistan's economy, law and order, and gender inequality, to international ones, including foreign policy and the War on Terror. Aziz appeared to be at his ease responding to everything. He was suave and urbane, but also disinclined to small talk and lingering; when he was done answering questions, he was done.

The interview over, I ventured a word with the Prime Minister about my moneylending bill. "Prime Minister Sahib," I said, "I've been working on a bill that aims to prohibit private moneylending because usury, besides being anti-Islam, is a societal ill. I wondered if I might ask you to take a look at this file. Perhaps the federal government might consider this issue worth looking into?"

The Prime Minister took my file, glanced at it fleetingly, and set it aside. "You know, Humaira," he said, "I've been following your work with interest, particularly the human rights resolutions you have campaigned for in the Punjab Assembly. You have been doing some good work."

I knew somehow to brace myself for the "but."

"But the problem is that this country already has too many legislations pending," Aziz said. I felt my stomach tighten. "We don't need another one." He stood to indicate that our conversation was over. I understood from the look in his eyes that he, once a career banker, could not possibly throw his weight behind a measure that ultimately called into question the very foundation of the banking industry. Banning even private moneylending would pose a threat to an entire economic system.

During our drive back to the hotel, Ednan nudged me gently. "Don't look so glum, Humaira," he whispered. "Look, you've been working on this bill for so long now. You didn't expect the Prime Minister to wave a magic wand, did you?"

"I didn't," I said, defensive. "I did expect him to show at least a degree of interest, however. He didn't even bother to glance at what was in the file! This bill isn't about me, Ednan. I'm not looking for a personal favor. This bill is about Pakistan. This bill is about a scourge afflicting this country, and our Prime Minister couldn't be bothered!"

I was still very upset when we reached the hotel. Ednan, long an expert at navigating through one of my storms, knew to steer clear for a bit. After an hour or so, he returned to ask me to join him for sandwiches in the hotel restaurant. He said nothing further about my exchange with the PM, and I didn't bring my disappointment up. I was glad just to eat, glad to have Ednan there with me, and glad to be returning to Lahore. I missed our children, and I wanted to put this wasted trip to Islamabad behind me. As soon as we landed in Lahore, Ednan sent me home with the driver, and he went straight to the office with his father. *The Post*'s launch was just days away.

SINCE BEGINNING WORK on the new paper in January, Ednan had been spending less and less time at home, more and more time at the office. I had become used to his coming home in the wee hours. Once, when he had projected that he might be home early—by eleven o'clock—so that we could do the unheard of thing of dining together, he called at ten minutes to the hour, full of regrets. He had been overly optimistic, he said. There was no way he would make it home by eleven. It was rare for me to protest, but I did. "No!" I said. "You promised! Ednan Shahid, I'm beginning to think you are secretly married to someone living under your desk!"

"It seems that you really, really want me to come home," he said.

"I do! And you're a beast to have disappointed me in this way. I will exact my revenge," I said, realizing that I half meant it; I was sorely disappointed.

"Perhaps if you wish for me to be there, if you really, really want me to be there," Ednan said. "Make a wish. Let's see what happens!"

"Now you're just toying with me," I said. "Let me go to bed. I'm exhausted."

"Just try it. Just wish aloud, in your clearest voice, for me to be home. Let's see what happens," he said.

I gave in, declaring in a tone that was one part stentorian, one part supplicant, "I pray to Allah to send my husband home!"

At that, Ednan burst through the bedroom door, giving me the fright of my life. We were both laughing too hard to speak for a long time. It had been many months since we spent an evening, even the last hour of one, together. I was elated.

If he could play a little trick with my affections, Ednan did not take his absences from our children lightly at all. By July, I had resorted to bringing them to his office in the evenings just so that Ednan could give them a kiss goodnight. This tore at him. He spoke often during that time about his boyhood and missing Zia, his indefatigable, workaholic father, and he did not want his children to pine after their father, too. We began discussing the idea of moving to be closer to the office, but where to? We shelved the question for the time being and focused on the mission at hand: launching *The Post*.

At dawn on the fourteenth of August, Ednan returned home from the office. He hadn't been home in the previous two days. I was asleep when he walked into our bedroom. "Look, Humaira!" he said, waking me as he sat on the bed. "This is testimony to the fact that dreams do come true!" Ednan placed a copy—a real one—of *The Post* on the pillow next to me. The paper had launched.

I propped myself up on a pillow and looked at the newspaper. It took a few moments to focus my eyes. Ednan had written something on it, the very first copy of his newspaper.

> For my love, my life, my best friend, my solace.
> If I am something, I would never have been without you.
> I owe you much, and I love you for always and forever.
> Yours, Eddie.

CHAPTER THIRTEEN

The Most Unmanageable Woman in Pakistan

SEPTEMBER IS THE MONTH when I press RESET on the year, when I take stock and resolve anew to get it done, whatever "it" is. January, with its obligatory intentions and high-minded resolutions, has always struck me as a bit late to get started with the business of meaningful change; the best months, in my opinion, are behind it. This thinking is a holdover, perhaps, of my girlhood in Kuwait, when all of the excitement and anticipation of advancing to a new grade converged on the head of a pin that was the first day of school. Part of my fondness for September has always been the novelty it brings. When I was a girl, it was simple: new teachers, new lessons, new books. All those years later, September's allure still lay in the new: Hafsa had just turned one and was walking with the determined abandon of a kamikaze pilot; *The Post* was up and running and working out its kinks; and I had a new platform from which to holler about the now old issue of my moneylending bill.

On the second of September 2005, I published an editorial in *The Post* called "From Extension to Extinction," an anticipatory obituary, of sorts, for my moneylending bill. I recapitulated my arguments, recounted the delays, and lay the blame for the bill's languishing on life support squarely on the Revenue Committee.

A week later, on the ninth of September, *The Post* published a very lightly fictionalized account I had written of an average

Revenue Committee meeting. Written as a short one-act play, *Between Off the Record and On the Record* was set in a well-appointed committee room and brought together Bibi, who was moving a bill to end moneylending; the chairman, who checks and rechecks his watch as though in danger of missing a pressing engagement; an MPA absorbed in a text-messaging exchange but otherwise not engaged in the conversation; and senior members of the Law and Government Departments who only stop yawning long enough to sip their tea and to defend their departments' inaction. The sign-in form bears more signatures than actual attendees; the group waits for two hours for enough members to show, during which time Bibi lays out her case point by point. The chairman confuses money-laundering with moneylending, orders more tea and sandwiches, and then declares the meeting inquorate, meaning that none of Bibi's arguments are put on the record. By the end, Bibi finds herself complaining to an empty room about the phantom signatures on the sign-in form, because everyone has left.

Taken for the exposé I intended it to be, my farce caused a bit of a sensation in parliamentary ranks when it appeared in *The Post*'s op-ed section. My phone rang incessantly. The Governor of Punjab, Khalid Maqbool, was the first to call. "Oh my God!" he said, laughing. "I am convinced of your writing skills now! What an insight you have given into how our system works."

"Or doesn't work," I replied.

Maqsood Malik called next. "Humaira Bibi, oh my God! I can't believe you wrote this!"

I said, "Well, tell me, is it an exaggeration?" He admitted that it was not.

"I am sick to death of hearing people complain that legislators do nothing," I said. "I am trying to do something, and look what is happening!"

Having laid it all out there for my colleagues to absorb in their morning paper, I decided to go to Chief Minister Chaudhry Per-

vaiz Elahi before the start of that day's parliamentary session.
Like the men in the ranks beneath him, Elahi was too much of
a career politician to betray his true feelings about me or my
bill one way or the other. I knew better than to ask him. What I
needed to know was whether Elahi, as head of the ruling party,
sanctioned what had been happening in Revenue Committee
meetings. It was not an easy question to ask, but I asked anyway:
"Our Chairman Mian Majid Nawaz is rude and demeaning, and
of late, he refuses even to call a meeting to discuss my bill, so it
goes from one extension to the next. Chief Minister Sahib, have
you directed Chairman Nawaz to conduct himself this way?" My
heart was pounding in my chest; just by posing the question, I
was implying Elahi's complicity.

Elahi assured me, emphatically, no. He had received multiple
complaints about Nawaz, he said, and would have never issued
a directive for the chair of a House committee to flout rules and
procedures, let alone mistreat another MPA. I was reassured, but
only somewhat; Nawaz was such a company man that I knew he
wouldn't behave with such impunity if the guy at the top hadn't
at least tacitly expressed his approval. But I could only take Elahi
at his word. I decided that if he hadn't sanctioned Nawaz's antics,
then he wouldn't mind my calling the chairman out about them
on the floor of the House, which is precisely what I did next.

My bill was up for another extension. When Chairman Nawaz
stood to request that it be granted, I stood, too. "These are delay
tactics to prevent my bill from coming to the House," I said,
calmly but with force. "This is an issue that concerns the poor. It
is a problem on every street in every town and village that is represented by every member in this Assembly, but still, no action!"
I spoke quickly because I expected that any second, the Speaker
would give the subtle nod to his staff to cut off my microphone.

Then something unexpected happened. Rana Sanaullah
Khan, leader of the PML-N opposition party, and the man who
years ago had complimented my work to Ednan, stood to speak

in my favor. "It is unfair that so much money should go into these meetings when nothing happens," he said. He was joined next by members of the other opposition party, MMA, who also stood in support of me. One member said, "It is unfair to take one extension after the other if there is not even a committee meeting held in between!" Next, Mohsin Leghari broke ranks from the other, silent members of our party, the National Alliance, and stood to demand accountability of the Revenue Committee. "One woman alone has stood up against this usurious system. How many of us had the courage to do so? And look what the system is doing to her! The power of this House becomes a joke if we cannot stand up for our friend and colleague who is fighting in the committees all alone!"

Speaker of the House Sahi issued my bill its tenth extension. Chairman Nawaz, embarrassed by the spontaneous and unforeseen protest in the House, turned spiteful: He again refused to call the next Revenue Committee meeting, thus ensuring that the entire spectacle would repeat when my bill was next up for an extension, the twenty-third of November. That time, even more members of the opposition would stand to demand that the Revenue Committee explain itself, and my bill would receive its eleventh extension.

Shortly thereafter, I went to meet with Nasrullah Khan Chattha at his Revenue Board office. I had to divine the source of such staunch opposition to my moneylending bill. He had been the first to oppose it, and his efforts to deceive the committee about the existence of records proving that his department had tried to implement the 1960 law had held my bill up for nearly a year. I figured Chattha was a good place to start.

"Why are all of you opposing me so fiercely?" I asked.

"It is nothing personal, Humaira Bibi," Chattha said. "But no matter what, under no circumstances should this law be passed. And it will not." He urged me to give up.

"I will not," I said. "I will fight this to the end."

"You should have thought of something other than usury, some other reform. Don't touch the economic issues of the province."

I replied that as a legislator, it was my duty to address the issues that hurt people. "Usury is forbidden in Islam! It is a curse!" I said.

"This won't happen," he said, as dispassionately as if he were telling me that we had run out of tea. "It is beyond my control. I am there just to express the view of the department."

That went well, I thought as I stormed out of his office.

I WAS DETERMINED that the Revenue Committee should meet before the thirty-first of December, when the current extension was set to expire. I enlisted Maqsood Malik, whose job, among other things, was to enforce the proper carrying out of rules and procedures in committee meetings, to write to Chairman Nawaz and demand that he call a meeting. Nawaz acquiesced, but when the committee convened on the sixteenth of December for its fifteenth meeting in two years, he was ready with a new delay tactic: He presented three pre-partition laws, one dating to 1938, that were peripherally related to the issue of debt and revenue collection. Nawaz claimed that the committee had to vet the laws for contradictions to my bill. I challenged him. "Your sole intention here is to waste the time of this committee," I said.

The chairman smiled broadly at me. He appeared to relish the moment. "Perhaps I should send your bill to the Federal Shariat Court," he said. "Don't be surprised if it takes them seven years to return an opinion!" He succeeded in wasting the entire meeting, but not before I had the chance to remind the chairman and the committee that in our previous meeting on the second of May, I had requested that Safdar Javaid Syed, the Senior Member of the Revenue Board, join us to explain why my bill had not been brought before the cabinet of ministers. I was told that

Javaid was ill and unable to attend, but that he would join us next time.

THAT DECEMBER, ZIA FELL ILL. He had been working in Multan when he had what his doctors thought was an appendicitis attack. One appendectomy and three days later, he was back in a hospital in Lahore, his condition and pain worse. It was the beginning of a disorienting time for our entire family; Zia had always been the strong one, the indomitable force with the unlimited stamina and drive, the one you take for granted will always be there.

A medical team in Lahore discovered that Zia's sudden illness hadn't been caused by his appendix, but by a blockage in his intestines. They operated, but his incision wouldn't heal because of his diabetes. What we all thought would be a routine surgery ended up being anything but, with Zia's pain compounded by further medical complications. Thus began a period of months during which we all took turns caring for him. To no one's surprise, Zia was not an easy patient. We were all shaken by this sudden turn.

Meanwhile, during the run-up to *The Post*'s launch the previous summer, we began to feel guilt over having the children spend so much time at work with us. It flared up again that January, when our hours grew even longer as we added some of Zia's responsibilities to our own. By then, both of our offices, but mine especially, had become filled with children's books and toys. I even had a crib in mine. It was not at all unusual for me to conduct a meeting in my office while Hafsa played under my desk. Our two oldest children made like free-range chickens, roaming the corridors of the newspaper's offices. Nofal did a deadpan impersonation of his father on the phone: "What's the lead story? The superlead? When will I see the draft!" He and his sister Fajr had become versed at playing "reporter," telling on each other with a startling alacrity and attention to detail.

A paradoxical side effect of having our children with us at work was the growing feeling of being unavailable to them— present in body but not mind—and it ate at us. We also feared that so much time spent in our offices would deny them something we wanted so much for them: a sense of home. We decided in earnest to move.

The top floor of *Khabrain*'s headquarters was vacant. I didn't love the idea of giving up our stand-alone villa with Zia and Yasmine for an apartment above the office, but thinking of it as a penthouse with sweeping views of Old City Lahore helped. I began meeting with an architect and designers to plan what Ednan called our "dream home." From January on, I would slip out of our fourth-floor offices, ride up to the eighth floor, and huddle over blueprints with the builders who would begin renovating the cavernous, 8,000-square-foot space.

IN FEBRUARY, THE EUROPEAN consul in Lahore invited me to visit the European Parliament. Given all that was happening on the home front, between Zia's failing health and a massive home-building project underway, I did not give serious thought to going; I didn't see how anyone could spare us. Ednan disagreed. Not only was he adamant that I go for the experience and the exposure it would offer me, he wanted to go with me. It was an appealing proposition. We hadn't been away without the children since before we had them—our brief honeymoon in 1997. Nine years later, a week away in Europe, just the two of us, sounded like a dream. Even though I fretted about the logistics of leaving home and work for a week, I didn't even consider mounting a counterargument, lest Ednan think twice and change his mind.

The thirteenth of February, we flew to Brussels, leaving our children with my parents and relying on Ednan's sister, brother and mother to look after Zia. I remember holding my breath— and Ednan's hand—as we took off from Lahore's Allama Iqbal International Airport. As the plane gained altitude, delivering us ever higher into the heavens, I prayed, among other things, for Zia's condition to at least hold steady while we were away. How terrible it would be, I thought, if there were an emergency and we were not there to help.

It was a whirlwind seven days during which I visited the European Parliament, whose Vice President I met, and the European Commission, whose Director General welcomed me. In conversations with journalists and politicians about my legislative efforts and the reserved seats, I had an epiphany similar to the one I'd had during our visit to London, when my television appearances led to such an outpouring of support: People respected my work. It was gratifying to learn that issues so specific to my part of the world—acid attacks, vani and private moneylending—mattered to my colleagues in Europe. And it was useful and inspiring to compare notes on concerns we shared in common, such as improved education and access to health care for women and girls, and matters relating to the prevention and prosecution of violence against women.

Outside of these meetings, Ednan and I made like flâneurs, strolling through the streets of Belgium and nearby Strasbourg, taking in the novelty of freshly fallen snow, and doing what we almost never did back home: holding hands as we ambled through the markets or shared a coffee, because there had never been time for aimless wandering or idle pursuits in Lahore. On the eve of our return home, news that Zia was suffering from renal failure made us glad to be going back so that we could be there to help, but also glad to have stolen those seven days away; who knew what we would be returning to?

THE ENTIRE SHAHID FAMILY gathered at the hospital on the fifteenth of March to meet with doctors about Zia's condition. We decided that a trip to a London nephrologist might be the best course of action, and we began making plans for Ednan and his sister to travel there with their father later in the month.

In order to be able to attend to the hospital business, I missed the parliamentary session that day. I learned that evening that Chairman Nawaz had taken advantage of my absence to request another extension for my moneylending bill. It had become embarrassing to him to have to contend with my challenges to his committee leadership on the House floor. Mohsin Leghari, who had risen in my bill's defense in September, stood in my stead this time and demanded to know what was going on in these meetings such that my bill needed a twelfth extension. I knew what was at stake for Leghari in doing so; defying our party to go on the record as being in my corner wouldn't earn him any favors with our leadership. I was grateful to him for his courage, which stood in such stark contrast to Nawaz's cowardice.

Shortly thereafter, on the twenty-first of March, I published an article in The Post's weekly magazine, Vista, about all of the resolutions presented in the first three years of each of the four Provincial Assemblies in Pakistan. In "Legislatures' Resolutions: A Mere Formality," we showed the range of resolutions proposed, how many of them had led to legislation that had been implemented, which ones yet demanded action, and which, like my acid attack resolution, remained in legislative limbo in federal departments.

I intended for the article to hold up a mirror to the government in general and to Musharraf in particular. He had come out so strong at the start of his presidency. Though he never had the legitimacy that comes from being directly elected, he enjoyed enormous popular support at home and goodwill abroad, not to mention a surge of foreign aid. His pledge early in his presidency to create a more democratic, more tolerant Pakistan set him apart from his civilian predecessors, Benazir Bhutto and Nawaz Sharif, neither of whom had made reform a priority; indeed, their regimes were famous for corruption scandals. But now, three years into Musharraf's presidency, his grip on power was slipping, his popularity waning. It is a trend of democratic leaders in Pakistan to turn autocratic as their power fades, to cling more desperately to it. That spring, the indications were beginning to show that that was what Musharraf was doing. As calls for impeachment mounted, and in the face of increasing protests in the National and Provincial Assemblies, Musharraf began to walk a vexatious line between democracy and autocracy. In the end, he would never commit fully enough to one or the other to be able to see his promises through.

That *Vista* article exposed widespread apathy and ineffectiveness in governance, a return to and proliferation of the very corruption that Musharraf had promised to weed out, and a system that was failing. His promises to establish rule of law, rule of merit and accountability had gone unrealized. If I could have had another audience with the President at that time, I should have liked to ask him: Is this the government you had in mind?

My small staff of curious young men and women at *Vista* also produced articles on, among other topics, women's and children's issues. In the process, they became ardent activists for their causes. Over the course of just a few months, we published reports that ranged in focus from a woman's right to alimony postdivorce and the ramifications of female infanticide on the gender ratio in Pakistan, to the peril posed to children by webcams in an age of online predators. We examined the problem of women's mobility in modern Pakistani society, where we are forbidden from riding bicycles and scooters and, as such, have limited commuting options. And we looked at what the repeal of General Zia-ul-Haq's 1979 Hudood Ordinances would mean for Pakistani society. The Hudood laws criminalized adultery and consensual, nonmarried sex, and made rape victims liable to charges of adultery and imprisonment. The National Assembly would repeal them in a landmark vote to come in November 2006, replacing them with the Women's Protection Bill. Our coverage anticipated this historic break with a repressive legacy. And eight months after an earthquake that devastated northern Pakistan and claimed upward of 75,000 lives, *Vista* reporters returned to the region to offer an assessment of the rebuilding effort. My young team was cutting its teeth on stories of pure substance, and I was proud of their work.

ALL THE WHILE, *The Post* was coming along. The majority of our staff was young and inexperienced, which made for a surfeit of energy that, at times, was a challenge to focus. They needed training, and so a good deal of what Ednan and I did during that first year at the paper was mentor. We also tried a more democratic approach than what was practiced at *Khabrain*, where Zia reigned and the rest of us, his subjects, spoke only when spoken to. Whereas his father's approach to management relied on more than a bit of fear and dread to spur on his underlings, Ednan set himself apart by getting the results he wanted by nurturing. Rather than call meetings in our offices, Ednan and I joined the reporters in their carrels and held what felt like open forums, where everyone was encouraged to contribute and brainstorm. Ednan ran his newsroom like a beneficent patriarch bestowing wisdom, kindness and, when necessary, tough love on his most dear. His staff repaid him with an abiding loyalty that they extended to me.

The Post also became an informal gathering place for some of my fellow MPAs, a group of young, Western-educated intellectuals who practiced a rebellious brand of patriotism. The eldest of us, Mohsin Leghari, was born in 1963. Together with the brilliant Syeda Sughra Imam, who received her bachelor's degree from Harvard; Abid Hussain Chattha, a lawyer with degrees from Boston University and Columbia who had a terrific mind for judicial and constitutional reforms; Muhammad Yar Hiraj, an engineering and computer whiz educated at Brown University, and the aforementioned Muhammad Mohsin Leghari from the Punjab city of Dera Ghazi Khan, who had found his way to the University of Oklahoma, we shared a deep suspicion of government and a desire to make it accountable. We had long conversations about how we wanted to contribute to building a new Pakistan.

All of these MPAs became good friends of mine and of Ednan. In time, I might come to work to find that one of my colleagues from the Provincial Assembly had just dropped in to say hello to Ednan. He developed an especially close friendship with Mohsin Leghari, who by then was my most ardent defender on the House floor.

As a group, we would stay up late into the night dissecting ills that afflicted Pakistan and dated to partition. We explored why tribal, linguistic and ethnic identity remained so important in Punjabi politics, and we looked at our own families for answers to why clan identity remained so strong in modern Pakistani politics and society. Imam was Syed; Chattha was Jatt; Leghari was tribal Baloch; Hiraj and I were Rajput; and Ednan was Arain. While such classifications might seem irrelevant given all that we desired in common for Pakistan, as long as clan identity still mattered in Pakistan, we had to be aware of it, too.

So much of Punjabi humor revolves around the caste system, so when evenings ran long and humors turned punchy, we would tease Ednan about coming from the clan thought to be the most materialistic. Rajputs were known as warriors, and Ednan liked to cite my disposition as proof. I was also a Bhatti, which Ednan considered wonderful fodder for teasing me, because Dullah Bhatti was a great warrior hero of the Punjab who rose up against the Mughals. Whenever I was particularly fired up about something, Ednan liked to say, "Here comes Dullah Bhatti."

IN LATE MARCH, with Zia's renal failure acute and the added complication of an eye infection, Ednan and his sister flew with their father to London in the hope that a specialist there could help. They left on the twenty-fifth and were gone for two weeks. Between late March and June, they would take three such trips abroad, each intended to seek another opinion about Zia's worsening health, and each lasting a little longer than the one previous. It meant that Ednan was away on average more than he was home during a three-month period.

It was strange to be without Ednan, and difficult. I wasn't prepared for how much so. I felt as though I were separating from a part of myself. In the swirl of deadlines and meetings and domestic obligations, we were almost never apart. For nearly a decade, Ednan's constant presence had come to feel as normal and right as having a right hand. To my delight, time hadn't dulled Ednan's enthusiasm for demonstrative—and usually silly—expressions of love. In a group he might suddenly drop to his knees and say, "Tell her to marry me again!" while I, mortified but happy, bid him to stop—"Oh God, Ednan! Get up!" I would say. Even when our days took us in different directions, he would always find the time to call me. I might answer the phone to hear Ednan's rendition of "Is You Is or Is You Ain't My Baby?" or, in his horrendous French accent, "You set my soul on fire!" impersonating Pepe Le Pew, the amorous cartoon skunk who is forever forcing himself on that poor black cat. We sent text messages with updates on this and that, and just to say hello. There was never an hour in the day, really, when we weren't in touch. And when we were apart for a few days, it was never longer than that. Since my brother Muhammad had moved to Dubai for his studies a year earlier, Ednan enjoyed a long weekend with him there now and again. When he did, he was in such frequent touch with us back home that I would urge him just to enjoy himself and not worry about calling.

I struggled with Ednan's being half a world away and five

hours behind. Caught up in meetings with doctors and with Zia's care, he was able to send only the briefest messages. More often than not, we missed each other when he called, because on my end, I juggled caring for our children with everything else, which now included riding herd on contractors. The extent to which I missed my husband both reassured and unsettled me; since when did one person become the deciding factor in whether or not I woke and went to bed happy? Was this a blessing, I wondered, a great gift from Allah that only made me stronger, or was it a dependency, a crutch, that risked making me weak? I was glad not to have the luxury of time to ponder this for too long.

In his absence, I took over Ednan's responsibilities at the newspaper while managing my own. I found this difficult, too. He counseled me to be "strict and assertive." He warned me against being "overly friendly," even though his entire management style was rooted in his inherent warmth and kindness. Ednan was that rarest of workplace hybrids: the demanding boss that everyone loved. Whenever I filled in for him, I struggled to establish such benevolent authority and felt that I was coming up short.

When Ednan was away, however, I reaped the rewards that his bighearted leadership had sown. Several of his reporters and editors, knowing that I alone was steering the ship while checking in on progress on the eighth floor and helping the children with homework, jumped in to help me. They distracted Hafsa when she was fussy and I needed to edit a story. They were solicitous of and indulgent with Nofal and Fajr, inviting them to watch what they were doing and sit at their desks like grown-up journalists, tapping at their keyboards as though on deadline. We became a family at *The Post*, and the credit for that went to Ednan.

Newspaper and parliamentary business made for frightfully long days. I was loath to go too long without being with my children, though, and so I had the children brought to the office in the evenings, and then I brought as much work as I could home with me when it was time to feed them and put them to bed. Just as some on the newspaper staff got a bit antsy while Ednan was away, our children acted up, too. I made the mistake that parents everywhere do, promising grave consequences when their father returned home if they didn't behave. I wasn't fooling anyone. The children knew better than anyone that Ednan was the softie in the family.

In the midst of all of this, Dr. Akbar Chaudhry from Sir Ganga Ram Hospital had called to share the excellent news that, one year after receiving funds to break ground, construction on the new burn unit was complete. He urged me to come for a ribbon-cutting ceremony that the hospital planned for April. I told him that I would, but only on the condition that the hospital open the unit right away and begin treating victims. I didn't want pomp to delay lifesaving treatment. He agreed, and the unit began accepting patients immediately.

On the third of April, I attended a modest opening ceremony for three new wings of the hospital, including the burn unit. While there, I reflected on the fact that my acid legislation had vanished into the legislative tar pits that were the federal Law Department, and felt gratified to have pursued the burn unit on my own. If I had waited for the legislative process to secure the funds, it never would have happened. It wasn't often that I thought of Raja Basharat warmly, but on that occasion, I had to allow a debt of gratitude to him for green-lighting the funding for this project.

THE NEXT REVENUE COMMITTEE meeting took place on the thirteenth of April, and it was more of the same: we squeaked by with a quorum of three, the pitiful minimum; my bill had yet to be sent to the cabinet of ministers for an opinion; the Senior Member of the Revenue Board did not show—and neither did anyone from his or any of the other relevant departments. I demanded that the committee send my bill to the Chief Minister of the Punjab, Chaudhry Pervaiz Elahi, and his cabinet of ministers for their opinion in the next ten days.

By then, Chairman Nawaz had begun to fear me, not because I was particularly fearsome, but because the House leadership was pressuring him to shut me up. My bill had become an embarrassment for the ruling party, and the order from above was to make my bill go away, however Nawaz had to do so. He began calling other MPAs on their cellphones, urging them to come to the meeting so that the committee could reach a majority decision with the maximum number of members. I heard him spluttering into the phone, "She won't spare me if we don't have more members present!" When I heard him say, "She is like a mountain! She doesn't move!" I could barely suppress my laughter. Thereafter, when committee members saw me coming, I would hear them say, "The mountain is coming." Yes, all five feet two inches of her.

If only to make me go away, Chairman Nawaz agreed to send my bill to the cabinet of ministers. We would meet again on the twenty-ninth of April. I made it clear that I expected Safdar Javaid Syed, the Senior Member of the Revenue Board, to be there.

When the day of the meeting arrived, only Nasrullah Khan Chattha, not his boss, Syed, turned up. I asked Maqsood Malik to phone the secretariat to find out where the Senior Member of the Revenue Board was. I was polite but direct in addressing the committee. "Chattha Sahib and Chairman Sahib, I refuse to carry on with the meeting without the SMRB in attendance." When told that Syed was again indisposed, I stood up. "I am walking out."

By then, a few reporters from the Assembly's press gallery had been following my story with interest. I opened the committee room door to find them standing there, surprised to see me—shouldn't the meeting have lasted longer? I took advantage of their presence to hold an impromptu press conference. "This is how the bureaucrats treat representatives of the Punjab," I said. "When we bring up the issues, this is how cavalier and insensitive they are to the cause of the people they supposedly represent. The press keeps saying that we don't do our work, so let me tell you who creates the obstructions." I named Safdar Javaid Syed. "We have requested his presence since May of last year, and never once has he bothered to show. Syed Sahib thinks he's too good to lower himself to report to the committee. Well let me be clear: As long as the SMBR deigns not to show, I will walk out of these meetings."

The story of my battle with the Revenue Committee got prominent placement in most of the region's news dailies, which roundly called Syed to account. Editorials decried the do-nothing bureaucrats, and I got a new title: "The Most Unmanageable Woman in Pakistan." Reporters had overheard bureaucrats saying that I could not be managed, and so they anointed me with this epithet. I didn't mind at all. At home, Ednan said, "Tell me something I don't know."

My bill received its thirteenth extension in June during a parliamentary session that I missed, again because of the priority of attending to Zia's situation. And on the twenty-second of July, the Revenue Committee reconvened for the eighteenth time. This time, in addition to four MPAs plus the chairman, Safdar Javaid Syed was in attendance. Stung by press coverage that characterized him as arrogant and disinterested in the problems of the people of the Punjab, Syed was contrite. He apologized for not having attended previously.

I had never met Syed before, and almost immediately, I found him slippery. He protested to believe in my bill, which I doubted, and he promised to seek and deliver the Cabinet of Ministers' opinion on it. Syed might truly have thought he could do so; there was no way to know. But I knew that his promise about procuring the Cabinet of Ministers' opinion was far-fetched. For one thing, the ministers rarely met; it could be months before they did again. For another, years of corruption and vying for control on the part of the House bureaucracy had inverted the power relationship between bureaucrats and elected ministers, reducing the latter to mere yes men for the ruling party. All MPAs were hostages to the bureaucracy. As I learned in my battles to draft legislation that would be accepted by the Law Department bureaucracy, if bureaucrats didn't want to help an MPA, there was little she could accomplish without putting up a mighty fight. The same held for the ministers, many of whom appeared to me to have given up. Besides, I knew that the Cabinet of Ministers would never go on the record with their opinion about my private moneylending bill. If they came out in favor of it, the ruling party, which wanted the matter to go away, would be unhappy. If they came out against it, they would reveal themselves to be unmoved by an issue that plagued their people. Knowing all of this, I made it clear to Syed that the opinion was important only to the committee, and not me. Nothing that I did would be influenced by their judgment. I merely wanted it done so that the committee could at last prepare a report on my bill and send it to the House for a vote.

Syed also conceded that there was nothing in the Revenue Board's records to show that the 1960 Ordinance had been implemented. This was not news, but I appreciated the admission. I tried to be gracious, and I thanked him for joining us. It wasn't much, but it felt like progress.

THROUGHOUT THE SUMMER, Ednan divided his time between the paper and taking care of Zia, whose condition had improved only somewhat. The cause of his chronic renal failure remained a mystery. There would be more trips to more doctors abroad, the family decided. Ednan began researching nephrologists in the United States, but for the time being, he was able to stay put. He had given me carte blanche to design our new home—"happy wife, happy life," he would joke—and so I spent what extra time I had picking out fabric for window treatments and stone samples for the mosaics I planned to have underfoot. I intended for our new home to be comfortable but not grand, well appointed but not lavish, and to have white marble floors that would not absorb the punishing summer heat, because we all loved to be barefoot on cool stone.

I had designed the apartment's layout so that family and workspace abutted but did not intersect. That way, Ednan could conduct a meeting in our round sitting room, with its sweeping views of pre- and post-Raj architecture, and then slip out to help with homework or just muss a little head and administer a loving kiss to the forehead. I planned our move for the end of September, just before the start of Ramadan. When Ednan told me that he and my cousin Ziad planned a quick jaunt over to Dubai to see Momi, I wanted to kill him. I called Ednan, Momi and Ziad the Three Musketeers for their devotion to one another, and sometimes the Three Stooges, too. I also chided them for leaving me out of their fun. They often spent their weekends together playing cricket or soccer, often with a delighted Nofal in tow, and free evenings were for watching those infernal *Lord of the Rings* movies. I envied their bond, even as I rejoiced that three of the most important people in my life adored each other.

"And leave me here to pack up our home and three children?" I said, marveling at the obliviousness of his timing.

"I just need a break, Humaira," Ednan pleaded.

"What about me?" I said. "What about my break?"

Ednan looked frightened. He couldn't tell whether or not I was genuinely upset. Neither could I, really. "Oh, go," I said at last. "Miserable toad. Go, because you are a man, and men have all the privileges. Go, but know that I curse this trip!" I was kidding, but only somewhat. Ednan approached to take me in his arms. "Don't even think about it," I said. "I am tempted to change my mind!"

Ednan traveled to Dubai, and I packed up our home. When he returned, everything was ready for our move on the first of October. The new space was beautiful, serene. Ednan had been following its progress with only a fraction of his attention; he seemed awed by what I had done. The children ran through bellowing, taking full advantage of the acoustics of empty rooms. We settled in with remarkable ease; it already felt like home.

Not long after moving in, we gave in to the children's requests for doves. We had a covered outdoor space where we could raise them, and from the other side of a sliding glass door, the children observed their progress. They were delighted when, in a little nest the doves had built in a potted plant, three tiny eggs appeared. They began making videos of the nest. One morning, they discovered three scraggly hatchlings in the place of the eggs. Fajr named them Tu Tu, Chu Chu and Tin Tin. Hafsa was the most taken of all with the little avian kingdom. She dragged her mattress to the window so that she could be the first in the morning to report on their doings. She sang lullabies to them as she went to sleep.

Tin Tin died, and Nofal and Fajr were crushed. We removed the lifeless body from the nest and buried it, saying prayers for the little bird and the rest of his family. Hafsa cried when her older siblings did, but she continued to think the chick would wake up. Ednan protested. Dr. Samia Amjad, a fellow MPA who had become a close family friend, had joined us for dinner, and Ednan looked at us both with an intense gaze and said, "I'm not sure this is such a good idea. How do I explain death to them? I don't want them dealing with death while they're still so little." I assured him that no harm would come to them from learning in such a small way that there is a cycle of life. The children carried on their nest-side vigil, making videos of their tiny charges and squealing over how fluffy Tu Tu and Chu Chu were becoming.

WHEN LEGISLATIVE BUSINESS continued that fall, my bill received its fourteenth extension on the fifth of October while I was absent from the House. The Revenue Committee met again on the eleventh of November, and Safdar Javaid Syed returned to say that he had no news, which was exactly what I expected him to say. He vowed to try again to get the cabinet's opinion on my bill. I wanted to roll my eyes but remained composed.

When my bill was presented for its fifteenth extension on the twentieth of November, I did not stand to protest it. I wanted to give Syed the chance either to make good on his promise, or to reveal himself to the rest of the committee to be as ineffective as I suspected he was. I looked forward to the next Revenue Committee meeting, which had been set for the twelfth of December, to see which way it would swing with Syed. At long last, he had something different to say. The cabinet ministers had met for the first time in many months, he said. Alas, my bill did not make it onto their agenda. For me, that was the last straw.

I was beyond fed up, and I told the committee so. My bill, I said, would go back to the House for voting, with or without their recommendation. I demanded that the next meeting be held on the twenty-eighth of December. "Try one more delay tactic," I said, "and during the next House session, I will stand, and at least one hundred others will stand with me, and we won't sit until the Speaker has ruled on my bill." I felt on the verge of a fit of apoplexy.

Two days later, Ednan and I flew with the children to Dubai to visit Momi. It was a short break, just five days in all, but it was a relief to get away. Zia's health had declined steadily since the spring, and Ednan had decided that he would take his father to the United States in January. Ever since he announced the trip, I'd had a powerful foreboding about it. I was dreading being without him again, especially as I entered such a critical time for my bill in the House. I had come to rely on Ednan to help me maintain perspective during periods when I was doing battle with recalcitrant colleagues, and to shore me up when I was certain I couldn't go on. I wouldn't dream of asking him to stay behind for me, though. Doctors at the Johns Hopkins School of Medicine had suggested that they might be able to offer alternate diagnoses for Zia's condition if they could perform a biopsy of his spine, because the infection had spread from his kidneys, and we all hoped they would be right. We were desperate for a turnaround. We had not been rudderless, exactly, without Zia at the helm; Ednan and his brother Imtinan had done well to fill Zia's shoes, each in his own way, Ednan managing contact with doctors and keeping the *Khabrain* staff apprised of developments with Zia's health; and Imtinan, who was so much more like his father, emulating Zia's penchant for running a tight ship.

ON THE TWENTIETH OF DECEMBER, Ednan and I marked ten years of marriage. When I awoke to begin the day as I always do, washing, dressing and praying before rousing the children from their beds and to the breakfast table before rushing myself out the door, Ednan stopped me. "There is a car waiting for you downstairs," he said.

"Are you sending me away? Trading me in for a newer model?" I said.

In fact, it was an elaborate and loving scheme. Primping never ranked high on my list of priorities, but back then, with all that was going on, I sometimes felt burdened by the time commitment of basic grooming. Ednan saw this and wanted, if only for a day, to remedy that. He had felt so awful for me when my hair began falling out, and worse when I'd had to submit to a course of painful steroid injections directly into my scalp to halt it. That morning, Ednan told me, I was going to a spa.

Above my embarrassed protests, Ednan was adamant. "You do nothing for yourself, so today I am seeing that you do!"

When I arrived at the salon, ten young women holding a lush

bouquet each, one for each year of our marriage, greeted me with a card from Ednan. A banner on the wall read, HAPPY ANNIVERSARY MY WIFE. The owner greeted me and said, "I have very specific instructions from your husband." I thought I might die of mortification.

All at once, I was set upon by eager beauticians who would transform me, by day's end, into a massaged and manicured, plucked and blow-dried version of myself. Throughout, Ednan called me almost hourly. "How do you feel now?" he would ask. "And now?" I had to admit: I had no memory of ever having felt so relaxed.

That evening, Ednan picked me up and we went for a long drive, just as we used to do when we were courting. It was the first time in a long while that we had an entire evening to ourselves. No children, no in-laws, no colleagues requiring our attention. As indulgent as the spa day was, that was the true luxury: having my husband to myself. Over a candlelit table at an elegant restaurant for dinner, Ednan set one condition. "Not a single word about work." I was glad to comply.

We spoke then about matters long untended. We spoke to each other the way lovers do. Ednan told me what he used to think of me and why he had wanted to marry me. "You are so much more than my expectations," he said. Our feelings were mutual. I told him that I could never have imagined finding such peace and happiness in life with one person. While we'd endured some terrible sadness in a decade together, there was so much joy, as well. Three healthy, funny, beautiful children, two closely knit extended families, bustling careers and professional lives and bright futures. Ednan was thirty-seven, and I was thirty-four, and we marveled at and expressed gratitude for so much good fortune. "I have everything in my life that I could have hoped to have," Ednan said. What a rare and wonderful thing, I thought, that we both felt the same way, and that we were still so young, with so much yet to come.

WHEN, ON THE TWENTY-EIGHTH of December, the Senior
Member of the Revenue Board, Safdar Javaid Syed, still could not
offer anything new, I announced that it would be my last meeting. I did not get angry. I simply announced an end to the spectacle of bureaucracy. "It is time to act according to conscience," I
said. "The Qur'an prohibits usury and likens it to a war against
Allah and His messenger, peace be upon him. You will receive
no pressure from me one way or the other. Ask yourselves what
the right thing to do is, and let your choice stand before God." I
stood to leave and said, "I know my privileges as an MPA, and
I know that the rules of the House permit me to take my bill
directly to the House for a vote, whether this committee recom-
mends it or not. So that is what I am going to do: I will take my
bill to the House with or without you. I hope you will submit
your findings on my bill as soon as possible." I turned to look at
Maqsood Malik, and said, "Please Malik Sahib, if there is a delay,
then inform me. Otherwise, I will see you all in the House."

As I turned to go, each committee member, one by one, stood.
Samina Naveed said, "We will support you. This farce must
end." Another said, "We stand with you, because usury is haram
[forbidden in Islam]. It is cruelty, and we believe in you."

I could not believe what I was hearing. The bureaucracy's
antics had been an insult to the legislature, a rebuke to an august
House. Rather than further abet a ploy between Chairman Nawaz
and the Revenue Department and thus be used as pawns, the
Revenue Committee members revolted. They were also swayed by
their collective conscience—they knew what harm the practice
of usury brought to many in their constituencies, and they were
at last moved to stop it. Enough was enough, they said, emboldened, perhaps, by their knowledge that they had the teachings
of the Qur'an on their side. The last to stand was the chairman.
He understood that if he didn't go along with the committee, the
members would defy him, too. "We will recommend your bill
without changing a comma in it," he said, because he really had
no choice.

I was stunned. It was the last outcome that I expected. It hadn't occurred to me that it was even possible. I had felt hostage to a cycle of obstructionism and resistance over the past three years. I realized in that moment that I wasn't the only prisoner; we all were. Syed's inability to work on the committee's behalf with the Cabinet of Ministers only underscored the feeling that had been growing in the House that the bureaucracy was pitted against politicians. In a sense, I think that Syed's failure helped me.

With the threat of political retribution from above, the committee members had been afraid to act. By declaring their support, they were joining me in defiance of party leadership. I knew this was not easy for them; the leadership would make sure of that. But in choosing to stand with me, they were putting the common good over political gain. I wanted to be elated, and a part of me was. But I also knew better than to dispense altogether with caution. Either way, with or without the committee's backing, I was going to see that my bill be put to a vote in the House.

I couldn't wait to hear Ednan's take on this development. I had just completed my afternoon prayers and heard Ednan's footsteps as I sat on my prayer mat. He had come upstairs to find out what happened. "I don't know what to think," I said when he came into the room. "I suppose I'll believe it when my bill goes back to the House."

He gave me a kiss on the forehead. "Humaira, no one else could have done this," he said. "You are doing this for others, and you will get the reward from Allah."

THERE IS A SUFI CONCEPT that holds that separation revives love, that in absence, one's beloved is actually more present. Even before I knew firsthand what that meant or what it felt like, I thought it an appealing notion. Once I had fallen in love with Ednan, I also found it to be true. His absences in the previous year had only made me love him more. But in anticipation of his upcoming trip to the United States in January, there was something different about the way I was preparing myself for his departure. It was the first time that his going away had filled me with a kind of dread. In those weeks before he left, I felt as though a plumb weight had been attached to my heart. Ednan, too, seemed afflicted by some kind of trepidation.

A few days before he left for America, Ednan took my hands, turned them over, and remarked upon the abrupt end of my palm's life line. "It is so weak," he said, sounding a bit crushed at the discovery. He was right. Where the trajectory of most people's lines arches and extends, mine simply stops. It is common in Pakistan to dabble in a bit of palmistry, and I had long known that my life line, if you believe in this sort of thing, didn't suggest longevity. The question was always whether I believed in that sort of thing. I examined in turn Ednan's. "Look!" I said. "So strong and healthy, and with a star on it. I am so glad I am going to die before you."

I was teasing him. "It will be fascinating to see you full of regrets: Why didn't I do this for her? Why didn't I do that for her?" I told him to forget about marrying again. "My ghost will come back and hound you." I also told Ednan that should I die in the morning, he must see that I am buried in my white dupatta, that diaphanous veil that is my favorite headscarf, by the afternoon. "Don't keep my body in a freezer," I said. "I want to go back to the earth."

"Humaira, you are so morbid. Cut it out," Ednan said. When he was courting me, he used to say that I was a sprite with a death fetish. "And anyway, what if I die first?"

I told him it wouldn't happen in that order; just look at that life line.

A day or so later, Ednan and I were watching a movie in the evening when all of a sudden he got up and said, "There is something I have to tell you." He stopped the video, and I said, "You are actually pausing the TV to talk to me?"

"Be serious," he said. Then he took me in his arms, looked me in the eyes and said, "You are the most important thing in my life, and I love you more than I have ever loved anything in this life. I love you more than my kids. I love my kids because you are their mother. I love you more than my mother, my father, any relative, any relation. More than my career. More than anything."

I asked if something was wrong with him.

He said, "I don't know if I will be able to say this to you again, and I won't ask you the same question, because I know I can't compete, because children are a part of your flesh. It is not fair to ask a mother to choose from her husband and her kids. But Humaira, I knew you were the woman of my life from the first moment we met."

"Ednan, calm down," I said. "Have you found another woman and now you are trying to pacify me with these bubbly words of love?" I had to deflect because the intensity of the moment caught me so off guard. It also exacerbated the feeling that I'd been harboring but not expressing that I didn't want him to take this trip.

"I don't find peace without you, Humaira," Ednan said. "You are my solace."

MY GOODBYE TO EDNAN before his trip to America was distressing. "I wish I could stop you from going," I said. "I know you have to take Zia for the biopsy, but . . . "

Ednan reassured me. "You will be able to manage without me, I know you will."

He was referring to the newspaper, but that's not what I meant.

"How will I cope in your absence?" I said. "How will I sleep without you? You know, your pillow is a poor substitute."

Ednan held me close and told me he loved me.

He went next to find Fajr and Happy and kissed them goodbye. His last stop was Nofal's room, where the boy was on his

PlayStation. Ednan said, "While I am away, you are the man of the house. You are going to take care of your mother and your two sisters." Our nine-and-a-half-year-old son seemed quite puffed up to have the responsibility.

"Yes, Baba," he said.

"And no complaints about your spending too much time on your computer games." Ednan kissed Nofal, my little man of the house, and we all said goodbye one more time as Ednan turned to walk toward the elevator.

Ednan flew with his mother and father to Washington, D.C., that night, the fourteenth of January. The text message I received the next day read: "I am only trying to sound ok. I am miserable without you. Everything reminds me of my wife. The cinema, the car park, the tickets, the movie theatre, the trees, the air, the coke, the popcorn, the drive back home, the TV, the woolen gloves, the cold weather, the sports channel, the kitchen, the home-cooked food, the after-dinner gupshup, the TV channels like E TV, you name it honey. Does that tell you EXACTLY how much I love you?"

The next message read, "Humaira, I am missing you so much, it has started to hurt."

CHAPTER FOURTEEN

Devotion and Defiance

AT DUSK ALONG the Lawrence Road in Lahore, the sky resembles a pair of hands outstretched in invitation to the slowly descending sun. It's a view that never fails to draw my eyes heavenward during my evening commute, offering momentary respite from the fret of life and the growling motorcycles at street level. One glance up past the towering sheesham trees that shimmer in the day's waning light, and I am calmed.

That Friday evening in February 2007 was no different. I was driving with the three children west along the road that still bears a British imperial statesman's name, past the magnificent botanical gardens that no longer do. When he was Viceroy of India in the mid-nineteenth century, Sir John Lawrence commissioned the gardens now named for another statesman, Mohammed Ali Jinnah, the founder of modern Pakistan. Bagh-e-Jinnah, or Jinnah's Garden, was modeled on London's Kew Gardens. Today, with a mosque, a cricket ground, and a library housed in a Victorian building, the garden is a crossroads of homegrown and colonial influence. The two have not always melded to such splendid effect.

London was much on my mind as I drove home that day, because that is where Ednan was. As I took in the familiar sight of Jinnah's Garden and the view of the evening sky, I said a silent prayer for his safe return. It was the ninth of February, and

Ednan was due home in two days' time. I had been missing him powerfully since he had left for the United States with Yasmine and Zia in January. The doctors at Johns Hopkins had performed a biopsy on Zia's kidney; it seemed that a fungal infection was the culprit, and it had spread to his spine, which explained Zia's deteriorating health. Now, with a twenty-four-hour layover in London, Ednan had decided to take Zia to see one more doctor for one more opinion, just in case.

I had just spoken with Ednan at my mother's house, where the children had gone after school. I rang him at his cousin's in London. When he picked up, he sang, "Hello my baby, hello my darling, hello my ragtime gal . . . " I laughed and asked if I had reached the wrong number. The afternoon light bathed my mother's sitting room in its golden light, and I clutched the receiver. I wanted to share Ednan's levity—he was so happy to be coming home. But I had been dogged for weeks by a sense of dread that I had kept from him. That afternoon, I confessed at last that after three weeks of his absence, I'd had enough. The heart-sinks, as I called them, that I had felt in advance of his departure had grown more intense as the weeks had passed. Ednan's text messages to me during that time had only deepened them. I received a message with no content one day and replied, "Did you just send me a blank message?" For some reason, Ednan's response gave me chills. "The blank message means that I will love you till the day I am no more and that you are my most precious, my life." During his previous trips abroad, his messages to me had more to do with Zia's condition and whether or not he was keeping crackers down. During this trip, every other message was an ardent declaration of love.

Talking with Ednan that day at my mother's, I felt an intense longing. It was more than the happy ache of anticipation that I had come to know so well in the last year. It had caused me to fear the worst. I told Ednan that I feared that something terrible might happen. Terrible in the world? he wanted to know. At the newspaper? I couldn't say, but I knew with eerie certainty that it would hit much closer to home than that.

"I love God," I told Ednan, "but He is going to test me."

There is a passage in the Qur'an in which Allah says, "We shall certainly test you with fear and hunger, and loss of property, lives, and crops."* If it were true, as I believed, that the believer should be tested in accordance with the degree of her faith, then I trusted that I would face a mighty test. I thought of the day almost ten years earlier, when we lost our son.

"Don't sit alone in your room and speculate and think too much, honey," Ednan said. "I will be back."

"It will be someone close to me," I told Ednan. "Someone who gives me great contentment and a sense of well being." I worried aloud that it would be Fajr. She had turned six the day after our tenth wedding anniversary in December, and she was radiant, already the kind of person whose presence seemed to cause everything around her to shimmer. Her birth and the ease of caring for her had contrasted so greatly with that Nofal's. The very fact that she had brought such relief and joy to me caused me to fear that God would take her away. I had begun to fixate on the idea of losing her, and I told Ednan so.

Ednan was shocked. He told me to calm down. "Humaira, you must stop having these thoughts," he said. "Nothing is going to happen to our daughter. Nothing is going to happen to anyone."

I thought of another awful possibility. "It can't be you," I said. I had already been tested that way when he was in that awful car accident at the end of 1998. No, I decided, God wouldn't test me like that twice.

Ednan redirected our conversation, as he had learned to do whenever I lingered for too long in my dark places. He talked about how exhausted he was from the trip with his parents. In one phone message that had made me laugh because of how

---

*The Qur'an, trans. Haleem, 2:155, pp. 17–18.

very much like an exasperated little boy he sounded, Ednan bewailed the hours that Yasmine and Zia spent watching the Bollywood awards on satellite TV, while he waited impatiently to watch basketball. Their push-me-pull-you dynamic wore on him. "They have an argument every half an hour," he said in the same message. The scary prospect that his father might not get well no doubt troubled him, too; Ednan revered his father.

Our conversation turned to Ednan's imminent return and how he'd spend his last hours in London. He would upgrade their tickets so that his father would be more comfortable on the flight home. He also wanted to buy gifts for the children and me. "I'm picking up chocolates for the children," he said. He knew that the first thing they would want to know when he walked through the door was, *Where's the candy?* For me, with Valentine's Day approaching, he wanted to pick out diamond earrings. "But I told you, I want that book," I said. I had asked Ednan to look for Peter Watson's *Ideas: A History of Thought and Invention, from Fire to Freud.*

"Of course you do," he said. "You're an odd piece, Humaira. Only my wife would prefer a philosophy book on Valentine's Day. So I'll get you both."

"Just bring yourself home to me," I said. "You're all I want."

Ednan planned to go next to the Lord's Cricket Ground. "I want to get a ball for Nofi," he said.

"Why would you go all that way for a cricket ball? A ball is a ball," I said. "And anyway, you know he'll lose it."

"Don't come between a father and a son and a cricket ball," Ednan said. His tone was teasing and warm. He asked after the doves. Were the children still filming their every move?

I hadn't wanted to tell him while he was away that another chick, Tu Tu, had died. He had been so bothered by seeing the children upset by Tin Tin's death. He heard my hesitation.

"What is it?" he asked.

I told him that the week before, Happy had woken up, pressed her nose against the window and said, "Tu Tu's not moving." She ran with great purpose to wake her older brother and sister. The three of them returned to confirm the sad finding: Tu Tu was dead. Nofal and Fajr burst into tears and asked to stroke the little bird's corpse, which we later buried. Happy didn't understand, and that, somehow, made it all the more poignant.

Ednan sounded distressed. "Oh, Humaira!" he said. "You know I did not want them to go through this! They are too young to understand death." He made me promise: no more doves. I promised.

And then he had to be off. "We have just fifty-two hours between us, honey," he said. "And then I will be back on your nerves." His voice filled me up and gave me strength. I decided to try to push the discomfiting thoughts I'd been having from my mind, and to focus instead on his return.

We hung up, his voice still in my ears. I thanked my mother for her help with the children, and then I gathered them and their little mess of things for the short drive home. From the back seat, the children sang along to one of Ednan's homemade CDs. They had recently discovered "Seasons in the Sun" by Terry Jacks, and already they knew all the words.

Driving home that February day, I wondered if perhaps our recent wedding anniversary and the rare pause it had offered from our otherwise breakneck lives had left us both wistful for the simple pleasure of each other's company. As I struggled to rationalize Ednan's text-message declarations and my own sinking sensations, I thought to myself that maybe that's all it was: This is what it meant to miss each other. Ednan gave voice to his yearning, as was his wont, while I retreated into myself and harbored grim fears, as was mine. The notion offered me momentary comfort, but the truth of it was: I had become convinced that someone I loved was going to die.

As TERRY JACKS blasted from the car stereo and my little chorus of three kept time from the backseat, my BlackBerry buzzed. It was a text message from Ednan. "Call me as soon as you are home," it read. I clicked on a link and up popped that singing, dancing, top-hatted Looney Tunes frog crooning the Howard and Emerson ragtime ditty, "Hello! Ma Baby."

I realized he must have sent the message before I had called from my mother's. *So that's why he answered the phone singing that ridiculous song,* I thought. I tried him again once we arrived back home, but there was no response. I pictured him walking around Lord's Cricket Ground, Nofi's ball in his hand, and I smiled.

IT WOULD BE A NIGHT of leave-takings. Momi was booked on a late flight out of Allama Iqbal International Airport, destination: Melbourne, Australia. He was twenty-four and headed to Monash University to complete the bachelor's degree in accounting that he had started at the American University of Sharjah in the United Arab Emirates. Far-flung study agreed with him, and so to the chagrin of those of us who appreciated the relative proximity of Dubai, where we could visit, he had decided to go even further afield.

Two days before my brother's departure, Momi came over so that we could call Ednan on his last day in the States. It would be their goodbye. Ednan was disappointed not to be in Lahore to see Momi off, so I assured him during that call that I would do so on both of our behalves. He told Momi that he'd travel to Australia in the coming year to go to a Formula One race with him, and I dared him from the background to plan that trip without me.

When Momi passed me the phone, I was almost overcome with sadness. Ednan remained light and positive, urging me to get outside and do something nice for myself. When he asked me to put Momi back on the line, however, he sounded very worried.

My brother would later tell me that Ednan had said: "Try not to leave her alone. She is too speculative. Between your departure and my return, she will have just one day on her own. Stay with her as much as you can."

BACK HOME FROM MY MOTHER'S, I set about getting the children settled for the night before leaving again for the airport. Nofal and Fajr were in the high spirits that come with Friday nights—no homework, a later bedtime, and the always thrilling prospect of testing their nanny's limits once I was gone. I fed them a dinner of chicken and noodles and gave Happy, who was two and a half, a long cuddle before putting her to sleep. Then it was on to arbitrating the latest round of sibling mischief. Nofal was obsessed with Hulk Hogan and The Rock; the room he shared with his middle sister was filled with World Wrestling Federation belt replicas and figurines. A favorite impish pastime of his had become acting out "smackdowns" between his hard-bodied dolls and his sister's considerably softer ones. Fajr had become so distressed by this that she had taken to hiding her dolls so that Nofi wouldn't find them. Except that he always did, and as any big brother worth his salt will tell you, provoking his little sister was always well worth the trouble it landed him in.

If my time in the Provincial Assembly had taught me anything, it was how to make my way around warring parties. Now, as I had done countless times in my day job, I endeavored to get my children to see their way to a mutually beneficial solution. In their case, I proposed that they sign a peace treaty. Finding my approach wanting, they made like little parliamentarians and joined forces against me, insisting that only their Baba, their father, could give them justice. I was curtly informed that they would wait for his return the day after next to adjudicate the matter, and that was that. I nevertheless considered it a triumph that they were sitting contentedly together in front of *Home*

Alone by the time I made it out the door, and that I was on time for the airport to boot.

The temperature outside had fallen. The night sky had clouded over, and a light drizzle fell. Rain is so rare during a Pakistani winter that it comes almost as a relief. I thought then of Ednan and London, which in my mind's eye is forever enveloped in gray mist, and wondered what the weather had been like. I hadn't thought to ask him when we had spoken earlier.

It was just after ten o'clock when I arrived at the airport. My father and cousin Ziad were already there, saying their goodbyes to Momi. I asked them to wait for me so that I could sit for a while with Momi and then ride home with them. As an MPA, I had the security clearance to accompany my brother all the way to his departure gate.

Perhaps it was being in the airport—air travel always makes me a little bit anxious—but I found that I could not sit down. "Momi," I said. "I don't want you to go."

"Why are you saying that?" he asked. Muhammad's enormous dark brown eyes narrowed as he studied my face. He is tall and slightly built, and his wide set eyes have a long fringe of jet-black lashes. I stood on tiptoes to take his gentle face into my hands and tell him that I loved him.

"Humaira, what is wrong with you?" he said. "Your face has lost its color—you're all white."

My heart was beating fast in my chest. I needed to sit down. I felt panic. "Momi," I said. "Who is it? Something bad is going to happen—are you going to die? Is this the last time I am going to look at you?" I squeezed his hands.

"Humaria, what is wrong with you?" he said, alarmed. "Why are you thinking about this? Repeat after me: Ednan is coming back."

"I hope that God gives you a long, healthy life, and that this is not the last time that I am seeing you," I said. My heart was pounding so wildly that I put my hand to it.

"Are you well, Humaira?" Momi was upset. "Look," he said, "you go home. Give my love to the kids. Ednan will be home the day after tomorrow, and I will call you as soon as I land."

I kissed my brother, squeezed his long hands once more, and turned to leave the airport. My heart palpitations made me feel as though my chest would explode. Any hope I had that the night air might calm me vanished when I stepped outside. The damp only chilled me.

THE DRIVE HOME with my father and cousin was virtually silent; we were all sad to see Momi go. Still, I couldn't imagine that my brother's departure would leave me this disconsolate. By the time my father pulled up to the base of my building, my heart had stopped thumping, but my sense of panic remained. I said goodnight and stepped out of the car. From a distance, I saw Imtinan. It was eleven-thirty and he was just wrapping up his day at the paper. I waved good night and went upstairs.

The children were asleep, and the report from their nanny was good—they had managed to keep the peace, treaty or no. Exhausted, I removed my eye makeup, washed my face, did my ablutions, and prayed. When I finished, I saw in the mirror's reflection that my face looked very white, as though aglow. *I must be happy*, I thought to myself, *because Ednan is coming back. Yes, Momi is right: I have to focus on Ednan's return.* As I got into bed, I told myself to stay very busy in the next twenty-four hours. *Don't give yourself time to think*, I thought, *and then he'll be back home.*

THE TELEPHONE'S RINGING woke me an hour later, around one o'clock. It was Imtinan, his voice hoarse. "What's happened?" I asked.

"Can you open the door?" he said. "I am standing downstairs, and I want to come see you."

"What is wrong?" I said.

"Let me just come upstairs," he said.

My children were asleep. My apartment at the top of the building was dark. The stillness unsettled me.

I rushed out of bed and opened the door to find my brother-in-law, his eyes red and swollen. My first thought was that he had been punched. He came inside on shaky legs and I realized that, no, he hadn't been hit, he'd been crying. What on earth was going on? I ran through more possibilities in my mind: Zia? A fight with my sister? With someone else? Had there been a fire in the building?

"Sit down," he said, his tone gentle but his voice barely a rasp. I sat across from him, and he said, "No. Come sit with me," and gestured to the spot on the sofa beside him. I joined him there, and he took my hands and said, "I am struggling to find words." After what felt like a long pause, he said, finally, "Ednan has had a heart attack."

I leapt up and felt a gush of pain in my heart. I thought of the palpitations I had at the airport and couldn't stop rubbing my chest. "Is he alive? Are they trying to resuscitate him? How did he have a heart attack?" I was pacing back and forth. "Do you know something you're not telling me?"

Imtinan told me that he wanted me to speak with his father. "I will put you on the line with my dad," he said. "He is in the hospital now."

"I have to leave!" I cried. I told him that I wanted to be on the next flight to London. "Yes," he said, "you will leave in a minute, and we will find the next available flight." He was repeating what I said, trying to soothe me.

I was numb. I scanned his face for a hint at the rest of the story as he got on the line with Zia. He handed me the phone, and I heard Zia say, "Just pray, Humaira." And then he began to cry. In all of the time that I had known my father-in-law, even through the recent ordeal with his health, I had never known him to cry. That he was weeping in a hospital in London told me everything. I looked at Imtinan, whose cheeks were wet with tears. I was in a state of shock. The line to London went dead.

The phone rang and Imtinan answered. Zia was back on the line. Tears rolled down Imtinan's cheeks. He put the phone down and turned to me. "He is gone," he said. "He is gone."

I don't remember what came next. I couldn't see. I couldn't hear. I just knew that it was a test. I recognized it as such right away—that was the only clarity I had in that moment. *It is God*, I told myself. *This is between me and my God.* I claim to love Him, and here He is saying to me, "So what is your future strategy now? What are you going to do now that I have taken Ednan away?"

My parents and sister arrived. My cousins came next. Ziad, his eyes red and haunted, ran toward where I sat on the sofa shaking but unable to move. I buried my face in his chest. He knew this devastation, had lived it when his father died when he was just a boy of Nofal's age. Ziad loved Ednan so much. Ednan had been like a father figure to him. I sobbed as Ziad held me so tight, the way I had held him all those years ago. I said, "I feel a dagger has been put in my heart. It is dripping blood, and it hurts so much. How will I live without Eddie?" He just continued to hold me, whispering in my ear, "I am with you, and I will help you raise these kids. I know this pain, I know this pain . . . "

The apartment filled with *Khabrain* and *Post* staffers, some expressing their confusion. Surely it was Zia who had passed, they said. Was there some mistake? I was aware of their presence and that they were speaking to me, that they were crying, too, but their physical forms and voices were blurred. I was aware of only one voice, God's. "You have always claimed to love me," He said, "so love me now that I have taken your heart away. Can you love me now?"

I knew in that moment that I would either submit to His will, or not. I collapsed at the doorway to my bedroom and I fell into prostration, saying, "I am submitting to what You have done to me. If this is Your will, then let it be. If you think You can test me, then you will remember who you tested."

It was the most difficult moment of my life. My spirit demanded that I submit and accept Allah's will, prove my devotion. My agonized heart reminded me that I am only human. "Why did You do this to me?" I cried. With my forehead on the floor, I shook with sobs and said, "Allah, it hurts! It hurts too much! How will I live without him?"

The words I said next changed me. "I submit to you unconditionally. I love you more than anything." All at once, I felt Allah's love and compassion alongside the piercing pain of loss for my Ednan.

I BID THE NIGHT never to end, the morning never to come. I knew that the worst was ahead of me. I thought of my aunt all those years ago, and I heard with a new and terrible recognition the shrieks of her anguish when my Chacha was killed. Here I was, the same age, also with three children who were the same ages that my cousins had been when they lost their father. How would I tell the children? I wished that I would never have to do so.

In the morning, my parents took my children to their home. I wasn't ready to tell them yet. I went to Zia and Yasmine's home and stayed all day in our old rooms. The next day, Ziad brought my children to me. He stood with me as I told Nofal, Fajr and Happy that their Baba had gone to the other world to be with Allah. I had no idea how to make them understand death. I had been unable to explain it when a hatchling died; this was their father.

"When is he coming back?" Fajr asked.

The most difficult thing that I have ever done was say, "Never."

"Are we never ever going to meet him again?" Nofal and Fajr asked, the gravity of it sinking in and tears rolling down their cheeks. Fajr wanted to know if she could join Ednan where he was. I had no answer but the tears in my eyes.

Nofal said, "You mean I can never play cricket with my dad? Or watch Formula One with him?" I was silent.

Happy did not know what I was saying. I remember watching her with her pacifier in her mouth, fidgeting about the way toddlers do, oblivious to the fact that she would never find out who and what her father was.

After that, I don't remember. For the next six days, I felt as though in a trance. I would go into prostrations and pray for Ednan, bargain for him. I relived what he went through before he died. I learned that he died at 5:30 P.M. London time, or 10:30 in Pakistan. My heart was beating out of control at the airport at the precise moment that my husband's heart stopped.

In the week between his death and his burial, so many people came to me. There were friends, family acquaintances, some I didn't even know. All of them told me stories about Ednan. Some told me he had been secretly helping them. He had helped some escape land mafias, he had given others money for their daughters' weddings. He had paid school fees, intervened on behalf of a woman whose in-laws were threatening her. Each story reminded me of Ednan's pure heart. Without even telling me, my pious love, my gentle soul, had gone quietly about the business of making people's lives a little easier. All these people wept as if they had lost their own son or brother.

My friend Sughra Imam reminded me of the day a few weeks before Ednan left for America when I complained to him in front of her that too much was on my shoulders, from managing *The Post* in his absence to doing it all on the domestic front. I had accused him of taking me for granted. She said, "The moment you stepped out of his office, you know what he said? He said, 'Out of six billion people in the world, I only want one. And that is her! And she doesn't get it.'"

Sughra said, "He loved you immensely, Humaira, and you

both argued as perfect lovers do, with too many expectations of each other."

EDNAN'S BODY ARRIVED in Pakistan the following Friday, and we buried him at three o'clock that afternoon. People who were with me that day have told me that I was constantly talking to God. I prayed to him for peace, eternity, the nearness of Him, the nearness of the Prophet, praise be upon him, and I saw Ednan. He was walking and talking to me. I felt him come to me and hold my hand, and I said to him, "Oh man, shame on you, Ednan. What kind of weak heart you must have!" Ednan had always said that when you see God, your heart stops. He said to me, "I saw God, and my heart stopped."

When I buried Ednan, I felt that he and God had merged. I considered all that I loved about him: His brow. His eyelashes. His lips. His ears. The color of his hair. The way he used to talk. The way he used to love me. But all of that was given to him by God. He was a manifestation of God's love and grace. Ednan had gone back to his source. It is very painful to love the invisible: It's nowhere and everywhere at once. That's how my love for God had always felt. Now, it's what my love for Ednan felt like, too.

THE MONTHS THAT FOLLOWED the burial were a time of great stillness. For the four months of iddat, or mourning, the only movement in my daily life was that of the sun as it crossed the sky outside the bedroom where I lay, immobilized by grief. As I gazed at the sun from my window, I found it blissful and cruel, wondering how it could shine when my world had gone black. I felt unable to receive its light from within the void where I now dwelled, where I had eyes but could see nothing, where I had ears and heard only silence, where I could feel but was numb. *Is this what the Sufis mean by empty vessel?* I wondered. *Where you experience the nothingness of nothing, where you root around in complete darkness, in order to prepare to receive the light?*

As I lay in my room, I thought often of my cousins' confusion and pain when their father was killed, and I knew to reveal nothing of my fear to my own children. That is the iota of strength that I mustered during that time: I held myself together in front of my children, who were too vulnerable to lose their surviving parent to her pain, and too young to comprehend that their father was not coming home.

His possessions did: The green and white sweater that I had given him on our most recent anniversary, which the paramedics had scissored down the middle in trying to revive him; his watch, his glasses, the London tube ticket that had been in a pocket. To have these things but not Ednan was unbearable. My mind's eye captured flickers of the face I loved, but nothing of his flesh remained in my physical world. And so I turned in time to his closets, forging the courage to go through them in search of what could help me conjure what was no longer. I found his scent, earthy and musky and sweet, and I unearthed love letters that I had written but not known that he had kept. I went through his shirts and his sweaters one by one. I gathered up the hairs I found on them and wrapped them in a tissue. They were all I had of his physical being. *So this is death*, I remember thinking. We vanish forever but our possessions live on. It seemed a terrible trade then, and it does still.

THROUGHOUT THE PERIOD of traditional mourning, I did not attend any House sessions. During that time, faithful clerks from the Provincial Assembly reached out to let me know that my bill had been put on the agenda. I was stunned. It seemed that not even a widow's mourning was enough to keep some in the

House from wanting to see my defeat. They knew that if I were not there to defend my bill, there would be no pressure to pass it. "Humaira Bibi," Maqsood Malik said when he called to tell me this news, "we know what you are going through. We will make certain that your bill is rescheduled for right after your mourning."

My iddat ended just before the start of the next legislative session on the eleventh of June. Because mine was a private member's bill, I would have only one afternoon on one day to bring it to the floor. That opportunity would fall on the Tuesday after my mourning, the twelfth. I knew that if it did not pass then, it was unlikely that there would be another extension, because the parliamentary term was nearly up. As I prepared to go to the House the morning of the twelfth of June, I prayed to Allah to see my bill through to passage, and I asked Ednan, wherever he was, to give me strength. My entire world that day consisted of three things: an awareness of Allah, vivid memories of Ednan, and the realization that my pain was evidence that I was alive.

From the back seat of the car on my way to the Assembly building, I took in the hustle along Charing Cross on our approach to the Mall Road, and the long line of cars tangled in the paralysis of unmoving traffic. I saw hundreds of people go past, and I thought, "Each one of them contains multitudes." I thought of the billions of hearts, the billions of destinies, the billions of losses that weigh on the world. It gave me goose bumps. "Oh, Allah," I prayed. "How do you manage them all? I find my own life so unlivable after losing a piece of my heart. I can't manage myself. How do You manage this universe?"

I reread the last sermon of the Prophet, praise be upon him. More than anything else, that sermon had inspired my work in the parliament. It had given me the courage to go beyond myself. It gave me strength.

"O People! lend me an attentive ear," it begins. Among its entreaties, the following most moved me:

Return the goods entrusted to you to their rightful owners. Hurt no one so that no one may hurt you. Remember that you will indeed meet your LORD, and that he will indeed reckon your deeds.

Allah has forbidden you to take usury, therefore all interest obligations shall henceforth be waived. Your capital is yours to keep. You will neither inflict nor suffer any inequity. Allah has Judged that there shall be no interest. . . .

O People, it is true that you have certain rights with regard to your women, but they also have rights over you. Remember that you have taken them as your wives only under a trust from God and with His permission. If they abide by your right then to them belongs the right to be fed and clothed in kindness. Do treat your women well and be kind to them, for they are your partners and committed helpers. And it is your right that they do not make friends with anyone of whom you do not approve, as well as never to be unchaste.

All mankind is from Adam and Eve, an Arab has no superiority over a non-Arab, nor a non-Arab has any superiority over an Arab; also a white has no superiority over black, nor a black has any superiority over white except by piety and good action.

As I reread the sermon, I reconnected with that original inspiration and felt fortified for the fight that I knew lay before me.

ALMOST AS SOON AS I was inside the parliament building, a member of the Assembly staff came bustling toward me. He seemed hurried, and he strode with all of the self-importance of a minion doing a higher-up's bidding. "The Law Minister would like to see you right away," he said.

Raja Basharat. I groaned inwardly at the summons. With the

exception of his help with funding the burn unit, the Law Minister had only ever worked against me. I wondered what he could possibly be up to this time.

A babble of chatter spilled from Basharat's chambers. I walked in to find that it was full of government officers absorbed in what seemed an urgent and animated conversation. I had that uncomfortable feeling of having walked in on a conversation that was about me. When the Law Minister saw me, he shushed the gathering.

"Please accept my condolences on your husband's death," Basharat said in Punjabi. He managed always to sound very refined, if not always sincere. "We were present at the funeral, but of course we didn't get to see you."

I felt a sharp pain in my heart at the mention of Ednan's death. I still couldn't believe he was gone. I felt the sting of tears come to my eyes and blinked to make them go away. I wouldn't show vulnerability to this crowd.

Basharat got to the point. "Your bill is on today's agenda," he said. "I'm afraid that we will have to oppose it until we get the opinion of the cabinet." His tone was diplomatic, his smile condescending.

"I will not let you do that," I said.

"You are our honorable member," Basharat said. "We have great respect for your work. I assure you that your bill will be passed in your name, but we first need the opinion of the cabinet."

I couldn't believe that he was resurrecting this tired ploy.

"Just give me five more days," Basharat said.

"You're asking for five more days after you've taken four years to let it get to this point? I have just buried my husband, and I am ready to bury this bill, too. If there is going to be another death, let it die on the floor of the House, and may everyone be a witness to it."

I turned to go. Basharat said, "Okay then. We will oppose it on the floor."

"Do what you want," I said. "If it has to die, let it die honorably, and let the historical record show that someone tried, and that it was smothered. See you on the floor." I was thinking, *If I can survive the death of Ednan, I can survive this, too.*

Basharat was saying something else, but I was already out the door, slamming it shut behind me.

I was shaky with grief and took a moment to collect myself in the hallway. The walk to the Assembly lobby from the Law Minister's office is a short one, but I was leaden, as though someone had flipped a switch, and I could move only in slow motion. It felt like it took an age and a million deliberate steps to pass the various ministers' rooms before I reached the bustle of the members' hall, just outside the House chamber.

Lobby speakers broadcast the perfunctory sounds of the House proceedings. I didn't feel like going in just yet, but I didn't fancy staying there, in the smoke-filled hall where echoes of laughter landed on my ears like affronts. I took in a sea of white dotted with color—men in their starched shalwar kameez, a smattering of women in bright dupattas. I thought of my first day in the Punjab Assembly in November 2002, when I took my oath. It had all been so new. The spectacle of it now was jarring; I had the disorienting sense of one who is passing through a hall of mirrors, where the familiar is distorted.

What a relief it was, then, when I spotted Mohsin Leghari. He was walking toward me, smiling. Leghari had been wonderful after Ednan's death. Like everyone who met my late husband, he had forged his own friendship with Ednan, and he loved him.

Leghari saw my face and his smile disappeared. He led me to a nearby sofa and insisted that I sit down.

"What's the matter, Humaira?" he said. He listened as I recounted the exchange with the Law Minister.

"He's just trying to stress you out," Leghari said. "Don't let him get to you. Let me get you a glass of water, and then you go inside the House, and you watch how your bill goes through."

"It doesn't matter," I said when Leghari had returned. "They are going to kill it anyway. They are going to rip me apart. I saw it in Basharat's eyes." He urged me to go in anyway.

"At the very least, witness the proceedings," he said. "You owe yourself that much."

I HAD LONG IMAGINED what kind of speech I would make to motivate my colleagues to support my bill if it ever came up for a vote. But that day, I had no prepared remarks. I had lost the center of my life. It was as though the core of my entire being had dropped out of my body. I was there in the parliament reconstituting myself as I went. I steeled myself to endure another loss.

The Speaker asked me to move the bill. I stood, and I said, "I move the motion of the Prohibition of Private Money Lending Bill 2007." The motion thus moved, it was open for debate. Any objection by the Revenue Minister to any of my bill's thirteen clauses would send it back to the committee. With our five-year parliamentary term drawing to a close, I knew that my bill would likely never make it out of committee again, so I prayed, literally, for my bill to go directly to a vote. "Allah, all that was in my power to do, I have done. I stand here now where my domain ends. I don't have the strength. My legs are weak. My eyes are holding back tears. Allah, if you are up there, then please, come down. You deal with these people, because I don't have any more strength left." All the while, my friend and fellow MPA Samia Amjad sat holding my hand, squeezing it and saying quietly to me, "We are with you."

Because I was deep in prayer, I almost missed it when Raja Basharat nudged the Revenue Minister, Gul Hameed Rokhri, and said, "Oppose it!" Because the bill fell under Rokhri's purview, only he had the authority to oppose it. Basharat didn't realize that his microphone was on and that the entire Assembly had heard him. Coercion like that is not allowed in the Assembly, and it should have fallen to the Speaker of the House to reprimand Basharat. When he didn't, the leader of the opposition, Rana Sanaullah, stood on a point of order.

"If the Law Minister and the ruling party have already decided to rule against this bill, then why persist in this mockery of democracy?" he said. "The bill has been moved in this House, and now the members should debate it or put it to a vote. If the ruling party has already decided, then this is not democracy, and it goes against the spirit of the House!"

Raja Basharat denied that he had tried to coerce a colleague's vote. Rana Sanaullah countered that the assembly should listen back to the audio recording of the previous few minutes. The threat quieted Basharat, who knew he would be proved a liar.

Sanaullah had given me his quiet support all along, complimenting me to Ednan when he had the opportunity, and now, he was going on the record as my ally.

Basharat was indignant. "Let the Revenue Minister decide, then. If he opposes the bill, the motion breaks and the law will be open for debate. But if he doesn't oppose it, the motion will be eligible for a vote." He spoke with righteous authority, the way bullies do.

To my and everyone's astonishment, Gul Hameed Rokhri stood and said, "I don't want to oppose it."

In an instant, the game changed. Basharat glared at him. And then one person stood for the bill, and then another, and all the while I hadn't said one word beyond moving the motion. As each of the bill's thirteen clauses was read out for approval, a chorus of yeas filled the House chamber. In a matter of four and a half minutes, the Assembly accomplished something it had not been able to do in four years. The supporters were loud, the opponents silent. Women MPAs stood to join me. The parliament voted its conscience, and my bill passed, making history as the first piece of legislation put forward by a private member in the Punjab Provincial Assembly to be made into law. One legislative step remained: The Governor of the Punjab, my longtime supporter Khalid Maqbool, would have to sign the bill into law. I would learn later that Raja Basharat had tried to dissuade him from doing so.

My friends in the assembly stood with me to hug me, and that is when I cried. Dr. Samia Amjad, another member on a reserved seat, said, "Humaira, it happened!"

I said, "Didn't you see God?"

The session was gaveled to a close. As I left the House, the sound of Raja Basharat berating Gul Hameed Rokhri faded as the doors closed behind me.

The journalists who had been in the press gallery had gathered in the cafeteria downstairs. They bid me to give them a statement. I spoke of my gratitude to the Provincial Assembly for passing the bill, and then I left to call my family and to return to the office.

At *The Post*, the entire staff was celebrating. One of my most dear editors, Taimur ul-Hassan, said, "Humaira, I told you that you would do this! You had the purest intention, and it is always difficult to defeat a pure intention."

I was in awe and full of gratitude, but I was unable to smile or to feel the victory in my heart. I thought of the day five years earlier when Ednan blessed my parliamentary bid. "A raging sea," he had called the Assembly. His assessment had been prescient. What neither he nor anyone would have predicted, however, was that Ednan wouldn't be there when I made it back to shore.

I felt that I had done my duty, fulfilled my responsibility. I thanked Allah, and then silently I said to Ednan, "I did it, Eddie. I could not have done it without you, but, my darling, I did it." My father had always told me that there is power in the individual. At last, I understood.

Legislative Postscript

HAD I ACQUIESCED to Raja Basharat's insistence that he take another five days to put my bill to the cabinet of ministers for an opinion, my bill would never have seen the light of day. That is because that Tuesday, the twelfth of June, would turn out to be the last Private Members' Day of the parliament's tenure. After the budget sessions that followed, the Assembly didn't meet again. It was dissolved the following November, when our five-year term was up. I considered the timing of my bill's passage a miracle.

ON THE THIRTIETH OF JUNE, just eighteen days after my bill became law in the Punjab Assembly, the Prohibition of Private Money Lending Law, which had been replicated by the North-West Frontier Provincial Assembly, known now as the Khyber Pakhtunwala Parliament, passed there, as well. During the debate in that House, MPAs attributed the bill to me and praised the efforts of all in the Punjab Assembly who had voted for it.

MY DRAFT ACID CONTROL and Acid Crime Prevention Act never made it out of the federal Law Department. It would not be until 2011 that an amendment to the existing criminal law would classify acid and burn violence as a crime against the state, exempting it from barter or diyat and other means of evading punishment. The new law imposed a fine of 1 million rupees on the perpetrator of acid and other burn crimes and mandated between fourteen years and life in prison as punishment. The movers of the bill in the National Assembly, the lower House, were Begum Shahnaz Sheikh, Marvi Memon and Anusha Rahmen Khan. The bill passed in May 2011, and was passed by the upper House, the Senate, the following December. The mover of the bill in the Senate was Nilofer Bakhtiar, who I had long admired and respected for her work on behalf of women, including her efforts to outlaw vani, as well.

Acknowledgments

THERE ARE MANY who made this book possible and to whom I owe a debt of gratitude. First and foremost, I thank my Almighty God, the original scriptwriter of my life. I thank Him for this journey of trials and opportunities. I could not have done any of it without my faith in Him. I thank every single victim of abuse, violence and injustice that I have met over the years in my work. They are why I continue. They taught me gratitude, mercy and courage.

I thank my parents, Abdul Hamid Bhatti and Musarat Hamid, for never accepting less than perfection from me, and for making me into the person I am today. I thank Kelly Horan, my gifted writer, for her magic with words and also her ventriloquism; in writing my story, she absorbed my experiences, lived the moments of my life and captured my voice. In Kelly, I found not just a brilliant work partner, but also a beautiful human being and soul mate whom I will cherish for the rest of my life. Words can't thank her enough; this book would not exist without her. I thank also my adorable children Nofal, Fajr and Hafsa, and Kelly's son, Dashiell, for their patience with mothers engrossed in this work for days and nights that added up to years. I thank them for their out-and-out love, the only thing that relieved their mothers of guilt for having to sacrifice so much time with them in order to see this book through to completion. One day, may each of you be proud of this effort and of your mothers! I thank also Kelly's husband, Anthony Brooks, for understanding why I had to steal so much of his wife's time from him. Thanks also to Olivia Musisi for her unbounded love and care of Dashiell while Kelly was spending long hours on the manuscript.

I thank my agent, Janet Silver, who first introduced me to Kelly and who found in my editor, Alane Mason, the ideal fit for this book. I thank Alane and her diligent staff at W. W. Norton for believing in this book. I am grateful to Alane, Anna Mageras, Denise Scarfi and the rest of their team for all of their hard work on this book's behalf. I thank also my brother Samir and his wife Saima, my brother Muhammad and my sister Aisha for always being there for me and for reminding me of all of the stories without which this book would not be complete. I thank them also for keeping me grounded, for reassuring me at every step, and for giving me their unconditional love, belief and support. I thank my cousins Ziad, Zain, Amna, Saima and Saadia for their enthusiasm for this book and their help in culling memories for it. Special thanks to Saadia for the photograph that is on the cover of this book. I thank my in-laws, Yasmine and Zia Shahid, and their son, Imtinan, for their constant support and encouragement. I thank my friends Saira, Iffat, Fia and Sahyl, who fielded my anxious mid-night calls about the book and never refused me their insights or kindness. I thank Ambassador Swanee Hunt, who was the first person to convince me that I should write this book. She has served as a great inspiration for me. I also thank the late Lindy Hess of the Radcliffe and Columbia Publishing Courses for convincing me that I had a meaningful story to tell and for helping me get over my fear of telling it. I miss her and wish only that I could share the final product of her inspiration with her. May Allah bless her beautiful soul. I thank Dean Barbara J. Grosz and Associate Dean Judith Vichniac of the Radcliffe Institute for Advanced Studies. Their constant support and encouragement enabled my work on this book. I thank the Radcliffe fellows from the class of 2009–10, in particular

Ravit Reichman, who gave me this book's title when she one day summed me up as all "devotion and defiance." Thank you, Ravit, for seeing me so clearly. I thank also Reuven Snir, another Radcliffe fellow whose eight months of persuasion helped me find the courage to tell my story. I thank Agha Jee, Mujahid Kamran, Ishtiaq Farooq, Saeed Qazi, Farhat Abbas Shah, Mohsin Leghari, Nawabzada Shams Haider and Shuja Khanzada, each of whom provided great suggestions for this book and who believed in it from the start. I thank the eagle-eyed and tireless teams at *Khabrain* and *The Post* who spent endless hours digging through the reference sections of those newspapers, aiding my research and sorting through stories and documents. I thank my colleagues in journalism and the parliament who have shaped my life in many ways and whose input and belief in this book motivated me to see it through to completion. I extend special gratitude to the staff members of Punjab Provincial Assembly who helped me with the details of the proceedings and the complete file and record of my bill and legislative work, the details of which were was so crucial to the writing of this book. I thank Ritu Sharma, President of Women Thrive Worldwide, and her magnificent team for their unflagging support of my work and the International Violence Against Women Act. I thank my dear friend Taimur ul Hasan for helping me piece the political events that are recounted in this book together; his tolerance for tedium is admirable, and his feedback and suggestions were invaluable to me. I thank Umar Vadillo, my mentor, friend and, now, husband, whose praise for my spirit and my work makes me proud of this book and gives me the strength to continue with my struggle more resolutely. Finally, but not least, I am indebted to Ednan Awais Shahid. He was the fortifying strength behind my work. This book is an acknowledgment of all that he gave me or guided me toward: beautiful children, the most meaningful work, a life's purpose. I treasure his love, his support and his ever-unshakeable confidence in me. May Allah reward him for any good that this book may bring. Amen.

Index